Tourism and Handicrafts of India

Tourism and Handicrafts of India

J.C. Dua

Kaveri Books
New Delhi-110002

First Published in 2013
ISBN 978-81-7479-148-1

Published by
Kaveri Books
4832/24, Ansari Road
New Delhi - 110 002 (India)
Tel.: 011-2328 8140, 2324 5799,
Fax: 011-2328 8140
E-mail: kaveribooks@vsnl.com,
kaveribooks@gmail.com
Website: www.kaveribooks.com

Laser Typesetting by : Deep Graphics, Delhi

PRINTED IN INDIA

Dedicated to
All the Handicraftsmen and Women
who have kept India's Culture
and Traditions Alive & Aloft

CONTENTS

Preface

The main objectives of this book are: Recognizing the importance of local handicrafts in tourism development and reciprocally the importance of tourism as an agent for the protection and preservation of traditional crafts, methods of production and cultural context; examining tourism related handicrafts; production technologies and design aspects and optimizing the sale of handicrafts among tourists and the tourism industry.

Tourists do visit a country or a tourist spot may not be for the express purpose of shopping, but shopping is a part and parcel of tourist activity. Tourists thoroughly enjoy buying things that are peculiar to that particular region.

Handicrafts are an important part of shopping. These objects are made by the skill of the hand which is an admixture of tradition and creative craftsmanship. Moreover, handicrafts as souvenirs arouse nostalgia, because symbolic of the place, event or activity, they are status symbol, often utility item or of aesthetic value and sometimes are decorative.

Handicrafts can be of several types. They may be designed for personal use like soap boxes. They could be religion oriented like *malas*, replicas of idols for worship, etc. Most places have specialized handicrafts like the puppets of Jaipur. Some handicrafts are steeped in tradition, like the carved miniaures available at Agra are said to be by the descendants of the makers of the Taj Mahal. All the types of handicrafts ensure employment to a large number of handicraftsmen and women.

Through these handicrafts, the tourists learn about the cultural heritage of the country. For example, when a tourist buys a statue of Natraj, the concept of Hindu religion somewhat becomes apparent to him. For the tourists, these handicrafts revive treasured memories of the tour which had been undertaken.

For the preparation of this book, I have received tremendous help from wife, Mrs. Anita Dua and childhood friend, Lala Bhagwan Dass Goel. I am grateful to them.

Dr. J. C. Dua
278, Kadambri Apparments
Sector–9, Rohini, Delhi-110085

CHAPTER-1

Introduction

Since time immemorial, Indian handicrafts have been popular throughout the world. India craft tours take you on an online tour to acquaint you with the forms of handicraft artifacts available in India.

The first reference to Indian handicrafts can be found from the Indus Valley Civilization. Works of art always portray the customs, traditions and beliefs of the people of that era. Being a work of art, crafts also exhibit religious beliefs and lifestyle of people.

Modern handicrafts evolved after much alteration in the traditional styles. The invasions during ancient periods led to cultural exchanges that in turn flourished the Indian art and architecture. The artisans and craftsmen warmly received new ideas of Persian and Arabic styles.

Indus Valley Civilization showed a remarkable artistic skill and technical excellence in pottery, jewellery, sculpture making and weaving, etc. The designs on the articles represented the activities going around at that time, for instance, discovery of trade routes and dances etc.

The influence of the Central Asian culture on Indian craftsmanship is reflected in the sculpture of the Kushan king Kanishka. The sculpture depicts him wearing leather boots and a heavy warm coat. The foreign influences equipped the Indians with the art of making jewellery, sculpture, textile making, leather products, metal working, etc.

Embroidery Work in India is carried out in Punjab, Uttar Pradesh, West Bengal and many other regions. Buttonhole or blanket stitch, running stitch, cross stitch, satin stitch and chain stitch are some of basic techniques of stitching used in Indian embroidery. It has also given way to machine stitching with the advent of the industrial era. There are diverse varieties of Indian embroidery.

Embroidery can be used in diversified manner according to the design that is stitched on top of or through the foundation fabric, and also by the relationship of stitch placement to the fabric. 'Mirror work', 'zari' work of Hyderabad, 'Gota' work of Rajasthan, 'zardozi' of Delhi, 'phulkari' of Punjab, 'chamba rumals', 'kasuti embroidery' of Karnataka, 'chikan embroidery', 'kantha embroidery' of West Bengal, etc are some of the significant classifications of Indian embroidery. In case of free embroidery, one applies the designs without paying much importance to the weave of the underlying fabric.

Moreover, another classification of Indian embroidery is the cross-stitch counted-thread embroidery. This particular type is basically used in foundation fabric. This type of embroidery can be more easily worked on a smooth weave foundation fabric including embroidery especially woven on cotton canvas, linen fabrics.

The embroidery on wool of Cashmere on loom-wrought along with the needle is universally famous. The cashmere shawl trade is an old art. The cone pattern, with its flowing curves and minute diaper of flowers characterise these shawls.

The ornamentation of the shawls is distinguished by different names. The border is disposed along the whole length and it may be single, double or triple. Pala means the whole of the embroidery at the two ends, or at the heads of the shawl. The chain runs above and below the principal mass of the pala.

The dhour is situated on the inside of the hashia and zangir. Mattan is the decorated part of the ground and the butha is the generic term for flowers specifically applied alone to the cone ornament. When there is a double row, the butha is called dokad, and as tukadar when above five.

Muslin is embroidered at Patna and Delhi in coloured floss silk. Rich embroidery is also seen at Hyderabad in coloured silk thread and gold and silver. The embroidery of Nauanagar, and Gondal in Kathiwar is in coloured silk thread. Gold is also used in embroidery which is a Persian style. The embroidered native apparel of Cashmere, Amritsar, Lahore, Delhi, Lucknow, Murshidabad, Surat and Mumbai, is prized all over India; and that of Vishakapatnam has an extensive reputation in the south. Carpets originated in embroidery and they were first used like embroideries for hangings and palls.

In many parts of India, muslin is beautifully embroidered with green beetle wings and gold. The embroidered leather work of Gujarat is well known.

Chikan embroidery of Lucknow is very popular; chikankari is now being done on various fabrics and are available in various colours too. Phulkari, an embroidery technique of Punjab is flower working on shawls and head scarfs.

Applique work is seen in Orissa and Gujarat. It is basically a patch work in which coloured pieces are cut and sewn on a plain cloth. Embroidery of Kutch known as

Aribharat is very attractive. Embroidery of Lambada tribes of Andhra Pradesh is worth mentioning here. It is done on fine cotton or polyester. Kantha stitch is practiced in Bihar and West Bengal. Here, the threads are picked from old materials.

The materials used in Indian embroidery like the fabrics and yarns vary from one place to another. Silk, wool and linen have been predominantly used for thousands of years for both fabric and yarn. In the recent times, the thread used in traditional embroidery is manufactured in rayon, cotton, as well as traditional wool, silk and linen. In the techniques of canvas work, huge quantities of thread are buried on the back of the work to use more materials but provide a sturdier and more substantial finished textile. Further, in surface as well as canvas work techniques, an embroidery frame is generally used for stretching the material as it ensures avoidance of any sort of pattern distortion.

Mughal period is also called the Golden Period of Art and Architecture. Mughals endowed India with a rich legacy of architectural and artistic heritage. The new occupations added during this era were glass engraving, carpet weaving, inlay work, brocades and enameling, etc.There's something undoubtedly magical about Indian handicrafts. Unique, intricate, eye catching and expressive, each item has a story behind it. It's impossible to come to India and return home empty handed.

Handicrafts of India broadly include:

Ceramics

Phulkari

India Painting Styles

Carpet Weaving

Handloom Textile Weaving

Tie-and-Dye

Papier Mache

Ornaments

The First International Conference on Tourism and Handicrafts was held from 13-15 of May 2006 in the seminar hall of Iranian National Broadcast in Tehran. This conference was organized by the United Nations World Tourism Organization (UNWTO) and Iran's Cultural Heritage and Tourism Organization (ICHTO) in order to discuss the role of handicrafts in promoting tourism industry which would result in job creation and earning more currency through attracting more tourists.

Nowadays, Indian handicrafts belong to the group of better-designed, high-quality products the country has to offer. Tourists who visit India take them back as souvenirs.

Just as there is a huge geographical diversity, from Kashmir to Kanyakumari and from North-Eastern states to Punjab and all the regions in between, there is a great variety of artisan products that make India stand out in the world. Our artisans exhibit the enormous creativity, imagination, ingenuity, and talent that characterize us.

In India, there are ornaments for almost all parts of human body. Some of these are worn regularly while others are worn at specific occasions. Some ornaments are woven for rituals and others for ceremonial purposes. For the ritual and ceremonial ornaments, even material is specified. The use of ornaments by women is universal but in many communities men also wear them. Let us give you a brief account of various types of ornaments worn on different parts of human body.

Ornaments used for the head are of three types. The first is what was called turban jewels. These were not in common use and were used mainly by royalty and chiefs on their turbans. These are called jigha or sarpati. Other two head ornaments are used by women. Of these one is for the forehead (tika). They come in various forms and shapes. The other one is for hair. This also comes in various shapes and sizes. In some regions, they are worn regularly while in some others, the head ornaments are worn only on ceremonial occasions like marriage.

Ornaments for ear and neck are most common. The ear ornaments are of various types. The most common are small tops and the dropping types with special bands or strings to support the weight. These are generally worn in earlobes, but in many regions and communities, a number of big and small ear ornaments are worn together.

Nose is the other part of body which is popularly used for wearing ornament. Small nose studs and a circular big ring (nath) are two common types. The different regions have variations in shapes and sizes. The large ring-type ornament is generally worn on the occasion of marriage and other ceremonies. In many communities, only married women are supposed to wear nose ornament.

Neck is adorned with a variety of ornaments. The most common ornament called necklace is the one that hangs in the neck through a gold chain or a thick thread. Another variety is the chocker (guluband) which fits tightly around the neck. The third variety is the pendant which can be put in any chain, string of beads or plain string. In the south, the necklace worn for marriage is called wall. Wearing of gold chain without any pendant is also quite popular. These chains are made in various designs. One specific neck ornament called mangalsutra is worn only by married women among Hindus. It is considered auspicious and great significance is attached to it. It is made with black and gold beads.

Ornaments for hands can be divided into three categories—fingers, wrists and lower arms & upper arms.

Armlets or bazubands are worn in the upper arm. These are mainly of two types, the one that is tied with strings and the other which fit around the arm with a locking mechanism. The ornaments for lower arms are bracelet, wristlets and bangles. The first two fit to the arm while the bangles are loose. The bangles are of two varieties thin (churhi) and thick (kada). The rings also have a large variety. There are separate rings for thumb and different fingers of hand. These are made as simple circular rings or with floral pattern on top or with stones fixed on top. Besides adorning the hand, these are worn for therapeutic or magical or ritualistic purposes or for warding of evil influences of planets. In a large number of communities, the rings are exchanged between man and woman on the occasion of marriage.

In a large number of communities, a thick waist ornament is worn. It is called kardhani (kamardhani). Generally, married women wear it.

The ornaments for the leg are of two types—the anklets and toe rings. Anklets come in various shapes. Some cling to the ankles while others are loose like bangles.

There is a specific type called payal which is worn around ankles by women and makes a musical sound when women move around. The toe rings are worn in the fingers of feet. In most of the communities, these are traditionally worn by married women only.

The basis of these products is the large amount of easily accessible natural materials offered by the land. Handicrafts are the maximum representation of India's idiosyncrasy and one of its better cultural expressions.

History of textiles in India is, perhaps, as old as Indian civilization. The earliest example of cotton fabric comes from Harappan excavations (c. 2500 B.C.). Rig Veda (c.1500-1000 B.C) refers to golden woven fabric hiranyadrapi. Greek records are also full of references on gorgeous paithani fabric from Paithan—the ancient Pratishthan. The author of the Periplus of the Erythrean Sea (A.D. 60-100) mentions the presence of Indian dyed cotton in Rome. Kautilya refers to the superintendents (adhyakshas) of weaving during the Mauryan period (c.300 B.C.).

Bengal was the chief centre of fine cotton production. Dacca Muslin in 16th-17th centuries is said to be the best cotton textile made in India. Gujarat was another centre of cotton production.

With the coming of the Turks and Mughals, many new features were introduced in the field of textile production with the fusion of new culture and new technology. They exposed Indian craftsman to spinning wheel. Earlier women used to spin the yarn with single spindle (takali). Many new varieties of cloth were also introduced during this period. Fine quality velvets belong to the Mughal period. Mashru and himroo, a mixed fabric also appears to be the contribution of Muslim weavers. Kalamkari of Golconda has a very strong Persian influence. The rich weaving tradition of Kashmiri shawls with its twill-tapestry weaving seems to have been introduced in India by the Central Asian weavers.

Carpet weaving also reached new heights under the Mughals.

Similarly, tanchoi was introduced in Surat by three Parsi brothers who brought the art from China.

Nagaland, Manipur, Tripura, Mizoram and Arunachal Pradesh are the most important centres for back strap weaving. Since the body is used for creating the tension, weaving is quite strenuous. Besides, cloth's width is also highly restricted (it can not go beyond 50-60 cm) on account of the fact that the warp is attached to the body. That's why you will find Mishimies' woven jackets are prepared by putting two pieces together; Lotha Naga shawl is woven in nine parts.

The arts and crafts of a nation reveal its culture and heritage and India is one such nation which is quite affluent in awe-inspiring works of craft. Almost all the Indian states have their own ethnic craft traditions and most of them have been passed from generation to generation as legacies. The ingenuity of the craftsmen has lent an unending appeal to the various craftworks and craft in India is valued by tourists frequenting this country.

Orissa is one such state that has kept its age-old tradition and culture alive by their inimitable craftworks and some of the tribes such as Kondhs, Koyas, Bondas, Santals, Gadabas, Juangas, are known for their fine craft works. Every tribe is known for its unique art forms that range from weaving of handloom, saris, basket, stone carving, painting, metal work are popular the world over. The stone carving on the walls of the Jagannath, Konark and the Lingaraja temples reveal the superiority of the artists. Each stone has been brought to life with the endeavor and art of the artists.

Every region and every craft have their workmen. They are known by their names of their crafts in different regions carrying different names. Jewellers, potters, ivory makers, perfumers, glodsmiths, weavers, carpenters, braziers, panters, blacksmiths, agricultural instrument makers, coppersmiths, glass makers, cutters of crystals, inlayers, stone cutters, embroiderers, paper makers, lace workers, bamboo workers so on and so forth. The list is endless. Babar in 1526 was amazed to see large range of workmen in India.

Many a time, a number of specialised artisans are involved in a single trade. Weaving for example has different artisans for almost all stages of cloth making, cotton carders, yarn makers, weavers, dyers and bleachers, printers, etc.

The craftsmen carried different names in different regions. The ironsmith in North India is lohar; in Bengal he is called kamaker or kamars, while metalsmith in the South is kammalar. The metalsmith in Ladakh is sergar. Bharatias do casting of metals in U.P., while thateras work with brass in Moradabad (U.P); in Gujarat kansaras are metalsmiths; the icon-makers in Tamil Nadu are called Sthapati.

The artisans and craftsmen mostly work with simple tools and implements. The organisation of production is mainly individual and family based. Most of the times, the whole family is involved in the craft. Children also start working at early age and learn the craft. Because of this, most of the crafts run in the same family generation after generation. In many cases, the commodities produced are also marketed by individual craftsmen. In some cases, they sell their produce to some traders who market these for earning high margins. The craftsmen work with small capitals, therefore, they are at times dependent on the traders. Now, government and some non-governmental organisations have taken initiative in helping craftsmen to form their cooperatives. These cooperatives help them with capital and also market the end product. A number of establishments have also been created to help craftsmen to directly market their art work thus eliminating the middlemen.

Traditionally, the artisans and craftsmen are assigned a lower place in social heirarchy in almost all regions across different religions. In earlier times, there were rigid caste structures with restrictions on practicing particular crafts by people of particular regions. These restrictions are no more there but still some sort of caste basis of artisanal crafts continues. Another significant feature is large scale participation of women in different crafts.

Crafts tourism in India has gained immense popularity and is quite valued by not only the domestic but also the foreign travelers from all parts of the world. As far as handicraft tours of India are concerned, Orissa occupies a prominent place among all the other states of India and its craftsmen are specialized in the production of exquisite hand-made trousseau sarees. The craft in India is incomplete without a mention of earliest traditional weaving villages of Orissa and Nuapatna.

Apart from Orissa, the craft show in Rajasthan is also very popular and is valued by the tourists who are the true appreciators of craft works. The handicraft shops in Rajasthan are huge in number and house a large number of incredible craft items such as antiques, pottery items, durries and carpets, fabrics, furniture and wood carving items, gesso works, jewellery and gemstones, leatherware, metal crafts, paintings, puppets, stone carvings. Moreover, the paintings and the hand-made royal furnishings found in the royal mansions and also in the shops are quite famous.

The level of excellence and intricacy depicted through the various craft works is simply unparalleled and catches the attention of the most discerning aesthete. Craft in India is surely going to bring in something special for the tourists and they can surely take back some of the best craft works as souvenirs after their tour to India.

Today, modern India is filled with diversity of dresses. Rajput women wear voluminous ghagara, brief choli and orhna; the tight pyjamas and long kurta is worn by U.P. Muslim women while salwar and kameez by Punjabi women. But, saree is the traditional and most common of the Indian dress worn by a peasant woman to a most modern urban lady almost all parts of India. Maharashtra women wear nine gaz saree while sarees of South India varies from seven to ten yards in length. In the North, saree varies from 5 to 6 yards. Generally in Maharashtra and South India (except Kerala) women draw pleats to the rear through the legs. The Bengali women displays the decorative crosswise border, half in front and half on the hip. In North India and Gujarat, the border shows wholly on the front. The front pleats are tucked into the peticot. The Santhal women of Bihar wear six yard saree and worn to fall just below the knee. The saree does not go over the head and part of the right breast is exposed.

Generally speaking, brides wear red colour saree, preferably Banarasi. Nowadays, ghaghara is also in fashion and urban girls like to wear richly adorned ghaghra and odhna. But Punjabi brides wear bright colour richly embroidered salwar-kameez with embroidered odhna. Similarly, Muslim bride also prefers salwar-kameez-odhna, garara, and sharara.

Kashmiri women wear salwar and long tunic (pheran). A sleeveless jacket of embroidered velvet of a dark shade is occasionally used over the pheran. A scarf similar to the odhna completes their outfit. Women generally tuck their scarf into the cap. A skull cap with tiny embroidery is the typical head-dress. Dresses of both Muslim and Hindu brides are the same, but the head-dress shows a slight difference. The Hindu bridal cap (tarauga) is more decorative than the Muslim LAP (kasaba). The long pheran and salwar used in Kashmir are also popular in Himachal Pradesh.

Tribal people have their own distinctive costumes. The Assam woman still wears her traditional mekhla or sarong and chador. The mekhla is a straight cut skirt worn around the wrist reaching to the ankles. The lower half of the skirt is richly embroidered. The chador is embroidered and of a lenght of three yards. It is worn by unmarried women. After marriage the bride has an additional piece for the middle part—the riha, which is just a scarf wrapped around the waist.

Not only exports, handicrafts in India are a major attraction for tourists. All Indian states have their unique native skills that result in creation of exotic crafts. The traveller comes across works of art and crafts all over his route.

For instance, those on tours to Kerala or Rajasthan states are likely to discover and be impressed by Indian handicrafts since these are popular destinations. In popular tourists states, an infrastructure has been laid down in bringing forth all elements of tourist attractions.

But as rest of India opens up to tourism, more and more states are gearing up to display and promote the local talent which produces unique works of arts—be it jewellery, wooden statues, brass works and designer dresses. Those on travel to India must read and know beforehand about the craftsmanship popular in the parts of India they are visiting.

Of late, tour operators offering package tour to Kerala and Rajastahan include visit to handicraft fairs or villages in these states which produces handicrafts unique in nature. Other travel agents are following in their footsteps.

The government has taken a lot of steps forward to encourage exports and exposure on crafts from India. EPCH has been set up for this very purpose.

EPCH full form Export Promotion Council for Handicrafts under Development Commissioner of Handicrafts, Textile Ministry, GOI was set up under EXIM policy in year 1986-87. It helps create infrastructure and encourages marketing by offering information to member exporters and importers.

It offers professional advice in areas of technology up gradation, quality and designing in improving standards and specifications, development of products and encourages creativity.

- EPCH organizes visits of members to foreign countries to explore overseas marketing potential.

- Participating in International Trade Fairs of Handicrafts & Gift.
- Organizes Indian handicrafts and gifts fairs.
- Acts as intermediately between exporters and Govt. at Central and State level. It represents all the committees/ panels of the Central govt.
- EPCH creates awareness through workshops on "Export Marketing, Procedures and Documentation", Packaging, Design Developments, Buyer Seller Meets, Open House and other such programs.
- EPCH disseminates notification, orders, information on trades, etc. issued by GOI.

The deeply entrenched tradition of Indian craft echoes the true colour of India whilst impressing generation after generation amidst their varied forms and styles. For people around the world, India is synonymous to exotic arts and handicraft traditions.

A wide range of traditional Indian handicraft reflects the richness of Indian ethnic art and culture. The designs and finishes represent the excellent artistic skills of the craftsmen. Traditional Indian art is inspired by a variety of functions, which can be meaningfully understood only through a comprehensive study of the social, cultural and religious contexts of Indian arts and handicrafts.

The history of Indian crafts comes from one of the established civilizations of the globe while going back to almost 5000 years from present. The primal references of Indian crafts were found in the remnants of Indus Valley Civilization (3000 B.C.-1700 B.C.).

Beginning its journey in the age old days, the craft tradition in India has witnessed enough alteration. Prehistorically, Indian handicrafts were basically made for day-after-day use, the yearning for aesthetic application soon saw development of flooding designs and motifs. The incalculable artistic and ethnic assortment has enabled a fusion of motifs, techniques and crafts to increase on this land.

The tradition of Indian craft has whirled around religious values, confined needs of the commoners, as well as the special needs of the clientele and royalty, along with an eye for overseas and home trade.

Each state of India has its own tradition and legacy of handicrafts. Whether the fragile beauty of the Phulkari art of the North India or the dizzying artistry of the silver filigree work, famous in the eastern India, whether the colossal impact of the stone craft of South India or the artistry of the bidriware of the western India—all demonstrates the elegance and brilliance of Indian craft. From pottery, metal craft, woodcraft, stone works, gems and jewellery, textiles, leatherwork to mesmerizing paintings and awe-inspiring sculptures and statues—India has perfected almost all the arts and handicrafts known to humanity.

The types of Indian crafts are varied each standing as the logo of the rich Indian heritage. It is amidst the myriad tradition of Indian craft, the varied traits and the true character of India can be ideated. Be it the sheer brilliance of the brocades of Varanasi or the warmth of the Kullu shawls of Himachal; be it the elegance of the namdhas of Kashmir or the artistry of the meenakari and kundan works, the charm and originality of each Indian craft reverberates the heritage of India, unswayed by time.

Indian crafts amidst their elegance, brilliance and originality thus symbolizes the very essence of Indianness whilst reflecting its rich heritage in its past and present.

Every tourist place is having some unique items of art and handicraft associated with, however the potential of amalgamation of the tourism and handicraft has not yet been understood, explored & developed in manner it should have been. The craft has the ability to create jobs, socio-economic opportunities, and enhanced quality of life in local communities; this gives an added recognition to the tourist spot as well.

The main objectives of this book are: Recognizing the importance of local handicrafts in tourism development and reciprocally the importance of tourism as an agent for the protection and preservation of traditional crafts, methods of production and cultural context; examining tourism related handicrafts; production technologies and design aspects and optimizing the sale of handicrafts among tourists and the tourism industry.

Visit India and discover the unbelievable assortment of handcrafted articles that this country proposes to the world. India Tourism enhances your knowledge regarding India Crafts.

CHAPTER-2

Tourism and India

India has fascinated people from all over the world with her secularism and her culture. It is endowed with historical monuments, beaches, places of religious interests, hill resorts, etc. that attract tourists. Every region is identified with its handicrafts, fairs, folk dances, music and its people.

The Departments of Tourism promote international and domestic tourism in the country. The Tourism Advisory Board recommends measures for promotion of tourist traffic in India. Indian tourism is adversely affected by terrorism, tours and pollution. Sincere efforts could help to further develop the Indian tourism industry.

Tourism is one of the fastest growing industries of the world. It plays vital role in the economic development of a country. India is one of the popular tourist destinations in Asia.

Bounded by the Himalayan ranges in the north, and surrounded on three sides by water (namely, Arabian Sea, the Bay of Bengal and the Indian Ocean), India offers a wide array of places to see and things to do. The enchanting backwaters, hill stations and landscapes make India a beautiful country. Historical monuments, forts, etc. add to the grandeur of the country. They attract tourists from all over the world.

Tourism is the second largest foreign exchange earner in India. The tourism industry here employs a large number of people, both skilled and unskilled.

Hotels, travel agencies, transport, including airlines, benefit a lot from this industry. Apart from this, tourism promotes national integration and international understanding. It promotes cultural activities and also traditional handicrafts sector. The tourists get an insight into the rich and diverse cultural heritage of India.

India has a composite culture. There is a harmonious blend of art, religion and philosophy here. Though, India has been subjected to a serious of invasions in the past, yet she has retained her originality even after absorbing the best of external influences.

Religions like Christianity, Buddhism, Islam, Hinduism, Jainism, Sikhism, Zoroastrianism and others have co-existed in India since long. Her culture and adherence to secularism have been appreciated the world over.

The diverse geographical locales of India delight the tourists. The monuments, museums, forts, sanctuaries, places of religious interest, palaces, etc. offer a treat to the eyes. Every region is identified with its handicrafts, fairs, folk dances, music and its people.

Some of the places that attract a huge number of tourists are Agra, Jaipur, Jhansi, Hyderabad, Nalanda, Mysore, Delhi, Mahabaleshwar, Aurangabad, etc. Hardwar, Ujjain, Shirdi, Varanasi, Allahabad, Puri, Ajmer, Amritsar, Vaishno Devi, Badrinath, Kedarnath, Rameshwaram, and the like, are places of religious importance. While Srinagar, Kullu, Manali, Dehradun, Nainital, Darjeeling, Ooty and many others serve as famous hill resorts.

The Department of Tourism was formed to promote international and domestic tourism in the country. It provides infrastructure and carries out publicity campaigns. It provides information aimed at promotion of tourist sites in the world market. It formulates policies and programmes for the promotion of tourism in India. It has its employees both in India and abroad. Organisations such as the Indian Institute of Tourism and Travel Management, The National Council for Hotel Management and Catering Technology, and many others provide professionally trained personnel to the industry. The Tourism Advisory Board recommends measures for promotion of tourist traffic in India. It reviews the tourist trends and suggests appropriate measures. Some of the palaces, *havelis* and castles have been converted into heritage hotels. In these hotels, the tourists get the experience of the exotic lifestyle of the bygone era. The exotic train 'palace on wheels', which travels through Rajasthan, attracts a lot of foreign tourists. The Indian Tourism Development Corporation (ITDC) organizes entertainment programmes like folk dances and songs and even provides shopping facilities to the tourists. Today, many private companies, like Sita Travels, Club Mahindra, etc. arrange domestic as well as foreign tours.

With the growth of urban professional middle class, the tourism in India began flourishing. Many states have taken necessary steps to promote tourism. Goa promotes water sports like sailing, scuba diving and rafting. Kashmir offers the pleasure of winter sports like skiing and mountaineering. Kerala has introduced the concept of houseboats in its lagoons. Himachal Pradesh has developed winter sports in the state.

In 2005, The Indian Tourism Development Corporation (ITDC) stared a campaign called 'Incredible India' to encourage tourism in India. For better growth, the organisation divided different places in different sections like 'spiritual tourism,' 'spa tourism', 'ecotourism' and 'adventure tourism'. Things have now started looking bright for the Indian tourism industry.

However, Indian tourism industry has been hit by pollution. The effluents emitted by the Mathura Refinery has led to the decolorization of the Taj Mahal in Agra. The condition of many of our monuments is deteriorating due to the negligence of the concerned authorities. On the other hand, beaches have become dumping grounds of garbage and waste left by tourists. This nuisance should be properly redressed. Terrorism, nowadays, has become a global problem. Our country is also not an exception. The terrorism in Jammu and Kashmir, Maoists attacks in West Bengal and Bihar, Bodo agitations in north-eastern hill areas greatly affect the tourism in our country. Kashmir is the paradise for domestic and international tourists. The terrorism in this valley not only affects the life of the common people but also the tourism, which is very important for the economy of this state. Necessary steps should be taken by the state government as well as central government to prevent this menace.

The tourist infrastructure in India should be strengthened. Airports and railway stations should provide information to the tourists about the tourist destinations. Government-owned hotels should be properly managed. The Government should also take steps for the maintenance of tourist destinations. Steps should be taken to restore the ancient splendor of the monuments. Sincere efforts could help to further develop the Indian tourism industry.

It will not be an exaggeration to state that India has the right tourism potential and that is what makes it attract all types of tourists from all over the world. The Foreign Tourist Arrivals (FTAs) in India during 2010 were 5.58 million with a growth rate of 9.3 percent as compared to the

FTAs of 5.11 million and growth rate of minus 3.3 percent during 2009. The 9.3 per cent growth rate in FTAs for 2010 is much better than UNWTO's projected growth rate of five to six per cent for the world during the same period. Foreign Exchange Earnings (FEE) from tourism during 2010 were USD 14,193 million as compared to USD 11,394 million during 2009 and USD 11,747 million during 2008. The growth rate in FEE in USD terms during 2010 was 24.6 per cent as compared to a decline of three per cent in 2009 over 2008 with this year being even more promising. Foreign Tourist Arrivals (FTAs) during the month of January 2011 was 538,000 as compared to FTAs of 491,000 during the month of January 2010 and 422,000 in January 2009. There has been a growth of 9.7 % in January 2011 over January 2010. The trend of significant positive growth in FTAs observed during the year 2010 continued in January, 2011. Without a tad of doubt, it can be said that Indian tourism is growing in leaps and bounds. With Government of India's pro-tourism policies, there is strong growth and development expected in the near future. One of the major contributors to this significant rise is India's adherence to the principle of 'Unity in Diversity'.

Despite the global economic downturn, medical tourism in India has emerged as the fastest growing segment of tourism industry. High cost of treatments in the developed countries, particularly in the USA and the UK, has been forcing patients from such regions to look for alternative cost-effective destinations to get their treatments done. Indian medical tourism industry is presently at a nascent stage, but has an enormous potential for future growth and development.

According to the new market research report, "Booming Medical Tourism in India" of RNCOS, India's share in the global medical tourism industry will reach around 3% by the end of 2013. Moreover, medical tourism is expected to generate revenue worth US$ 3 billion by 2013, growing at a CAGR of around 26% during 2011–2013. The number of medical tourists is anticipated to grow at a CAGR of over 19% during the forecast period to reach 1.3 million by 2013.

Medical Tourism

Today India is emerging as a favored place of medical treatment. Our country has witnessed a remarkable growth in the service by hospitals and well-qualified doctors which has not only attracted the patient population from neighbouring counties but also from the Middle East and the West. As the concept of medical tourism continues to gain momentum in India, the Ministry of Health and Family Welfare, with the help of the Ministry of Tourism, is taking numerous initiatives in order to maintain international standards in medical facilities. With some of the best hospitals in the world, Delhi is competing with foreign countries. Even there are countries where critical patients may have to wait for months. But in Delhi, any kind of treatment is available in the shortest possible time. The cost of treatment is substantially less than those in developed countries. Besides personalized nursing care, Delhi is superb place to rejuvenate. Our country also integrates traditional medical concepts of Ayurveda, Unani and Homeopathy with complementary therapies like Yoga, Acupuncture and Aroma so as to progress the process of healing. Tour operators are now offering attractive packages in collaboration with city hospitals for a perfect health vacation. Thus, the land of nirvana has also become a favored place for medical treatment.

India represents the most potential medical tourism market in the world. Factors such as, low cost, scale and range of treatments provided by India make it preferable to other medical tourism destinations. Moreover, growth in India's medical tourism market will be a boon for several associated industries, including hospital industry, medical equipments industry, and pharmaceuticals industry.

In addition to the existence of modern medicine, indigenous or traditional medical practitioners are providing their services across the country. There are almost 3,400 hospitals and around 755,000 registered practitioners catering to the needs of traditional Indian healthcare. Indian hotels are also entering the wellness services market by collaborating with professional organizations in a range of wellness fields including offering spas and ayurvedic massages.

A day long workshop on "Promotion of Golf Tourism" was organised by the Ministry of Tourism, Government of India sometime back. The Ministry of Tourism aims to create a comprehensive and coordinated framework for promoting golf tourism in India, capitalising on the existing work that is being carried out, and building upon the strength of India's position as the fastest growing free market economy. India has several golf courses of international standards. Further, golf events held in India also attract domestic and international tourists. With international tourists expected to grow in the next few years, it is important that India has the right product and facilities to meet the needs of the visitors.

Recognising this potential to develop Golf as a niche tourism product for attracting both international and domestic tourists, the objective of the aforesaid workshop was to evolve a road map for formulating strategies for development and promotion of golf tourism in India. During the workshop, four working groups comprising golf clubs, corporates, travel trade representatives, professional golfers and golf event managers discussed and came out with suggestions which will guide the Ministry of Tourism in its future course of action to position India as a leading golf destination in the region. The four major broad subjects discussed in the workshop include:

- strategy for marketing and promotion of international golf tourism,
- strategy for marketing and promotion of domestic golf tourism,
- identification and improvement of golf infrastructure, and
- linkages with hotels, travel trade, MICE segment, etc.

Inaugurating the workshop, the Minister of Culture & Housing & Urban Poverty Alleviation (HUPA), Kumari Selja lauded the Ministry of Tourism's efforts to position India as a year round destination. She remarked "it is our priority to develop multiple tourism products to attract all segments of tourists round the year. This will enable us to break the October to March syndrome that affects India Tourism particularly in the case of foreign tourist arrivals". Shri, R.H Khawja, Union Tourism Secretary, outlined the important initiatives and achievements of the Ministry, including development and promotion of niche tourism products to bring in a variety of such products to attract all segments of the tourism market. Rao Inderjit Singh, Member of Parliament, was the guest of honour at the inaugural session.

Based on the recommendations of this workshop, the Ministry of Tourism would look at a mechanism of supporting international & domestic golf events, professional events, golf shows, training for caddies, production of publicity materials, etc.

Important Steps being taken by the Government of India

Recognizing that tourism plays a vital role in the economic development of a country; tourism is the second largest foreign exchange earner in India; the tourism industry employs a large number of people, both skilled and unskilled and it promotes national integration and international brotherhood, some of the steps taken by the government of India in the under mentioned fields are as follows:

•*Hotel Management and Food Craft Institutes*

The Ministry of Tourism has accorded high priority to the development of manpower to meet the growing needs of Hotels, Restaurants and other Hospitality-based Industries. For this purpose, 21 Institutes of Hotel Management and Catering Technology and 10 Food Craft Institutes (3 of these are now also State IHMS) have been set up in the country. In addition to the above, four more Institutes of Hotel Management are in pipeline at Uttarakhand (Dehradun), Jharkhand (Jamshedpur), Chhattisgarh (Raipur) and Haryana (Kurukshetra).

These Institutes conduct Degree courses in the fields of Hotel Management, Catering Technology and Applied Nutrition and Craft Courses in Food and Beverage Services, Accommodation Operations, Dietetics and Hospital Food Service, Food Production and Patisserie, House Keeping, Front Office, etc. IHM's Mumbai, Bangalore and New Delhi Institutes have started 2 years M.Sc Hospitality courses also.

Food Craft Institutes conduct Craft Courses for duration ranging from six months to one year for operational staff. All these training Institutes are affiliated to the National Council for Hotel Management and Catering Technology and Applied Nutrition (NCHMCT) at apex level which regulates academics for all these Institutes.

•*Capacity Building for Service Providers (CBSP)*

In the year 2002, the Ministry launched a programme called CBSP to train the persons engaged in small hotels, *dhabas*, eating joints, restaurants, etc., and also handling tourists like Immigration staff, airport staff, security/Police personnel, guides, taxi operators, bus drivers, etc. The objective was to provide short-term training to improve their etiquette, behaviour and attitude towards tourists.

The scope of this scheme has been further enlarged and training programmes of 3/6 months duration have been added for skill development of existing as well as fresh service providers. Under this scheme, a new programme called 'Project Priyadarshini' was also launched in 2005 aimed at imparting training to women in taxi driving/operation, entrepreneurship like setting up souvenir kiosks, etc, to adopt tourism as their profession.

• *Hotel Accommodation*

The hotel sector forms one of the most important segments of the tourism industry with high potential for employment generation and foreign exchange earnings. To give impetus to this sector, the government provides concessions under EXIM Policy and other incentives. The Industrial Policy has now placed hotels and tourism-related activities as a priority industry. Foreign investment and collaborations are now facilitated under the new economic policy. Automatic approval is available for foreign direct investment upto 100 per cent in hotel and tourism sector.

• *Travel Trade*

The Department of Tourism has a scheme of approving Travel Agents, Tour Operators, Adventure Tour Operators and Tourist Transport Operators. During 2005, keeping in view the spurt in domestic tourism, a new category for the recognition of domestic tour operators has been introduced. The aims and objectives of this scheme are to encourage quality, standard and service in these categories so as to promote tourism in India. The Travel Trade Division also interacts with the travel trade associations like Travel Agents

Association of India (TAAI), Indian Association of Tour Operators (IATO), Indian Tourist Transport Operators Associations (ITTA), etc., and other agencies like India Convention Promotion Bureau, Pacific Asia Travel Association (PATA), etc.

The Travel Trade Division also deals with all matters pertaining to the regulation and training of tourist guides at regional level and also co-ordinates with other Ministries such as Civil Aviation, Culture, Railways, Surface Transport, External Affairs and Home Affairs on various issues to improve the facilities for the tourists visiting various destinations in India.

•*Celebration of Various Tourism Events*

A number of events and roadshows have been organised during 2005-06 for spreading awareness about India tourism in domestic and international tourism markets to attract more tourists to India. The major events organised by the Ministry of Tourism in collaboration with various State Tourism Departments are: Golf open tournament, Srinagar; Sindhu Darshan at Leh; Heritage Festival, New Delhi; All India Crafts Mela, Hyderabad; Heritage International Festival, Jaipur; India International Boat Show, Kochi; Paragliding Show and Tourism Conclave in Himachal Pradesh; Mega Folk Festival "Virasat" in Dehradun; Prithivi 05-Global Eco-Meet, Kochi; Domestic and International Photo Exhibition "A Confluence of Cultures" and Essay and Photographic competition on "What Tourism Means To Me" on World Tourism Day on 27th September (every year); India National Tourism Day on 17th March 2006; Designer's Night Bazar, Surajkund Crafts Mela, Haryana; 3 Global Interline Golf Championships, Photo Exhibition, Eco-Tourism Marketing Meet; Mussorie (Uttarakhand), WTTC, Himalayan Run and Trek and Photo Exhibition on Hindu, Buddhist and Islamic monuments of Kashmir.

The Ministry of Tourism also participated in various travel and tourism events, trade fairs and exhibitions in India and abroad. The important fairs and exhibitions are Tourism Travel Fair in New Delhi, Mumbai, Bangaluru, Chennai and SATTE (South Asia Tourism and Travel Expo), New Delhi. India Tourism offices located in 20 cities in India also participated at local important fairs.

The Ministry of Tourism participated in several overseas travel and tourism trade fairs, notably World Travel Market, London; ITB (International Tourism Bourse), Berlin; Arabian Travel Market (ATM), Dubai; EIBTM, Spain; IMEX, Frankfurt; Pata Travel Mart, Malaysia; FITUR, Spain; and World Travel Fair, Shanghai. India Tourism offices located in 13 overseas cities also participated in various travel and tourism fairs.

•*National Tourism Policy, 2002*

A National Tourism Policy, 2002 was announced by the Government with, *inter alia,* attempts to position India as a global brand to take advantage of the burgeoning global travel and trade and the vast untapped potential of India as a destination.

•*Tourism in 10th Five Year Plan*

In order to further accelerate the development of tourism in the country, the thrust during the 10th Five Year Plan has been to:

- Position tourism as a major engine of economic growth;
- Harness the direct and multiplier effects of tourism for employment generation and economic development;
- Provide impetus to rural tourism;
- Provide major thrust to domestic tourism which will act as a spring board for growth and expansion of international tourism;

- Position India as a global brand to take advantage of the burgeoning global travel and trade and the vast untapped potential of India as a destination;
- Acknowledge the critical role of private sector with government working as an active facilitator and catalyst;
- Create and develop integrated tourism circuits based on India's unique civilisation, heritage and culture in partnership with states, private sector and other agencies;
- Ensure that the tourist to India gets physically invigorated, mentally rejuvenated, culturally enriched, spiritually elevated and "feels India within him".

The Pacific Asia Travel Association (PATA) has recently announced the winners of the 2011 PATA Gold Awards. These awards have long been supported and sponsored by the Macau Government Tourist Office. This year, the awards recognised the achievements of 21 separate organisations and individuals. Therefore, the year 2011 sees 26 PATA Grand and Gold Awards presented, with multiple awards going to Kerala Tourism as well as the Ministry of Tourism, Government of India.

The awards ceremony took place on Monday, April 11, 2011 at China World Hotel during the PATA 60th Anniversary and Conference, Beijing, China.

Just in time for the ITB 2011, India Tourism Frankfurt has published the new India brochure. This 60 page colourful Brochure provides the tourists a good overview over all travel destinations in India. The brochure not only presents the different regions – North, East, North-East, West, and South of India but also provides special options how to spend a holiday in India. Whether one would like to visit wildlife sanctuaries, have fun with sports and adventures, or simply relax at the beach, the brochure informs about various travel destinations all over the subcontinent. Wellness resorts, cruises, or mountain holidays are also mentioned.

Furthermore, the booklet delivers useful information about climate, clothing, health care, opening hours, and many more. The absolutely beautiful designed brochure provides many pictures and raises the desire of travelling to India.

Even the names of the trains sound enchanting: Palace on Wheels, Golden Chariot, Maharajas' Express or Royal Rajasthan on Wheels. A journey across India in one of the luxury hotels on rails is a truly royal treat. The new brochure of the Indian Tourism Office in Frankfurt informs about luxurious train journeys and invites you to travel in style. Also a less expensive train journey is presented: the Buddhist Train visits important places of the Asian subcontinent. It travels from Delhi across Uttar Pradesh and Bihar until Nepal. The brochure invites you to explore Budhism in a new way.

CHAPTER-3

Tourism Products

The tourism product today is developed to meet the needs of the consumer and techniques like direct sales, publicity and advertising are employed to bring this product to the consumer. The country's natural beauty, climate, history, culture and the people, or other facilities necessary for comfortable living such as water supply, electricity, roads, transport, communication and other essentials serve as vital means of this product.

The tourism product can be entirely a man-made one or nature's creation improved upon by man. In modern times, these products, whether traditional in nature, like culture and pilgrimage; or modern, like adventure, conventions and conferences, health, medical, etc. are being packaged, promoted and priced appropriately.

Tourism products can be classified as under:

Natural Tourism Products

These include natural resources such as areas, climate and its setting, landscape and natural environment. A few of them are:

i. Countryside

ii. Climate–temperature, rain, snowfall, days of sunshine

iii. Natural Beauty–landforms, hills, rocks, gorges, terrain

iv. Water–lakes, ponds, rivers, waterfalls, springs

v. Flora and Fauna

vi. Wildlife

vii. Beaches

viii. Islands

ix. Spas

x. Scenic Attractions

The climate of a tourist destination is often an important attraction. Good weather plays an important role in making a holiday. Millions of tourists from countries with extreme climates visit beaches in search of fine weather and sunshine. The sunshine and clear sea beaches have attracted tourists for a very long time. In fact, development of spas and resorts along the sea coasts in many countries were a result of the travellers' urge to enjoy good weather and sunshine.

Destinations with attractive winter climates, winter warmth and sunshine are also important centres of tourist attraction.

Around these winter resorts, winter sport facilities have been installed to cater to the increasing needs of tourists. People from warm climates travel especially to see snowfall and enjoy the cold climate. Hence, climate is of great significance as a tourism product.

The scenery and natural beauty of places has always attracted tourists. There are landforms, like mountains, canyons, coral reefs, cliffs, etc. There are waterforms, like rivers, lakes waterfalls, geysers, glaciers, etc.

Vegetation like forests, grasslands, moors, deserts, etc. have all been developed as tourist products. Flora and Fauna attract many a tourist. Tourists like to know the various types of plants and trees that they see and which trees are seen in which seasons. Thick forest covers attract tourists who enjoy trekking and hunting activities. Fauna attracts tourists who like to watch birds, wild mammals, reptiles and other exotic and rare animals.

While most parts of the world have their own therapies and treatments that are effective in restoring the wellness and beauty of people, yet health tours have their own significance. New kinds of health tours are gaining popularity, of late, called as spa tours. Spas offer the unique advantages of taking the best from the West and the East, combining them with the indigenous system and offering best of the two worlds. Now various spa products are being combined with yoga, meditation, and pranayama, giving a holistic experience to tourists. Spa treatments are now combined with other medical treatments to treat blood pressure, insomnia, depression, paralysis and some other diseases.

Beach tourism is very popular among the tourists of all age groups today. Besides attraction and saleability, beach holidaying has lead to overall development of tourism in many parts of the world. The basic importance of beaches is that they provide aesthetic and environmental value of the beach such as beautiful natural scenery with golden sands, lush green vegetation and bright blue sky.

Beach tourism involves swimming, surfing, sailing, wind surfing, water scootering, Para-sailing, motorboat rides, etc. The land use has multifacets like sunbathing, recreational areas for tourists (parks, playgrounds, clubs, theatre, amusement parks, casinos, cultural museums, etc.), accommodation facilities (hotels, cottages, villas, camping sites, etc.), car and bus parking areas, entertainment and shopping complexes, access roads and transportation network. Due to its multidimensional requirements, the beach product needs special care. Environmental management should also ensure the support of the development on the coast to maintain its ecosystem.

Islands abound with natural beauty, with rare flora and fauna along with tribes. This tourist product has great scope as these islands are being developed as tourist paradises. The topography is generally undulating and they offer natural scenic beauty with exotic flora and fauna. As an added attraction, some of these islands have developed as tax havens thereby encouraging commercial development of these economies. They offer social and cultural attractions as tourists can experience the local lifestyle, local food, fairs and festivals, etc.

In short, breath-taking mountain scenery and the coastal stretches exert a strong fascination on the tourists who at the same time are enchanted by the magnificent mountain ranges that provide an atmosphere of peace and tranquillity.

Man-Made Tourism Products

Man- made tourism products are created by man for pleasure, leisure or business. Man- made tourism products include:

1. *Culture*

- Sites and areas of archaeological interest
- Historical buildings and monuments
- Places of historical significance
- Museums and art galleries
- Political and educational institutions
- Religious institutions

Cultural tourism is based on the mosaic of places, traditions, art forms, celebrations and experiences that portray the nation and its people, reflecting the diversity and character of a country.

A growing number of visitors are becoming special-interest travellers who rank the arts, heritage and/or other cultural activities as one of the top five reasons for travelling.

Today we can witness large masses of people travelling to foreign countries to become acquainted with the usages and customs, to visit the museums and to admire works of art.

The cultural heritage of a nation may not altogether be justified considering that the preservation of its culture is one of the basic responsibilities of any community. However, mass tourism can contribute unique benefits to the exploiting of the cultural heritage of a nation and can serve indirectly to improve the individual cultural levels of both citizens and travellers.

Cultural resources are such that many tourists want to experience the exotic. The tourists would like to visit and become acquainted with the ancient civilization in their quest for novel human knowledge.

Various museums also attract tourists such as the National Museum, New Delhi; Salarjung Museum, Hyderabad, etc. which are popular tourist hubs. Sites of archeological interest like remains of Mohenjodaro and Harrapan civilizations, tombs of various leaders and emperors, historical buildings such as Fatehpur Sikri (near Agra), Red Fort (located in Delhi), etc. are all popular with tourists. Even historical city like Varanasi in India draws a lot of tourists due to its status as one of the oldest cities of the world.

2. *Traditions*

- Pilgrimages
- Fairs and festivals
- Arts and handicrafts
- Dance

- Music
- Folklore
- Native life and customs

A pilgrimage is a term primarily used for a journey or a search of great moral significance. Sometimes, it is a journey to a sacred place or shrine of importance to a person's beliefs and faith. Members of every religion participate in pilgrimages. A person who makes such a journey is called a pilgrim. Secular and civic pilgrimages are also practiced, without regard for religion, but rather are of importance to a particular society too. However, large number of people have been making pilgrimages to sacred religious places or holy places. This practice is widespread in many parts of the world.

India is among the richest countries in the world as far as the field of art and craft is concerned. Tourists like to visit and see the creative and artistic treasures of various countries. India has certain traditional arts like gems and jewellery, tie and dye works, wood and marble carving, ivory, glasswork, hand block printing, sandalwood inlay work that are of particular interest to tourists.

India is famous for its classical dances. People who travel like to watch these dance performances and sometimes even take some introductory classes.

Music can be either traditional or modern. Traditional music like folk music, classical, and country music is specific to every region and country. Music also adds to the attraction of a destination.

Fairs and Festivals capture the fun-loving facet and bring out the joyous celebrations of the community. Festivals like Christmas, Eid, Ramadan, Diwali, and Holi and so on, also bring people to destinations where the celebration can be enjoyed. Some popular fairs which cater to fun and work are Pushkar Mela in Rajasthan, Mango Festival in Saharanpur, Surajkund Craft Mela (near Delhi), etc.

3. *Entertainment*

- Amusement and recreation parks
- Sporting events
- Zoos and oceanariums
- Cinemas and theatre
- Nightlife
- Cuisine

Tourist products that have entertainment as their main characteristic are many. Just to name a few, there are amusement and recreational parks like Fun and Food Village in Delhi, Essel World in Mumbai, and so on.

Tourists may come to attend sports events which also gives them an opportunity to explore the country. Many countries organise year-round sports events like swimming meets, athletic meets, weightlifting events, cricket matches, baseball and football events and many more such events which encourage tourism. India hosted the Commonwealth Games in 2010 and gave the tourism industry a big boost.

Nightlife is one of the prime attractions in a holiday. Tourists like to especially visit areas in cities where the night life activity is promoted. These are as are usually lit up with street stalls like flea markets and food areas. Bars, night clubs, casinos and very often open air bands attract and add to the psychological satisfaction and experience of tourists.

Cuisine is very often an understated but highly important part of any holiday. Now-a-days cuisine from all areas of the world is found at most of the tourist destinations. Specialty restaurants serve Indian, Continental, Chinese, Italian, Arabic, and so on. However, tourists usually like to eat the local food of the areas they visit.

4. *Business*

- Conventions
- Conferences

People who travel in relation to their work come under the category of business tourism. However, such travel for business purposes is also linked with tourist activity like visiting places of tourist attraction at the destination, sightseeing and excursion trips. Business travel is also related to, what is termed today as convention business, which is a rapidly growing industry in hospitality and tourism.

A business traveller is important to the tourism industry as it involves the usage of all the components of tourism. He travels because of different business reasons–attending conventions and conferences, meetings, workshops, etc. Participants have a lot of leisure time at their disposal. The conference organisers make this leisure time very rewarding for participants by organising many activities for their pleasure and relaxation. The spouses and families accompanying the participants are also well looked after by the organisers. The organisers plan sightseeing tours and shopping tours for the participants and their families. In India, visits to the craft bazaars are arranged where tourists see how artisans make clay pots and other handicrafts.

Conferences are events which require meticulous planning and efficient implementation, co-ordinating various activities so that the right things happen at the right time.

Symbiotic Tourism Products

Some tourism products do not fall into the above categories due to their being a blend of the nature and the man. In these types of products, the nature provides the resources while the man converts them into a tourism product by managing them. National parks, for example, are left in their natural state of beauty as far as possible. Yet, the core attraction is still nature in this category of product. These products are symbiosis of the nature and the man.

In case of adventure sports, tourists can be participants. The basic element of adventure is the satisfaction of having complete command over one's body, a sense of risk in the process, an awareness of beauty and exploration of the unknown.

Adventure tourism can be classified into aerial, water-based and land-based.

Aerial adventure sports include the following activities:

i. ***Parachuting***: It involves jumping off from an aircraft or balloon and descending by means of a parachute. The infrastructure required, includes an aircraft, parachutes and large landing zones.

ii. ***Skydiving***: It involves a skydiver jumping off an aircraft or balloon at a much greater height without deploying his parachute initially and opening it after some interval at a pre-determined height.

iii. ***Handgliding***: It involves running off a mountain or being towed by a winch and essentially flying like a glider where the directional control is achieved by a shift in his own weight by the pilot.

iv. ***Paragliding***: It is the latest aero-sport which has taken the world by storm. A paraglider is a specially designed square parachute, along with a harness attached by lines.

v. ***Parasailing***: It is a simple sport that involves towing a parachutist to a height of a few hundred feet in the air and then descending by means of a parachute. As a year-round activity, parasailing can be done on land and water.

vi. ***Bungee Jumping***: It requires no equipment except a 'bungee cord' made of nylon fiber of enough elasticity to be able to absorb the shock at the end of the jump. The jumper makes a headlong jump into empty space and the resultant rush of adrenalin makes the experience very exhilarating.

vii. ***Ballooning***: In this sport, a balloon is attached to a basket by steel wire ropes. By regulating hot and cold air, the pilot can steer the balloon along any charted course.

Water-based adventure sports include the following activities:

i. ***White water rafting***: It is one of the most important and exciting water sports, which involves riding down water rapids in an inflatable raft which is used to negotiate fast flowing rivers.

ii. ***Canoeing and Kayaking***: These are adventure sports which begin upstream where the water is wild and white. The gradient best suited for canoeing is the stage near the river's entry into the plains where the trip can be combined with a natural holiday in a forest. Kayaking is appealing as it enables innovation on the river by one or two oarsman seated in tandem.

iii. ***Adventure sports*** in the waters of the sea like wind surfing, scuba diving, snorkeling, yachting, water skiing, etc. also offer thrilling activities to the tourists.

Land based adventure tourist products include:

i. ***Rock climbing***: It originated as a means of practicing techniques for ascending high mountains. It was earlier provided as training to mountaineers but has now evolved into a highly developed sport. The climber moves up, using knowledge of rope handling, climbing, securing one to another, etc. Very sophisticated techniques and equipments are used now-a-days to ascend or descend on very steep terrain.

ii. ***Mountaineering***: It requires trained physical ability and suitable equipments. The higher peaks need better equipment which is also costly. The challenges which mountains, like the Indian Himalayas pose, attract mountaineers from various countries.

iii. ***Trekking***: The mighty Himalayas which spread across five Indian states form a sweeping arc and encompass in its expanse a wide geographical variety and contrasting cultures.

iv. ***Skiing***:It is the practice of sliding over snow on runners, called skis, attached to each foot. There are three types of ski resorts, the first are large towns, second type are alpine villages and the third are resorts built especially for skiing.

v. ***Heli skiing***: It is a type of alpine skiing where the skier is dropped to the top of a mountain by a helicopter and then he slides down on his own.

vi. ***Motor Rally***: It is a sport that tests the navigational skills of man and his endurance with the machine. Motor rallies, grand prix racing, hill climbing rallies, vintage car rallies, sports car racing, etc. are some forms of this tourism product.

vii. ***Safaris***: These were earlier taken on camels, horses and elephants as an excursion for hunting or a journey. As a modern tourist product, now safaris are taken on jeeps and in the form of caravans. Viewing and enjoying nature, meeting the local villagers, seeing their traditions, customs and lifestyle, entertainment and camp fires are some of the characteristics of modern safaris, eg. Egypt desert safaris. Horse and elephant safaris are arranged in most of the national parks and wildlife sanctuaries.

Event-based Tourism Products

Whenever an event is the main attraction, it called an event based tourist product. Events attract tourists as spectators and also as participants in the events, sometimes for both. The Dubai and Singapore shopping festivals, the camel polo at Jaisalmer, kite flying in Ahmedabad, attract tourists, both as spectators and participants.

Some events have a short time-scale, such as the Republic Day Parade, while others may last for many days, for example, Khajuraho Dance Festival and some for even months like the Kumbh Mela.

A destination which may have little to commend it to the tourist can nevertheless succeed in drawing tourists by mounting an event such as an unusual exhibition.

Site-based Tourism Products

When an attraction is a place or site then it is called a site-based tourist product. Site attractions are permanent by nature, for example, Taj Mahal, The Great Wall of China, Temples of Khajuraho, etc. Some new features have been added to the same product to keep the tourist interest alive in the products. For instance now visitors can see the Taj by night along with organisation of music shows as the backdrop at this site so that there are repeat tourists.

The above narration of different types of tourism products shows that a tourism product in its sense, could be a thing, a person, a place, an event or an activity that satisfies the need of leisure, pleasure or enjoyment of a tourist. The product which is offered should have an intrinsic value for consumer in terms of satisfying his/her needs.

Very often, the tourism product can be a thing like the ethnic garments of Rajasthan or Gujarat or marble statues from Jabalpur. It can be a place like Mumbai, Goa or London. It can be a person like a particular dancer, a musician, a guide or fictitious character like Walt Disney's Mickey Mouse. Events are also tourism products like the Snake Boat Race of Kerala, the Elephant festival of Jaipur or the Kite festival at Ahmedabad. The tourism prduct can also be an activity like paragliding or scuba diving or trekking. However, the examples given are of the products which are primarily intangible. They are service products or services.

CHAPTER-4

HISTORY OF HANDICRAFTS IN INDIA

In a large country like India, every region has its specific crafts where the skills and creativity of craftsmen provide a distinct colour to handicrafts. India has a rich tradition of crafts and artisan production. Prior to the industrial production through machines, all production was done through individual artisan production. With the coming of the machines and establishment of factories, mass production of articles of daily use started. Even after the introduction of machines, the tradition of production by artisans and craftsmen continued. At present, this production is of two types, viz. (i) the common articles made for functional use, and (ii) the articles made for decorative purposes. In both these, we witness the skills and art of craftsmen. At times, even the items of daily use are made with great skill and serve both functional and decorative purposes.

Craft is a special artwork involving artistic skills and creative acumen. Broadly speaking, it can be denoted as a profession, trade or pursuit that a group of professionals, namely, craftsmen, undertake in great exuberance. Craft refers to the creation of original objects through an artist's disciplined manipulation of material.

The prerequisite of producing crafts of high quality is manual dexterity nicely mingling with timely application, keeping its artistic fervor as it is. Thus, a whole lot of perseverance, care, diligence and ingenuity is what makes a craft more embellished and luxuriant.

There are salient characteristic that would perfectly identify crafts. First, it must be made significantly by hand. Any skilled craftsman spends prolonged hours in producing and giving concrete shape to any craft piece.

Craft is related to its past heritage and culture. Each of the craft disciplines embodies the trends and tradition of the multifaceted occurrences and events that were closely associated with them, rightly belonging to the past decades. Craft is medium-specific and it is for always identified with a material and the technologies used to make it.

For example, crafts prepared using manual labor and works of hands, are popularly known as handicrafts. Various things like wood, clay, glass, textiles, and metals are used to make a craft item. Secondly, craft is defined by use. How and where it is to be utilized is what makes a craft distinguishable. Some crafts are used as decorative items comprising of the fields viz. ceramics, furniture, furnishings, interior design, and architecture. They are used as traditional ornamental works, usually made from ceramic, wood, glass, metal, or textile.

Decorative arts, or furnishings, may be fixed (for example, wallpaper), or moveable (for example, lamps). Crafts practiced by independent artists working alone or in small groups are often referred to as studio craft. Studio craft includes studio pottery, metal work, weaving, woodturning and other forms of woodworking, glass blowing, and glass art.

The artisanal production was the only form of industrial production until the mill industries were established in India during the 19th century. There were broadly two types of goods produced in this sector:

1) Articles of mass consumption, which were used in everyday life and were cheaper and could be produced with much less skill.

2) There were refined and sophisticated items for the use of moneyed classes. The production of these articles required skills of very high standard and they could not be produced in bulk. Among these were fine muslins, silks, jewellery, traditional shoes, decorative swords and weapons, etc.

Both types of handicrafts faced decline during the British rule. The decline has continued even in the independent India for lack of adequate support. Suppprt from the government, development of marketing strategies and growth in tourism reinvigorate the traditional arts and crafts of India.

The majority of the handicrafts items are produced for exchange or sale. Production of handicrafts requires raw materials and labour. It is only by selling the products that the artisans can purchase the required raw material of production and perpetuate the tradition. The handicrafts items, therefore, have always been commodities in one form or the other. In fact, unless complete patronage from some source is provided, commoditization is the only channel through which the craft traditions can be maintained.

The history of crafts has a long tradition to follow. It traces back to almost five thousand years ago. The craft tradition in India has centered on religious beliefs and local needs of the commoners. Also, the special needs of the patrons and royalty with a keen eye on foreign and domestic trade became the foci of crafts of Indian subcontinent.

These craft traditions have resisted the onslaughts of time and several foreign intrusions. Till date, it is continuing to boom owing to the assimilating nature of Indian culture though highly accommodative nature of the craftsmen to accept and use new ideas also is responsible for this.

What is to be noted is that references to Indian crafts were found in the remnants of Indus Valley Civilization (3000 B.C.-1700 B.C.). The Indus valley civilization had a rich craft tradition. It had also got a technical brilliance in the arena of pottery-making, jewellery, threading, various sculptures like metal, stone and terracotta, etc. The craftsmen fulfilled basic needs of the locales and the excess items were exported to ancient Arabian countries mainly through voyages.

The rich heritage of Indus Valley civilization was perfectly incorporated in the Vedic era, starting from 1500 B.C. There is no dearth of references in the Vedic literature where instances of artisans involved in pottery making, weaving, wood crafting etc, are being duly mentioned. Especially, the Rig Veda refers to a variety of pottery made from clay, wood and metal. It also mentions about lot many weavers and weaving of the then period.

Artistic production of crafts, too, proliferated during Mauryan Empire, a landmark in Indian history, starting from 3rd century B.C. It is believed that during the time of Ashoka, 84,000 stupas were constructed in India. The "Sanchi stupa" is a part of it and has gained fame world over for its beautiful stone carving and relief work.

Wearing fashionable jewellries was in vogue. Several sculptures found in Bharhut, Mathura, Amravati, Vaishali, Sanchi regions depicting female figures decked up in beautiful jewelries bear a proof of this. The iron pillars of Vaishali and Delhi, created during the time of Emperor Ashoka, are a spectacle of metallurgical works.

The foreign invaders, leaving aside their tradition of cultural and traditional glories, ennobled the history of crafts of India. This happened between 1st century B.C to 1st century A.D The impact of these intrusions can be noticed in the Buddhist sculptures from Taxila, Begram, Bamiyan, Swat valley, etc.

A high degree of Greek influence is immensely found, especially in the statue of Buddha, bearing curly hair and wearing draperies. The same trend is maintained in the sculptures of the Kushan king Kanishka. These originated in the same period, depicting the influence of the Central Asian culture on Indian craftsmanship. Other exquisite craft pieces, namely, jewellery, textile-making, leather products, metalworking, etc. inherited these influences and also absorbed them in accordance with the then prevailing Indian scenario.

The Gupta (AD 320-647) age is not only regarded as the classical period in Indian history but also of history of Indian crafts. The rock-cut temples of Ellora and the Ajanta murals are perfect examples of it. These wall paintings depict a realistic view of the lifestyle of that time. Another interesting feature is that it underwent evolution under the patronage of Gupta kings, excelling in jewellery making, woodcarving, sculpture, stone carving and weaving.

The medieval period of Indian history is significant in the context of development of crafts. It expanded its influence to southern region after capturing the market of the whole of northern territories of India The craftsmen under the Delhi Sultanate period prospered in the fields of pottery, weaving, wood carving, metal working, jewellery, etc.

The contribution of the Cholas and the Vijaynagar empire in the field of bronze sculpture, silk weaving, jewellery, temple carving still remains unsurpassed. The fine example of stone carving from Central India can be seen in the form of the Khajuraho Temples, built by the Chandelas. Rich and ornate wood and stone carving can be found in medieval temple of Jagannath at Puri in Orissa.

The Mughal era was the golden period in the history of craft. The Mughals brought with them a rich heritage, which they had adopted from Persian territories. They imparted new techniques like inlay work, glass engraving, carpet weaving, brocades, enameling, etc.

The Mughal miniature paintings also showed influence of the traditions of many Indian schools of paintings like Rajasthani, Kangra, Pahari, etc. The famous Peacock Throne of the Mughals is one of the premium examples of precious stone decorative work and metal craft. They also laid the foundation for a host of many craft traditions and also the famous Mughal miniature painting. Petra dura, an inlay work is a unique example, perfectly beautified with jewellery.

In present times, growth and development of crafts in India is no less significant. Each and every Indian state has its own unique culture, their own designs, colours, materials in use and individual shapes and patterns, which is demonstrated in the handicrafts of that particular region. For instance, Kashmir is known for its Pashmina wool shawls as well as carpets, silverware, ivory works, etc.

Eastern states like Assam and West Bengal are far-famed for their exquisite 'Sholapith' and 'Shital Patti' works. Others regions are acclaimed for crafts pieces, for instance, Karnataka for its rosewood carving, sandalwood crafts. The engraved and enameled meenakari brassware found in Rajasthan, silk materials from Varanasi and Kanchipuram, colourful embroidery, mirror work, quilting and fabric painting from Gujarat, etc. are some of the exclusive crafts popularized not only in India but also abroad. Stonecrafts are too such things and few regions are popular for crystals and semi-precious stones.

Crafts are an indispensable part of Indian culture and tradition, nicely epitomizing the rich heritage of different regal kings of Indian subcontinent and also those of the foreign invaders.

Most of India's crafts have a long ancestry back to hundreds of years. There is at least one of them, namely, pottery-making whose continuity can be trced as far back as the Harappan Civilization. India's textiles reached the zenith of refinement during the Mughal period. Many of artisanal crafts also flourished under the patronage extended to them by the State and the nobility. During Gupta period, crafts like metalworks, ivorywork, jewellery, etc. were much in demand even outside the country. Under the Mughals, all kinds of weaving and silk spinning were brought to perfection.

The largest volume of artisanal production was integrated with the village economy under the *jajmani* system. In Deccan and Maharashtra, this was termed as *balutedari* system. The production included the articles of daily use, agricultural implements, commodities for local fairs, etc. The most crucial services were those of blacksmiths, carpenters, potters, weavers and shoemakers.

Slowly, however, money economy penetrated into the rural areas and, in the 17th century, we find some instances of payment in cash in the rural areas. By the mid 18 century, some of the rural artisans started producing for the urban markets also.

The artisanal production was done in the urban areas by individual artisans, mostly independently. Almost every craft had specialized artisans who manufactured articles for the market. In the medieval period, this specialization was very marked in the textile production. But, the individual artisan did not have much capital and the output was small. The quality also differed from artisan to artisan and from region to region.

In many parts of India, during the 17th Century, they also developed some sort of putting-out system of artisanal production. It was called *dadni*. In this system:

- the merchants advanced cash to the artisans for production,

- the artisans had to produce goods according to the specifications given to them by the merchants, and
- they had to deliver goods within the given time.

In this way, the artisans lost control over the quality, quantity and duration of production.

During the medieval period, the ownership of the *karkhanas* vested in the kings and high nobles. Skilled artisans were employed there to produce expensive luxury items for the the nobility. The production from these *karkhanas* was not for the market but for the personal use of kings and nobles.

The Indian states have a wide range of crafts, which have attained commercial proportions not only in India but abroad as well. They make excellent souvenirs for tourists and are sold through various handicraft emporiums. Craft making is an ancient tradition in India, which has withstood the test of time, and the tradition has passed on from generation to generation. The Indian craftsmen are still adept at making traditional crafts which have attracted the attention of connoisseurs of craft all over the world. The famous crafts of each Indian states are as follows:

The crafts of Andhra Pradesh are known for their aesthetic and utilitarian value and these are rich and flamboyant.

The crafts of Arunachal Pradesh are woodcarvings, weaving, carpet-making, pottery and jewellery-making.

The crafts of Assam bring out the artistic caliber of people living in the state. Weaving and embroidery are the chief crafts of Assam.

The crafts of Chattisgarh speak of the skill and artistic bent of the mind of the people living in the region.

The crafts of Bihar have their own patterns, styles and manifest the rich cultural heritage of the state. The crafts of Bihar include, stoneware, carpet-making, glasswork and wood inlays.

The crafts of Goa are a commercial success and reflect the perennial glory of Goa. The chief craft forms in the state are pottery and terracotta, woodwork, brass and metal work, crochet and embroidery, bamboo craft, fibre craft, batik prints and metal embossing.

The crafts of Gujarat have been deftly passed on from generation to generation and are replete with vibrancy. The major crafts of Gujarat are fascinating textiles, elaborately carved wooden and stone jharokhas, bandhini and intricately carved silver jewellery.

The crafts of Haryana have never been widely acclaimed and more than artistic showpieces they are utilitarian in nature.

The crafts of Himachal Pradesh have a relatively good demand in the market and some of the major crafts of the region include textiles, woodcarvings, carpet-making and pottery.

The crafts of Jammu and Kashmir are varied and diverse which range from woolen textiles, carpets to delicate designs worked on papier-mache.

The crafts of Jharkhand range from woodwork, bambooworks, pitkar paintings, tribal ornaments to stone carvings.

The crafts of Karnataka bear testimony to the dexterity, and decorative abilities of the craftsperson. The crafts of the state include woodcarving, ivory carving, kasuti embroidery, durries, pottery and cheennapatna toys.

The crafts of Kerala bring alive the rich cultural tradition of the people living in the state.

The crafts of Maharastra flourish mainly because of the royal patronage it received in the past. The state is famous for crafts like, bidriware, lacquerware, toymaking, weaving, printed textiles and Kolhapuri chappals.

The crafts of Madhya Pradesh have attained commercial proportions and are sold in emporiums and shops around the country.

Manipur is a storehouse of crafts and the people here are known to take a lot of interest in make new innovation in the craft.

The crafts of Meghalaya are unique in style and design and one of the famous craft of the state is weaving cane mats.

The crafts of Mizoram are made from locally available materials artistically and efforts are being made to promote the crafts.

The various **crafts of Nagaland** are woodcarvings, bamboowork, pottery, and blacksmithy, which have a commercial demand in the local and international markets.

The crafts of Orissa are a rare combination of utility and beauty and this makes Orissa one of the leading states in craftmaking.

The crafts of Punjab are distinctly colourful which speak of the vibrant spirit of the people in the state. The range of crafts in Punjab include phulkarl, woodwork, wood inlay, lacquerware, leathercraft, floor coverings.

The crafts of Rajasthan have received patronage from royal dynasties in the past. Today, the craft industry is a major source of revenue in the state.

The crafts of sikkim are as beautiful and magnificent as the scenic beauty of this mountainous state.

The crafts of Tamil Nadu include papier-mache, stonecraft, pottery, woodcraft, embroidery, durries and metal ware.

The crafts of Tripura range from cane and bamboo crafts, handlooms and basketry.

Craft making is integrally related with the lives of the people living in **Uttar Pradesh**. Each city in Uttar Pradesh specializes in one type of craft.

The crafts of Uttaranchal include woodcarvings and ornaments-making which have their own distinct style.

The crafts of West Bengal are so exquisite that they have a huge demand not only in the local market but abroad as well.

The crafts of Indian union territories are intricately beautiful and capture the fancies of tourists and locals alike. They bring out the artistic capabilities, dexterity and creativity of the people of the region.

Puducherry is famous for pottery, mat-weaving, papier-mache and clay dolls. It is also famous for weaving a variety of cloths like satin, twill, corduroy, poplin, chambray, oxford cambric and Khadi.

The crafts of Delhi have received royal patronage in the past and it was the hub of crafts in ancient India. Some of the various crafts of Delhi are jewellery making, toy making, zardozi embroidery and blue pottery.

The arts and crafts of Lakshadweep are made using the local resources that are available like coconut shells, seashells and tortoise shells.

The famous **crafts of Daman** are mat weaving, and that of Diu are tortoise shell and ivory carving.

The famous **crafts of Dadra and Nagar Haveli** are leather slippers and weaving of bamboo mats and baskets.

The islands of **Andaman and Nicobar** islands are famous for carpentry and woodwork, shell craft and basketry and mat-making.

India's crafts were traditionally produced by individual caste groups. Thus, while the *julahas* and *bunkar* (weavers) made clothes, shoes were made by *mochis* (leather workers); *sunars* (goldsmiths) were adept at making jewellery and *barhais* (carpenters) worked with tradition that still continues in most parts of India today. This closed nature of crafts production kept alive the traditions through of economic and political vicissitudes.

The urban artisan were organized in guilds. During the medieval period, we find two types of guilds in existence. On the one hand, there were craft guilds which were basically associations of the craftsmen from a particular caste group. On the other hand, there were merchant guilds which were loose organizations of traders and merchants.

In the pre-British India, the artisanal production was the second biggest source of employment.

History of Indian carpets dates back to 500 BC and draws influence from Persian invasion in India.

Carpets and floorings are an integral part of Indian homes and the history of Indian carpets features its development using mats and durries with a variety of material, ranging from wool, cotton, jute, coir, bamboo and grass.

History of Indian carpets, especially those of the woolen carpets, traces to a period as early as 500 B.C. References to the earliest woven mats and floor coverings can be found in ancient and medieval Indian literature.

Indian carpets are some of the most exquisite creations that date back to the age of Mughal era.

Indian carpets are made by weaving tight knots and displaying designs through bright, contrasting colours. These carpets are common in North India and used in order to avoid the chilling floor. However, with time, it has become a symbol of sophistication and interior decor. Carpet-weaving has strong traditions in India.

In the early stages, the motifs used in the Indian carpets were purely Persian. Later, various other designs were introduced from China, Afghanistan, Turkey, Morocco and Iran. The Mughals imported weavers from Persian countries, which were famous for carpet manufacturing. Under royal patronage, the artisans made beautiful carpets with aesthetically perfect designs and colours.

Each region developed a distinct style of carpet weaving. In the hilly and mountainous regions of India, from Ladakh to Darjeeling and Sikkim to Manipur, carpets are made of pure wool in glowing colours.

The predominant motifs are those of the dragon, lion and lotus. Patterns are also taken from Buddhist stupas with flag, the *kalash* (water-vessel) and the twin fish. These carpets essentially belong to Central Asia.

The history of Indian carpets entails that when Babur came to India, he was disappointed by lack of luxuries here. He missed the luxuries of Persia, which included the Persian carpet. In later times, Akbar laid the foundation of carpet weaving tradition in India, more specifically in 1580 AD, at his palace in Agra. With the support of these artisans, he established carpet weavings centers at Agra, Delhi and

Lahore to facilitate production of Persian styled carpets, which were inspired by designs of Kirman, Kashan, Esfahan, Herat and so on.

Mughals not only used the Persian technique of carpet weaving, but were also influenced by traditional designs and motifs from Persia. Mughal carpets were as obscure as their miniatures and usually depicted court life, animals and floral decorations. Mughal carpets were brightly coloured and the hand knotted silk carpets had 4224 knots per square inch. However, the most famous type of Indian carpets was the pile carpet, which came to India in the reign of Akbar in 16th century (around 1580 A.D.).

Akbar brought certain Persian carpet weavers to India and established them in India. The art grew and flourished here and it was modified as per the royal tastes and mixed with the Indian arts. The Persian carpets, were thus, re-created in Indian forms. These carpets spread to the whole subcontinent with each area having its own specialties

Since the beginning, wool or silk have been the essential material of the knotted carpets. The wool may have a diversity of origins according to the type of carpet being made. Silk knots are also used in Kashmir region. The patterns of Indian carpets varied from vines and floral patterns, animal and bird figures to geometric to calligraphic patterns.

Rugs from Akbar's reign (1556-1605) used cotton warp and wool pile and a variety of colour scheme had multiple shades of blue, green, and other colours on a red and peach base. The patterns were a reworked copy of Persian style but later modified to Indian tastes.

Indian carpets during Jehangir's reign (1605-27) were more superior. Materials like silk and pashmina were used that permitted greater number of knots to be included in the artworks. Patterns of these Indian carpets resembled miniature paintings. Subtle gradations and shadings with yarns were themselves artistic.

The patterns of these carpets were a reflection of manuscript paintings. The history of Indian carpets shows technically refined taste in both design and construction. The carpets had scrolling vines, flowering plants, and more naturalistic animals in pictorial or overall pattern.

During Shahjahan's reign (1628-58), the art of Indian carpets had reached new heights. Warps and wefts of fine silk yarns incorporated as many as 2,000 knots per square inch. Silk or pashmina piles gave the carpets a velvety-like texture. Yarn shading was as stylish as in Jahangir's reign. Flowers were still the primary elements of design.

During this era, the patterns were primarily floral all over with, at times, geometric or calligraphic trims. Chinese and European patterns also influenced the history of Indian carpets in their own way. Calligraphy influenced the carpet craft as it did the other crafts in India. Though like all other crafts, carpet making also saw a downfall for sometime, but the craft sustained in the traditional families.

Types of carpet weaving in India

High quality Indian carpets are available mostly in three varieties–Persian (Isfahan and Kashan), Turkoman and Aubusson (French). Designs in the Persian Isfahan variety are long leaf and floral. Persian Kashan variety is small with floral arrangement that are common.

In the Persian designs, seven to eleven shades are generally used. The Turkoman has only the Mohru Bukhara variety. The French Aubussan accounts for more than half the carpets manufactured in Agra.

Carpet weaving in Kashmir has Persian influence. Till today, most designs are distinctly Persian with local variations. Kashmiri carpets are more subtle and muted than elsewhere in the country where only chemical dyes are used. Kashmir is famous for its fine quality carpets, an average piece being made with about 324 knots per square inch. Kashmir has developed some of its own distinct designs based on shawl patterns, the traditional paisley, leaves and flowers. Kashmiri carpets are world renowned for their special two features. Firstly, they are hand made, never machine made. And secondly, they are always knotted, never toughed.

Fine quality carpets are also produced in places like Amritsar, Agra, Jaipur, Eluru and Warangal. The Mirzapur-Bhadohi belt in Uttar Pradesh represents the most important area of carpet weaving in the country as it has the largest number of carpet weavers. This area specialises in the lower, medium and low-fine qualities and accounts for nearly 90 per cent of the total production of carpets in India. The fineness of a carpet is judged from the number of knots per unit area, and the design, colours and quality of yarn. The firmness, thickness and appearance of the back of a carpet are the important considerations in determining the quality of the carpet.

Rajasthan is a traditional producer of fine quality hand-knotted woollen carpets. Jaipur was highly renowned for its carpets. Some of the finest samples of the old Mughal carpets are today in the city palace museum, the prized possession of the Maharaja of Jaipur.

The Indo-Heretic designs consist of smaller angular motifs enclosing little rosettes that are manufactured. These carpets are known for the boldness of the carving stems and the harmony of the colours.

Piled carpets in India are believed to have originated during the rule of Mughals. It is claimed that during the reign of Sher Shah, a nawab by the name of Dandi came to this region bringing with him some pile carpet weavers.

These carpets were patronised by the rulers, maharajas, rajas, nawabs, jagirdars and all classes of aristocracy; naturally, the industry grew and flourished. The Persians introduced the art of pile carpet weaving in silk and wool. Akbar' s successor, Jahangir, and later Shah Jahan, further encouraged the development of this craft.

Hand-knotted carpets of Kashmir made their appearance in India during the 15th century. In Kashmir, it attained a high degree of perfection especially under the Mughal emperors. Sometimes, silk or cotton is used for the warp with quality wool pile for weft.

The appearance and number of knots on the back of the carpet indicates the quality. Among the hand-knotted ones, the Bokhara carpets are one of the finest with about 125-500 knots in a square inch.

Namdhas are a type of Indian carpets that originated in Kashmir. The namdha is a speciality of Kashmir, which is so named because of the embroidery with woollen thread that completely covers the base of Hessian. Namdhas are either embroidered or appliqued.

Obra in Bihar is famous for carpet-weaving. Himachali carpets are brilliant in colours with traditional motifs. The Bhutias are the traditional weavers who make small bedside carpets (duns) and *asans*. The old alpana designs drawn on the floor on festive occasion are used. The geometrical pattern with floral motifs, like the two mythical Tibetan birds called the Dak and the jira, the dragon, the lion and the god of lighting with the zip zag lines.

The Indian carpets are considered most technically skillful classical craft. The carpet weavers throughout the history of India have grown artistically and are renowned for their exquisite designs, elegance, attractive colours and workmanship. In 1958, there were 14 factories with 350 looms and 80 cottage units with 400 looms.

According to a survey in India, there were about 3,500 carpet weavers in 1974. By the end of eighties their total number reached about 48,000. This remarkable expansion of the carpet industry is mainly due to the programme of massive training introduced and sponsored by the All-India Handicraft Board. Under this programme, numerous groups of girls have been trained that started a new development in job market of Kashmir. Another healthy sign of carpet industry's growth has been its movement from the city of Srinagar to rural and semi-urban areas.

According to the history of Indian carpets, the designs and patterns in Kashmir carpets continue to be inspired by Persian and Central Asian rugs through influences of Indo-Asiatic art are perceptible. Besides the widely celebrated designs like Kashan, Kirman, Ardebil, Bukhara, Qum, Ghoum, Tabiz, Hamadan, Senneh, peculiarly Kashmiri designs depict valley's scenic splendor; at the same time, some based on shawl patterns have also been evolved.

It is interesting to note that the Iranian masterpiece and the most well known Ardebil Mosque Carpet was made in 1536 AD by the artist Maqsud from Kashan and is now owned by the South Kensington Museum in London that was reproduced in Kashmir in 1902.

Kashmiri craftsmen have the remarkable ability to reproduce the most intricate designed carpets. It is said that a beautiful Kashmiri carpet once so charmed Maharaja Ranjit Singh that he rolled on it in great joy all day long.

While the Kashmir carpet craft has developed vastly during the middle of the twentieth century, it was felt that the quality in some cases had deteriorated. There was need for introduction of quality control measures. Apart from this, provision of adequate facilities for dyeing of the raw material used in the carpets and drying chambers for the finished products was very necessary. As such, the State Government took some steps to set up carpet washing and drying chambers in Srinagar. The need was urgent in the interest of the future healthy growth of the carpet Industry in India.

This policy resulted in increase of exports of both silk carpets and woollen carpets by 1980. However, there was an unhealthy feature in history of Indian carpets and that was the industry using 'staple silk' (viscose rayon) instead of pure silk. It was and is still sometimes called 'A silk', 'A' standing for artificial while it can also give the impression of 'A' quality silk.

The history of Indian carpets thus unveils the saga of the artistry of the Indian carpet weavers amidst their colour, pattern and style.

Gold Jewellery

Gold jewellery craft in India is deeply embedded to nation's history and intermingles with various changes having influenced by foreign cultures. The rich heritage and culture of India prompts the Indian inhabitants to decorate themselves with the rich variety of ornaments made from various metals especially from gold. India is supposed to be the only country where the jewellery plays a significant role in the adornment of personal embellishments.

The people of India, led by spiritual and superstitious beliefs, believed that the ornaments would help them to keep away from destructive forces. Gold jewellery art in India, since the remote past, therefore, played a major role.

At the early age, jewellery of stones, pebbles, and some other natural objects were used but after the initiation of the metals in India, the trend of wearing gold ornaments had been developed due to the glint and the durability of the metal. This further paved the way to the introduction of gold jewellery art in India whilst popularizing it to the core.

It is evident from various archaeological excavations that gold jewellery craft in India was prominent even in the ancient days. It had been discovered that in the earliest days the people, especially women, would use little clothing but they would bedeck themselves with ornaments.

A naked dancing girl, alluring, and bedecked with ornaments and bangles on one arm stretching from the wrist almost to her shoulder, had been found in the Harappa excavation. Almost a similar art of sculpture with minimum attire and a profusion of ornaments was found during the excavation of Gandhar and Gupta Empire. All these indicate the presence of gold art in India even in the days of ancient times.

During the later years, the Mughal emperors encouraged the gold jewellery craft in India. The Mughal jewelleries represented an incredibly high standard and quality. Mughal empire had amalgamated the Hindu and Muslim trends and made a fusion in the styles of gold jewellery craft in India. The Mughal emperors, by establishing *karkhanas* or workshops and employing artisans from different sects of excellence, encouraged this amazing art in India. The enamelling in gold jewelleries was also introduced by the Mughals.

Enamelling as a gold jewellery art has been well adored and is still practised in various parts of India like Nathdwara, Jaipur, Varanasi and Kolkata. Enamelling is categorised in to various types; in India, it is recognized as Champleve. An alternative of enamel is known as Tbewa, which is found in Pratapgarh district, Rajasthan in a small amount. After the end of the Mughal dynasty, the artisans moved to other places and the gold jewellery art of the Mughal period was merged with the crafts of the other places.

The gold jewellery art which was prevailing at that time gained a rich contour with the western influence in

Indian art and craft. The setting of gems in gold ornaments is an example of this western influence which became a famous gold jewellery art in 19th century India.

Although India maintained the tradition of the jewelleries that are engraved with gem stones and semi-precious gems from the early history of the ruling emperor, yet the western influence offered a rather contemporary touch to it.

The jewellery of different places differs from one-another and each type carries a speciality of its own. The original abode of the snake chain is Kilhapur in Maharashtra. The snake chain has gained its popularity in Hyderabad in recent times.

The ornaments such as odiyaanam (gold waist belt), jimikki (eardrop), vanki (armlet) are commonly used in all parts of South India. Some of the popular gold ornaments used in various parts of India are paambadam which are a great lump of gold and are in all one piece representing six earrings, worn by the rural Tamil women.

The earrings for Tamil men are known as Kadukkan. Kammal, Jimikki, Lolakku are some forms of earrings for women in Tamil Nadu. In Western and Southern India, Mangasutra, a gold pendant hanging from a necklace of black gun-metal and gold beads, is considered to be a symbol of the marital status of a woman and is considered as an auspicious sign of marriage.

Gold jewellery craft has evolved through the years and has attained great new level in India and is well admired for its dazzling Indian crafts that are highly acclaimed throughout the world for their aesthetic appeal and magnificence. The huge ethnical custom and cultural variety, has made possible for different types of crafts to accomplish. These are made up of different materials, themes, and proficiencies.

Indian crafts are highly acclaimed throughout the world for their aesthetic appeal and magnificence. The huge ethnical custom and cultural variety, has made possible for different types of crafts to accomplish. These are made up of different materials, themes, and proficiencies.

Works of woodwork, pottery, hand looms, terracotta, paintings, beadwork, jewellery, and embroidery, etc. have survived through centuries with fewer changes. With the advent of modernity, the craft materials have underwent sea change over the years and also the proficiency of construction have not altered to a great extent.

Articles of daily use like, chairs, bags, cushions, hats, purses, sofas, etc. are made from recycled materials like wire, plastic and tin that form part and parcel of crafts of India. Thus, the crafts not only meet the day-to-day needs of the people but are also utilized for decorative and religious ceremonies in India.

There are varieties of crafts available in India which are exquisite and delicate, providing new definitions to the Indian crafts and artifacts. These consist of several sub categories, which include bubblegram, glass blowing, glass bead making, stained glass, mosaics and pottery.

A bubblegram is a three dimensional image which is composed of points and remains suspended in a medium, usually a plastic block. Laser bubblegrams is also in vogue. Crossing lasers in 'appropriately-doped' plastic, which may cause a chemical reaction through heat or 'photonic' inflammation, make these images.

The art of sculpture is the poetic expression of stone craft. Sculptures of deities, decorative for house interiors, modeled on classical prototypes, continue to be made in nook and corner of India. In interior of India, such sculptures and exquisite figures are carved in relief with details engraved in fine lines. These objects are handmade artistic work made using hammer and chisels.

As early as 800 B.C., at the time when the Yajur veda was composed, glass craft was very popular. It is evident from the archaeological findings at Basti in UP that glassware is about 2000 years old. The way glass is prepared and transformed into various shapes is remarkable.

India is famous for its leather products. The state of Uttar Pradesh is an important source for finished leather and leather products. The tanneries in Kanpur are known all over the world for the finest quality leather tanned by them. Kanpur and Agra in U.P are two renowned production centres for leather items.

The tradition of the paper craft in India is fairly old. The paper industry was located mainly in Patna, Delhi, Rajgir, Avadh, Ahemdabad, Gaya and Shahzadpur (near Allahabad). Since the paper is one of the easily perishable materials, the traditions of the paper craft have been left unrecorded.

Under the British rule, the Indian artisanal production declined rather sharply. The British East India Company acquired political power in Bengal after the Battle of Plassey in 1757. Before 1757, the Company brought gold and silver into India in exchange for Indian hand-made textiles and other goods. After 1757, however, the situation changed. The East India Company financed its trade in India by the money acquired through plunder and Diwani rights in Bengal. It established monopoly over the produce of the Bengal artisans who were forced to supply goods at low prices to the Company. This created great hardship to the weavers and other artisans of Bengal and other parts of India.

Moreover, the British rule, by eliminating most of the Indian princes and nobles, destroyed the main market for the artisanal luxury products.

From 1813 onwards, the English machine made cotton goods started arriving in bulk in India. In the coming decades, this import increased phenomenally. These machine-made goods were cheaper compared to the hand-made Indian textiles. This caused a rapid decline in the production of Indian textiles thereby causing great misery to the weavers. From 1850s upto 1947, Indian handicrafts were subjected to the combined onslaught of the British as well as the Indian mills. This further eroded the already declining handicrafts market. The impact was most notable on the hand made cotton goods.

There are various handicrafts related associations in India to promote Indian crafts in the international market.

India, entwined with her rich artistic tradition has provided ample opportunity to make Indian handicraft to stand apart with its colossal pride. For the greater objective of taking Indian handicrafts to the next level of maturity, a number of handicraft-related associations in India have made their presence felt.

Whether to showcase the varied Indian handicrafts or to cater to the growth and overall mellowness of Indian handicrafts, the wide range of Indian handicraft associations have an immense contribution. The technical, marketing and even the financial aspects of Indian handicrafts are ideally being taken care by these handloom associations of India. The Handicrafts and Handlooms Export Corporation of India, also known as HHEC, the central cottage industries or the CCIE, The North-Eastern Handicrafts and Handloom Development Association are some of the important handloom-related associations in India.

The All India Handicrafts Board was established in 1952 to guide the Government on various problems of handicrafts and to provide measures for improvement and development of Indian crafts. The board also looks after other aspects of handicrafts like the technical, marketing, financial, organizational part and formulates plans in this direction. It also guides and provides assistance to the state governments for planning and executing schemes for the development of handicrafts.

The Handicrafts and Handlooms Export Corporation of India (HHEC) is a subsidiary of the State Trading Corporation of India, which was established in June 1962. The Corporation functions in the field of direct export and also helps in developing new markets and expanding the old ones. It also provides assistance to introduce new products for the consumers staying abroad. The Corporation undertakes and executes wholesale orders and conducts retail sale operations through retail shops abroad. It also takes part in various exhibitions that are organized throughout the world to promote Indian crafts. HHEC also helps private exporters by affiliating them as business associates. It also supports a number of publicity and promotional measures for the export of handicrafts and handloom products.

The Central Cottage Industries Corporation Private Limited is a registered society, which had absorbed the Indian Cooperative Union. The Central Cottage Industries Emporium (CCIE) is located at Janpath in New Delhi and is the first sales organization in Indian handicrafts. The CCIE has branches at Bombay, Calcutta and Chennai.

The North-Eastern Handicrafts and Handloom Development Corporation Limited (NEHHDC) located in Shillong was established in 1977 with the aim to promote and improve the sale of handlooms and handicrafts in the north-eastern region.

The National Handlooms and Handicrafts Museum (NHHM) was established in Pragati Maidan in New Delhi.

It comprises of fifteen structures, which represent village dwellings, courtyards and shrines from various states of India. It is spread over an area of five acres and has a rare and exclusive collection of Indian crafts.

CHAPTER-5

Types of Handicrafts and Textiles Produced in India

Indian handicrafts are always rich in variety owing to great diversity in the cultural set-up of Indian society. The handicrafts produced in far-flung regions of India are unique and possess great historical traditions and artistry.

Crafts in India present an array of exclusive Indian handicrafts culled from all the far and near corners of the country. From sculptures and statues, paintings, Indian home furnishings, home décor items to traditional games, toys and dolls, office accessories and more – crafts in India has it all. While some states and regions specialise in one kind of craft, the remaining in the other. In the hill states and Gujarat, every village has utensils and garments vibrantly alive with colour and ornamentation spontaneously created for their own pleasure.

Traditionally, craftsmen in India have always had the status of an artist, tracing their descent to Vishwakarma, the "Lord of many Arts".

For the novice tourist, the first overwhelming impact is of Kashmiri handicraft, papier mache, embroidery and carpets with vibrant flowing imagery and colour of foliage, flora and fauna of Kashmir's enchanted landscape. The glint of metal comes next. Brass, copper, silver and gold–hammered, beaten or cast, engraved, enamelled or *repoussed*–have been used down the ages.

Especially in Kashmir, walnut wood, blackwood, mahogany, redwood and ebony are used, whereas in the south and the cast, tcak wood is carved and ornamented in a variety of ways.

The *sadeli* marquetry work of Surat in Gujarat, the *tarkashi* brass wire inlay of Rajasthan and Uttar Pradesh, ivory craft and mother-of-pearl inlay in south, the brass sheet inlay *pittara* dowry chests and doors of Saurashtra, the *kamangiri* figurative painted woodwork of Jodhpur and Jaipur, the brilliantly coloured lacquer work of Sankheda, Nirmal and Sawantwadi, the lattice lace of *jaali* screens from Saharanpur; the flowers and foliage carved into the satin finish of Kashmiri walnut, the gesso and goldleat of Bikaner, are worth looking for.

No visitor to India should miss the sight of the village potter turning his wheel with his big toe and with a few flicks of his thumb, producing a shape identical to what his forefather would have made in Mohenjodaro some 5,000 years ago. Not turned on a wheel but moulded, is the famous blue pottery of Jaipur. Other lovely shapes are the blue and green cutwork pottery of Khurja, the blackware of Chinhat and Azamgarh in Uttar Pradesh and the huge teracotta horses of Tamil Nadu and Bengal.

Some of varied Arts and Crafts practised in different parts of India are mentioned below along with their details.

1) Applique

Applique is decorative work in which one piece of cloth is sewn or fixed onto another, or the activity of decorating a cloth using glass pieces, metals, wood or metal wires. The art of applique is mostly practiced in Orissa and Rajasthan giving rise to some of the most beautiful Indian fabric art. Exquisite bed spreads, lampshades, wall hangings and more are made using the art of applique.

Applique Work in Orissa

Orissa's applique work is one of the most fascinating handicrafts of India. The Pipli village in Puri district of Orissa is the main center of applique work. Rows of shops in Pipli flaunt applique handbags, bed sheets, wall hangings, purses, cushion covers, letter cases, pillow covers, canopies and garden umbrellas.

Patronized by kings and nobility of Orissa, applique work at one time had reached the artistic heights of excellence. The kings of Puri engaged craftsmen in the service of Lord Jagannath and set up village Pipli for them to live in. Though the art became popular after the construction of the Lord Jagannath temple in Puri, its origins go far beyond.

In olden days, Pipli craftsmen used to make canopies, banners, umbrellas and trashas (fans) for festivals held in Puri's famous temple. But as the craft's popularity spread far and wide through the pilgrims of Puri, the craftsmen started making other decorative and utility items also.

Process of Applique

This beautiful craft is usually practiced on dazzling red, purple, black, yellow, green and white fabric. The craftsman first prepares the base material in the shape of square, rectangle, circle or oval which forms the background for the pieces of art.

Applique motifs in contrasting colours are then cut in the shape of animals, birds, flowers, leaves, celestial bodies and geometric shapes. These motifs are then stitched onto the base cloth in aesthetic arrangements.

Raised motifs are prepared by giving several folds. The actual grace of applique craft lies in its intricate stitches namely, bakhia, guntha, turpa, chikan and other very delicate and esoteric embroidery techniques. Nowadays, small mirrors and bright metal pieces are used to enhance its beauty. After attaching the applique patches to the base cloth, the borders are then stitched.

Almost all the family members get involved in this craft. Skilled persons of the family go for beautiful intricate designs while the less experienced take up the simple works like stitching the borders and making the base clothes.

Applique Work in Other States

The traditional applique from Punjab is called 'phulkari'. The meaning of the word phulkari is flowering as the surface of the cloth begins to resemble flowering petals. Phulkari is generally made on shawls using the darn stitch to attach pieces of cloth onto the surface of the shawl. Apart from flowers, stylized figures of animals and plants are also made. Silk thread is generally used in creating phulkari, though occasionally cotton thread is also put in use.

In Andhra Pradesh, the blouses and headscarves worn by the Banjara tribal women are not only embroidered but also decorated with appliqu and mirror work.

Rajasthan is also known for its unique appliqu or gota, which is created by sewing edges of zari ribbon onto fabric, to create elaborate patterns. It is commonly used for making costumes for women. Khandela in Shekhawati is best known for producing these items.

Applique work these days can be seen on utilitarian items such as bags, lampshades, tablemats etc. Appliqu embroidery can also be seen on blouses, petticoats, gowns and other garments.

Applique work

The traditional homes of applique and patchwork are Kutch, Saurashtra, Orissa (Pipli), Bengal, Bihar, U.P., Andhra Pradesh and Tamilnadu. The people of Bahni in Kutch make a variety of dhadki, spread-cum-quilt by using the applique work technique. Similarly, Kathis, Mers, Kunbis use both applique and patchwork technique.

In applique technique motifs are cut out from colour red applied to a plain ground, normally white, to create a range of patterned spreads, quilts, costumes, etc. Motifs like human figures, animal, and flowers are also cut out and applied to the ground/plain cloth.

Applique comes from the French word applique, which means to 'put on'. In applique, one layer of fabric is placed over another layer of fabric and is sewn in place. Applique, a decorative work in white piece of cloth is sewn or fixed on to another, or the activity of decorating a cloth using glass pieces metals wood or metal wires. In India, the applique is mostly applied in Orissa, Rajasthan and Punjab giving rise to some of the most beautiful Indian fabric art, exhaust bed spreads, lampshades, wall-hangings and many more. Among the traditional textiles, the art of applique work occupies a distinguished place. Indian applique art is widely prevalent in the western states of India and especially in Gujarat, Rajasthan, and in the eastern coast of Orissa.

The roots of the applique art form is intertwined with the rituals and traditions of Lord Jagannath, the presiding deity of the Puri temple. The applique items are mainly used during processions of the deities in their various ritual outings. Items like chhati, tarasa and chandua are used for this purpose. Applique craft is traditionally practised by a caste of professional tailors known as *darjis*. Applique, the art of patch work, is an integral part of Gujarat and its world of folk art. The decorative needle work of Gujarat, has a distinctive style of its own. Applique is a craft, which has waste piece of cloth as its raw material. Articles produced by this craft were used by kings and emperors and the nobility in the past. The *shamiana* and *chandowa*, the two principal items of this craft, continue to be used today for all religious and social ceremonies.

Applique is a technique by which the decorative effect is obtained by superposing patches of coloured fabrics on a plain basic fabric. The edges of the patches being sewn in some form of stitchery. It is distinct from patch work in which small pieces of cut fabrics are usually joined side by side to make a large piece of fabric or for repairing a damaged fabric.

The basic material for applique is cloth. Flat motifs are first cut from cloth and specially prepared motifs are made separately. If more than one of the same cut motifs is required, than a stencil is used. These cut and specially prepared motifs are then superimposed on a base cloth in predetermined layout and sequence. The edges of the motifs are turned in and skillfully stitched on to the base cloth or stitched by embroidery or without turning as necessary. The specially prepared motifs may be coloured or white. Some of the specially prepared motifs have exclusive embroidery work and some have mirror work. The stitching process varies from item to item and come under six broad categories, namely,

(a) bakhia,

(b) taropa,

(c) granthi,

(d) chikana,

(e) button-hole, and

(f) ruching.

The layout of various motifs and patterns vary according to shape of the piece. The canopy has a large centre piece which may be a square. This centre piece is then bounded by several borders of different widths, one outside the other, till the edge is reached.

Gujarat applique is mainly based on patchwork, in which coloured and patterned fabric is finely cut in different sizes and shapes. It is then sewn together on a plain background to form a composite piece. The whole charm of an applique lies in the contours of each individual inset piece. The stitch done on each individual bit is not hidden, but adds to the art. Infact, gaudy colours of thread are used to show out distinctly. Generally two types of applique work is done by women in Bihar:

1) The first type is prepared by them for their personal use, and
2) The second for commercial purposes.

The latter is an interesting legacy of olden times when a variety of *kanatas* (walled enclosures), *samianas* (canopies and tents), with different types of brocades and patch-work were prepared. The *samianas* made with applique work designs, even today, continue this age old tradition. The designs and motifs are generally prepared on the *kanatas*. These are cut out of a piece of the desired cloth and stitched on to the basic material with the help of a few rough stitches. Then the edges are turned quickly and motifs stitched on to the background in a beautiful cloth in general manner. The background cloth is generally dark red or deep orange and the motifs are prepared in white with some portions in blue. The design of the *samiana* also is cut out of one piece of material which is usually the size of the background material. They carefully prepare and join both the pieces, and then nip and turn the cutout portions which are finally stitched with the original cloth. The men cut out the patterns to be stitched to *samianas* and *kanatas* and the women workers in the villages do the entire stitching. Applique is also done by women on their own garments. Here, stylised motifs are cut and stitched on to a fabric so that the pattern emerges in two colours. Energy and passion seem to find expression through vibrant scarlets, oranges, yellows, and provide the key to the mood and the tempo.

Originally the main applique items were built up around the temple and its festivals with large, highly decorated umbrellas, tents and pavilions. Now, they are used as beach and garden umbrellas, and as lampshades, canopies for parties, tents for public gatherings, etc.

The motifs used are fairly varied, yet fixed, and consist of stylised representations of flora and fauna as well as a few mythical figures. Of the more common of these motifs are elephant, parrot, peacock, ducks, creepers, trees, flowers, half-moon, the sun and *rahu*. Motifs in brilliant colours are cut out and stitched on to the material. These are usually peacocks with their tails unfurled, elephants with a rider, or a horse carrying a warrior, in addition to floral patterns. The applique work of Bihar called *khatwa* is famous for decorative tents and canopies used on ceremonial occasions. The designs on tents are the usual Persian type bearing trees, flowers, animals, birds, etc. The *kanats* (tented walls) carry stylised tree forms with juxtaposed animals at the base. All the basic traditional designs are collected on a piece of cloth as a master chart called *awalkhana*, from which the children begin to learn by copying figures like traditional umbrellas, canopies, saris, cholis, household linen, tents and pavilions, beach and garden umbrellas, lamp shades, shoulder bags, wall hangings, bed covers, pillow covers, letter pouches, torans, chaklas, chanderwas shamiana, chandowa, khatwa, cushion-cover, curtains, tea cosies, table cloths, blouse pieces, sari borders, etc.

2) The Art of Bandhej or Bandhni

Tie and dye is one of the most widely accepted and one of the most traditional methods of printing textiles in India. According to the design and the motif, each pattern has its special significance. The *chandokhni* and *shikhara* are specially created for the brides. The *barah baag*, when opened looks like a garden of flowers – a set of 12 (barah) beds of flowers. There was also a design called *bavan* (52) *baag*, but no one makes it now because it takes too much time and labour. The traditional design of bandhej are: (i) *Ambadal* – a network of branches and leaves interwoven with a variety of birds, that represent the branches of a mango tree; (ii) *Chokidal* – a pattern of squares with elephants and other animals; (iii) *Kambaliya* – a design with a dottedpattern in the center and a different design along the border; (iv) *Basant bahar* – representing the flowers of spring, and (v) *mor zad* – a peacock pattern, etc.

Origin of Tie-and-Dye

It is difficult to trace the origins of this craft to any particular area. According to some references, it first developed in Jaipur in the form of *leheriya*. But, it is widely believed that it was brought to Kutch from Sindh by Muslim Khatris who are still the largest community involved in the craft.

Bandhni was introduced in Jamnagar when the city was founded 400 years ago. This city has now become one of the principal centers of bandhni, creating new pattern and experimenting with modern colours.

The earliest reference to bandhni is in Bana Bhatt's *Harshacharita*, where he describes a royal wedding, "the old matrons were skilled in many sorts of textile patterning, some of which were in the process of being tied (bandhya mana)". This material was used to make the skirts for women.

A bandhni garment was considered auspicious for the bride. One also finds the maids in the Ajanta wall paintings wearing blouses of tie-and-dye patterns.

The tie-and-dye fabric is best produced in Gujarat and Rajasthan. In this technique portions of the cloth not to be coloured are plucked up in the finger nails of the maker and wound many times with waxed or starched string, and then immersed in the dye which does not penetrate the tied parts. Beginning with the lightest colour, this process is repeated one or more times according to the design.

Bandhani work is very popular handicraft all over India. After processing, Bandhani work results into a variety of symbols including, dots, squares, waves and strips. Bandhani work involves tying and dyeing of pieces of cotton or silk cloth. The main colours used in Bandhani are natural. In fact, all colours in bandhani are dark. Each state has particular areas, and each caste and each tribe, has its special design.

The term "bandhani" derives its name from the Hindi word bandhan which means tying up. Bandhani is an ancient art practised by people mainly of Rajasthan and Gujarat. Jaipur, Udaipur, Bikaner, Ajmer and Jamnagar are among the important centres producing *odhnis*, saris and turbans in bandhani. The wide variety was evolved over the centuries because of its close links with the religious and social customs of different people.

The work of bandhani has a rich history and the work was initiated exclusively by the Muslim Khatri community of Kutchh. Those Muslim Khatri women carried out the tradition from one generation to another and became the janitor of this art form.

The production of bandhani fabric is very tedious but appealing. Dyeing is accomplished by the tie-resist method as in *bandhana* and *laheria* where the patterns are made up of innumerable dots and weaves respectively. The manufacture of the bandhani work is usually performed both by men and women. Men do the dyeing while women do the tying, which is very intricately done, each dot is as tiny as a pin-head.

The cloth is first washed and bleached to prepare it for absorbing the dyes. After this, it is sent to the bandhani, the woman who does the tying, who inturn lifts a small portion of the fabric and tightly ties a thread around it. The tied textiles are then dipped in the light colour first while the tied areas retain the original ground colour. If a second dye is required, the areas to be retained in the first dye are tied for resist and the cloth dipped in a darker dye. This process is repeated, if several colours are to be combined.

Laheria in Bandhani is quite in style and refers to the wavy pattern of a fabric processed in the tie dye technique. The material is rolled diagonally and certain portions resisted by lightly binding threads at a short distance from one another before the cloth is dyed. The process of dyeing is repeated until the requisite number of colour is obtained.

For a chequered pattern, the fabric is opened and diagonally rolled again from the opposite corners; the rest of the process remains the same. The printing of residue on cloth with coloured powder, gold or silver dust, is known as *khari* or tinsel work.

Tying of the border in the bandhani is a special process known as sevo bandhavo. The border is tied according to the desired pattern by passing the thread from one end to the other in loose stitch so as to bring the entire portion together by pulling the thread from one end. The border portion is then covered up. This is process especially used to make sarees and has broad matching and contrasting borders. The style is applied to the pallus too. This tradition in India of bandhani print dresses is practised in Jamnagar (in the state of Gujarat), and Rajasthan.

Bandhani has become a popular tie-and-dye all over the country. The art work is used for various occasions and imparts new meaning. Bandhani woollen shawls are tie - dyed work which are presented by the khatris and worn by

Rabari women. *Suhagadi* – yellow dots on chocolate brown –is worn after marriage and before a woman bears child, while the *satbanteli* – red dots on black–is worn after her first child. The bagida pattern and colour combination is traditionally worn only by harijan women. The common design in bandhani is chains of grains represented by dots on the body called the dana pattern.

The work of bandhani has attracted not only women but it is popular among the men too. The women apparels possess beautiful bandhani work and the dresses of men also feature the opulence of the art form.

The garments that take in the gorgeous work of bandhani include sarees, woollens, shawls, scarves, handkerchiefs, dupattas, odhnis, turbans, suhagadi, satbanteli, bed-spreads, table cloths, jajams (floor-coverings), quilt covers, bed-covers, lungis, chunaries and pillya.

Tie-and-Dye Today

Today women and girls can be seen sitting in their homes in clothes of pieces of malmal (fine muslin), handloom or silk cloth. This cloth is first bleached and then folded into two or four layers depending on the thickness of the cloth. A *rangara* or designer marks the layout of the pattern on the material using wooden blocks dipped in *geru*, a burnt sienna colour mixed with water. The craftsmen then begin to tie the cloth, which is not to be dyed. The folds of the material within the small motif are lifted and tied together. The material with the first set of ties is dyed yellow.

There is also a process, mostly followed in Rajasthan, of dyeing parts of the material by hand-lipai technique. The material is then tied-and-dyed into red or green. If the border has to be darker, all the lighter parts are tied and covered with plastics foil and the edges are dyed with the required colours. Repeated tying and dyeing produces elaborate designs.

The raw materials required for bandhni are–muslin, handloom or silk cloth, ordinary thread for tying, starch and colours for dyeing. Traditionally, vegetable dyes were used, but today, chemical dyes are becoming very popular. The tools required are also very basic–wooden blocks for marking designs and the simple implements for dyeing.

The centres of tie-and-dye fabrics, especially in Gujarat, are Jamnagar (in Saurashtra), and Ahmedabad. The finest bandhani work of Rajasthan comes from Bikaner, Jaipur, Jodhpur, Barmer, Pali, Udaipur and Nathdwara. Rajasthan is well known for its *leheriya* pattern–literally meaning waves. These are harmoniously arranged diagonal stripes, which were originally, dyed in the auspicious colours of yellow and red. Pochampalli is also one of the three main traditional yarn-dyeing centers in the country.

The process of making bandhani varies in Gujarat and Rajasthan. Even the patterns, designs and craftsmanship vary in both the regions. The craftsmen from Rajasthan are easily recognized because they grow nail of their little finger so as to facilitate the lifting of cloth for tying, or wear a small metal ring with a point. The Gujarati craftsmen prefer to work without these aids. The flow is much better when one works with one's bare hands as it assures no damage to the cloth. The dyeing and printing of textiles has become a highly developed craft in Gujarat. Bandhani, a form of tie-resist dyeing and patola are two outstanding examples of the Indian dyer's art.

Colours Used in Tie-and-Dye

The colours commonly used in bandhani are–red, a symbol of marriage; saffron, a colour worn by a yogi who has renounced the world; yellow, which stands for spring; and black and maroon, used for mourning. Bandhani material is sold folded and with the knots tied. An intricate design in a sari may have approximately 75,000 dots.

What is essential in bandhani is the minute and skilful manipulation of the fingers for tying, extensive knowledge of colour schemes and skill in dyeing materials. It takes several years for a craftsman to perfect his skill.

Preparation & Process of Tie-and-Dye Weaving

The process of tie-and-dye weaving starts with preparing the warp and weft from the bleached silk yarn by spinning it. Squatted on the floor, women reel threads from primitive spinning wheels to load bobbins. Giant spinning wheels are employed to prepare the warp, which forms the length of the fabric. The warp is fastened between two poles set apart and marked according to the design.

For preparing the weft (which forms the width), a fan-shaped, spiked wooden frame is used. Strand upon strand of yarn is deftly wound between the spikes and the converging rod at the other end of the frame. The yarn is tied with threads and strips of rubber, in line with the predetermined pattern marked on it. The warp and weft yarns are individually knotted and wrapped tight enough to prevent the dye from penetrating into it when dipped in different colours. This is called double-tie-dye method.

The process of tying-and-dyeing is repeated several times depending on the number of colours required by the design. When the yarn has dried, the wrappings are carefully removed. The yarn, which is to become the length of the fabric to be woven, is stretched on the loom while the weft yarn is once again transferred to the fan-shaped wooden frame. At this stage one can see the patterns emerging, ready to be woven together.

The craft of tie-dyed weaving is known as *chitki* in Telugu. But its popular name, however, is *ikat*. The technique involves great skill and precise calculations by the textile artisans. The design is very colourful, intricate and attractive but at the same time very complicated. It takes nearly 15-20 days to weave a cloth of 20 metres–the maximum length a loom can take.

3) The Art of Batik Printing

Batik–The Art

Originated in India, the art of batik has come a long way from a mere handicraft. The word batik actually means 'wax writing'. It is a way of decorating cloth by covering a part of it with a coat of wax and then dyeing the cloth. The waxed areas keep their original colour and when the wax is removed the contrast between the dyed and undyed areas makes the pattern.

In the past, batik was considered as a fitting occupation for aristocratic ladies whose delicately painted designs based on bird and flower motifs were a sign of cultivation and refinement.

The beauty of batik lies in its simplicity and the fact that one need not be an artist to achieve results. Some of the best effects in batik are often achieved by chance.

History of Batik

Batik is very often considered a craft like ceramic, pottery or even needlework. Although it is a household word all over the world, batik is still overlooked by art critics who do not consider it an art form. There are several countries known for their batik creations, starting with India where it originated. From here, it moved to Indonesia, Malaysia, Sri Lanka, Thailand and the West.

The history of Indian batik can be traced as far back as 2000 years. Indians were conversant with the resist method of printing designs on cotton fabrics long before any other nation had even tried it. Rice starch, and wax were initially used for printing on fabrics.

India has always been noted for its cotton and dyes. Indigo blue, which is the basic colour for batik, is one of the earliest dyes. It is believed that after its initial popularity in the past, the tedious process of dyeing and waxing caused the decline of batik in India till recent times.

In the South, near Madras, the well-known artist's village of Chola-Mandal is where batik gets an artistic touch. Batik that is produced in Madras is known for its original and vibrant designs.

Process of Batik

The creation of batik is a three stage process of waxing, dyeing and dewaxing (removing the wax). There are also several sub-processes like preparing the cloth, tracing the designs, stretching the cloth on the frame, waxing the area of the cloth that does not need dyeing, preparing the dye, dipping the cloth in dye, boiling the cloth to remove wax, and washing the cloth in soap.

The characteristic effects of the batik are the fine cracks that appear in the wax, which allow small amounts of the dye to seep in. It is a feature not possible in any other form of printing. It is very important to achieve the right type of cracks or hairline detail for which the cloth must be crumpled correctly. This requires a lot of practice and patience.

Knowing how to use the wax is of prime importance. The ideal mixture for batik wax is 30 per cent beeswax and 70 per cent paraffin wax. For first timers, even the melted wax of a candle is adequate. It is the skillful cracking that is important. While applying, the wax should not be overheated, otherwise, it will catch fire. Correct knowledge of colours is also important. Practising on small pieces of cloth helps in the beginning. Patience is, of course, a very important factor too.

The cloth used should be strong enough to bear the heat and wax. Cambric, poplin and voiles are used besides pure silk. Synthetic fabrics should be avoided. Since ancient times, Indians have been known to wear vibrant colours and dyes which were made from barks of trees, leaves, flowers and minerals. Blue was obtained from indigo, while orange and red were obtained from henna. Yellow was derived from turmeric while lilac and mauve from logwood. Black was created by burning iron in molasses and cochineal from insects.

Since handmade batik is unable to meet with the consumer demands, very often, the answer is tjaping with a copper block. A tjap is a metal block made of copper strips into the required design after which it is stamped quickly and with great force.

Batik is created in several ways. In splash method the wax is splashed or poured onto the cloth. The screen-printing method involves a stencil. The hand painting is done by a kalamkari pen. The scratch-and-starch resist are the other methods.

From being a handicraft, batik has acquired the status of an art. Batik is a versatile medium that can become an ideal hobby for an amateur or a medium of expression for an artist. Batik, as an art form, is quite spontaneous and one can open up new vistas of creative form. Until recently, batik was made for dresses and tailored garments only but modern batik is livelier and brighter in the form of murals, wall hangings, paintings, household linen, and scarves.

Batik Sarees

The word 'batik' is an Indonesian-Malay word that has perhaps been derived from the word ' Ambatik' which literally means 'a cloth with small dots'. This form of art has been practiced in India for over 2100 years now. The textured art form of Batik is famous for the artistic freedom it offers due to its inherent style and technique. Multi-coloured and beautifully designed batik sarees are popular and attractive for their contrast colour schemes.

The charm of batik lies in each piece being individualistic and a fresh creation. It is an art wherein parts of cloth are covered with wax to make it dye resistant, and the other areas are dyed, to create coloured and uncoloured areas on the same piece. In the contrast between these dyed and undyed areas lies the inherent beauty of Batik Art. Batik is done on a large scale in Indore and Bherongarh.

Indigo was one of the most popular and frequently used colours for the dyeing process. The resist method of printing was widely used in India much before it gained popularity in any other country. However, the elaborate processes of dyeing and waxing caused the decline of this beautiful art.

The technique of batik is basically a three-stage process including waxing, dyeing and de-waxing. There are also several sub-processes like preparing the cloth, tracing the designs, stretching the cloth on the frame, waxing the area of the cloth that does not need dyeing, preparing the dye, dipping the cloth in dye, boiling the cloth to remove wax and washing the cloth in soap.

Batik is a resist process in which the fabric is painted with molten wax and then dyed in cold dyes. The surface of a finely woven fabric has melted bee wax and paraffin applied with a brush as a resist to block the parts which are not to be dyed or meant to be in light shade. After this, it is immersed in a cold dye which colours the background. The other remaining parts are dyed, part by part, shutting off the ones that are not to be covered. In the final stage, the entire fabric is cleared of wax with boiling water and soap.

As the fabric is handled, in the process, the wax coating breaks up into a kind of irregular network of thin hair-like cracks through which the dye finds its way and creates involuntarily a design of its own which gives the fabric a fresh-like quality and enhances its attractiveness.

4) Benarasi Saris of India

The Benarasi saris gained popularity during the Mughal era. During this period, all art was amalgamated to create a fusion of aesthetics. Persian motifs and Indian designs on silk studded with gold and silver remained the cue of Mughal patronage. There are mainly four varieties of Benarasi sari available today. They are – pure silk (katan); organza (kora) with zari and silk; georgette, and shattir. The sari making is more of a cottage industry for several million people around Varanasi encompassing Gorakhpur and Azamgarh as well.

Making the Sari

Most of the silk for the saris comes from South, mainly Bangalore, where sericulture is a unique industry. The weavers weave the basic texture of the sari on the power loom. In weaving the warp, they create the base, which runs into 24 to 26 meters. There are around 5600 thread wires with 45-inch width.

At the weaving loom, three people work. One weaves, the other works at the revolving ring to create lacchis (rolled bundles). At this juncture, another important process is initiated. This is designing the motifs. There are several traditional artists in Varanasi who, though not formally trained in designing, create wonderful designs for saris.

To create naksha patta (design boards), the artist first draws on graph paper with colour concepts. Traditional designs remain the base appeal for Varanasi saris. Once the design is selected, then small punch cards are created. These serve as guides for which colour thread has to pass through. For one design, one requires hundreds of perforated cards to implement the concept. The prepared perforated cards are knitted with different threads and colours on the loom. Then, according to the design, they are paddled in a systematic manner so that the main weaving picks up the right colours and pattern.

A normal sari takes around 15 days to one month and sometimes six months to complete. However, it all depends on the intricacy of designs and patterns to be created on the sari.

Weaving Benarasi saris is a functional art of India, which has been going on for centuries within a great fabric of Indian traditional weavers.

Maheshwari Sarees

Maheshwar, on the banks of the river Narmada, weaves fine cotton saris with tiny checks, which combine complimentary colours together. Very soft colours are used for dyeing.

Jamdani Sarees

The cotton saris of West Bengal are called jamdani and they follow the traditional patterns.

Gharchola Sarees

Gharchola saris mainly are weaved in Gujarat. These are, especially, traditional wedding sarees.

Sambalpuri Sarees

Sambalpuri, which come in a variety of colours and traditional motifs inspired by nature are the most popular among the people.

Venkatagiri Sarees

The cotton saris of Andhra Pradesh have variety. The best known amongst these are gadiwal, wainarpati, nainder and venkatagiri.

Paithani Sarees

Paithani sarees are used in special occasions only. These sarees are basically from Andhra Pradesh. The paithani became very popular during the Maratha period.

5) Hand Block Printing

Hand block printing, a craft handed down through generations is in the forefront of the fashion scene today. The ancient craft has seen a major revival over the last two decades and has moved away from its traditional rural centers to the metropolitan cities of Delhi, Mumbai, Chennai, and Bangalore.

History

India has been renowned for its printed and dyed cotton cloth since the 12th century and the creative processes flourished as the fabric received royal patronage. Though the earliest records mention the printing centers in the south, the craft seems to have been prevalent all over India. Surat in Gujarat became a prominent center for trade of painted and printed textiles. The major items produced were wall hangings, canopies and floor-spreads in rich natural colours.

Records show that as far back as the 12th century, several centers in the south, on the western and eastern coasts of India became renowned for their excellent printed cotton. On the south-eastern coast, the brush or *kalam* was used, and the resist applied was by the same method. In the medieval age, printing and dyeing of cottons was specially developed in Rajasthan. In Gujarat the use of wooden blocks for printing was more common.

Tents were created from printed fabrics and became a necessary part of royal processions. The seasons largely influenced the integration of the highly creative processes of weaving, spinning, dyeing and printing. Festivals also dictated this activity.

Trade in cotton cloth is said to have existed between India and Babylon since Buddha's time. Printed and woven cloths travelled to Indonesia, Malaya and the Far East.

In the 17th century, Surat was established as a prominent center for export of painted and printed calicos, covering an extensive range in quality. Cheaper printed cloth came from Ahmedabad and other centers, and strangely enough, Sanganer was not such a famous center for printing as it is today.

The idea of using an object to impress repeated designs on cloth can be traced to prehistoric times. The first application of colour to cloth was probably by hand. This progressed to twigs and brushes, then stamps made from clay, metal, and wood. Anokhi uses hand-carved wooden blocks to print cottons, silks, woods, and rayons. To ensure crisp carving and sharp detail, wood blocks are made by cutting into the end grain of dense woods.

Hand block printing is an inseparable part of cultural heritage of Rajasthan. Traditionally, Sanganer produced fine small floral motifs on white backgrounds for the royal court, whilst Bagru produced simplified graphic designs for the local rural people.

The process of hand block printing is very intricate and interesting. Once the teak block has been carved, the cloth to be printed is stretched out on a table five metres long and pinned at each end to fix it. A tray is filled with the pigment and the block is placed into it to collect the accurate amount of dye.

Once the design and colours have been finalised, they are given to the block-maker. He then marks the design out on a block, which is usually around 15 cms square. The number of blocks needed per design depends on the number of colours used. Colours are applied one at a time.

To ensure that each subsequent colour registers properly, blocks are often cut to shape or have registration notches cut into them. The block-maker may take up to 80 hours to carve a single colour block and the printer may require upto 30 separate blocks to complete a garment or quilt.

The tray, which contains a metal grid with layers of fabric laid on top, is filled with dye. The dye soaks through the fabric, which then acts as an ink pad against which the block is to be pressed. The block is then placed carefully on the fabric and struck with the heel of the printers hand. The process is repeated until the entire cloth is covered. This means that the cloth can be stamped over a 1000 times for three metres.

Each colour has its own block and each colour is lined up using tiny markers in the blocks. Colours can vary owing to the weather, and as it is printed in five metre, lengths can vary within a collection. Natural dyes are affected more by the weather and printing has to stop completely over the Monsoon season. The more are the colours used, the greater is the time and labour required for cutting the blocks and printing the cloth.

Different dyes react in different ways, and therefore, have separate process when applied to fabric. Indigo dyes, for example, are resist-printed with a paste made from clay, wheat chaff and gum. The resist paste is printed on the cloth with a block and left to dry. This blocks the indigo dye from penetrating the cloth when the cloth is later dipped into the indigo vat. Once the cloth has been dyed it is washed to remove excess dye and the resist paste. Hand block printed fabrics are best washed in warm water with a gentle detergent. This ensures the colours remain rich and vibrant.

We get the earliest references of printed cotton from Gujarat at Fostat. Traditionally, Pethapur in Gujarat was well known for its mud-resist prints, known as sodagiri which was made for export to the Far East. Wooden blocks with intricate patterns, using four colours, are prepared at Pethapur even today. The Persianised printed patterns, produced for export in the 17th century, are not seen any more in Gujarat today. Perhaps, it has got absorbed in the traditional, design. During the medieval period, there was large demand in the European market for Indian printed cotton cloth, commonly called *chintz*. It formed the major item of Indian exports to European markets.

Major Centers of Hand Block Printing

Cotton is also printed in Ahmedabad, Sanganer, Bagru, Farukhabad and Pethapur, the main centers in Rajasthan and Gujarat where hand block printing has continued to flourish.

In fact, the prints of these areas seem to be quite similar. The Bagru and Sanganeri prints cannot be easily distinguished but if one looks carefully each has its own typical characteristics. The Sanganer prints are always on a white background, whereas the Bagru prints are essentially in red and black. Farukhabad is famous for its artistry and intricacy of design. Pethapur near Ahmedabad is known for the finest block printing. Banaras block makers design their blocks to suit fine silk printing with each design sometimes having seven colours.

Block designs get bigger and bolder and the delicacy is lost as one moves towards the south or towards Calcutta.

Today, Andhra Pradesh is a large center for hand block printing. Hyderabad is the home of the very popular Lepakshi prints. It is quite amazing how the same motif can be interpreted in different forms. Ajarakh prints, popular even today, originated in Gujarat involving a resist print, primarily intended for garments for men.

The Process of Hand Block Printing

Block printing has become popular because the simple process can create such sensational prints in rich and vibrant colours. Originally, natural dyes were used, but now, they have been replaced by chemical and artificial colours. The main colours used are red, the colour of love, yellow the colour of spring, blue as in Krishna, and saffron of the yogi.

The main tools of the printer are wooden blocks in different shapes and sizes called *bunta*. Blocks are made of seasoned teak wood by trained craftsmen. The underside of the block has the design etched on it. Each block has a wooden handle and two to three cylindrical holes drilled into the block for free air passage and also to allow release of excess printing paste. The new blocks are soaked in oil for 10-15 days to soften the grains in the timber.

Wooden trolleys with racks have castor wheels fastened to their legs to facilitate free movement. The printer drags it along as he works. On the upper most shelf, trays of dye are placed. On the lower shelves, printing blocks are kept ready.

The fabric to be printed is washed free of starch and soft bleached if the natural grey of the fabric is not desired. If dyeing is required, as in the case of saris, where borders, or the body is tied and dyed, it is done before printing. The fabric is stretched over the printing table and fastened with small pins.

The printing starts form left to right. The colour is evened out in the tray with a wedge of wood and the block dipped into the outline colour (usually black or a dark colour).

When the block is applied to the fabric, it is slammed hard with the fist on the back of the handle so that a good impression may register. A point on the block serves as a guide for the repeat impression, so that the whole effect is continuous and not disjoined. The outline printer is usually an expert because he is the one who leads the process.

If it is a multiple colour design, the second printer dips his block in colour again using the point or guide for a perfect registration to fill in the colour. The third colour if existent follows likewise. Skill is necessary for good printing since the colours need to dovetail into the design to make it a composite whole. A single colour design can be executed faster, a double colour takes more time and multiple colour design would mean additional labor and more colour consumption.

Different dyes are used for silk and cotton. Rapid fast dyes, indigo sol and pigment dyes are cotton dyes. Printing with rapid dyes is a little more complicated as the dyes once mixed for printing have to be used the same day. Standard colours are black, red, orange, brown and mustard. Colour variation is little difficult and while printing it is not possible to gauge the quality or depth of colour.

It is only after the fabric is processed with an acid wash that the final colour is established. Beautiful greens and pinks are possible with indigo sol colours but pigment colours are widely popular today because the process is simple, the mixed colours can be stored for a period of time, subtle nuances of colours are possible, and new shades evolve with the mixing of two or three colours. Also, the colours are visible as one prints and do not change after processing.

Colours can be tested before printing by merely applying it onto the fabric. The pigment colour is made up of tiny particles, which do not dissolve entirely and hence are deposited on the cloth surface while rapid dyes and indigo sols penetrate the cloth.

Pigment colours are mixed with kerosene and a binder. The consistency should be just right, for if it is too thick, it gives a raised effect on the material, which spoils the design. Small plastic buckets with lids are ideal for storing the mixed colours over a few days.

Cotton saris after pigment printing are dried out in the sun. This is part of the fixing process. They are rolled in wads of newspapers to prevent the dye from adhering to other layers and steamed in boilers constructed for the purpose. Silks are also steamed this way after printing. After steaming, the material is washed thoroughly in large quantities of water and dried in the sun, after which it is finished by ironing out single layers, which fix the colour permanently.

6) The Art of Brocade

Brocaded Textile

Among the brocaded textile, jamdani textile is most important. The word jamdani is derived from 'jama of coat.' It means loom embroidered or figured. Weavers wove floral, animal or bird ornaments on the loom. The warp is, as a rule, unbleached grey yarn, the motifs being woven in bleached white yarn. Its woven both, on cotton as well as on wool.

The most important centres of jamdani weaving in the Gangetic plain are Dacca in E. Bengal and Tanda and Banaras in U.P. Banaras weavers use gold thread also. Dacca weavers use coloured cotton thread along with gold and white but the finest Tanda jamdani is woven only with white yarn. The ornamental figures are woven by two threads of yarn of the same count as in the background. The threads are lifted up by the weaver with his fingers. The weaver directly works on the loom and no naqshas are used nor the design is tied on the loom. Brocade technique is also used by the shawl weavers of Kashmir.

Brocades is known as "The Tradition of Bringing Silk to Life"

Brocade weaving, especially with gold and silver, has been an age-old tradition in India.

There are two broad classes of brocades. Brocades of pure silk or silk and cotton blends and zari brocades with gold and silver threads.

The most important material in brocade weaving is silk. It facilitates lovely weaves, is durable, strong, fine and smooth. There are several varieties of raw silk of which the chief ones used for brocades are tanduri, banaka and mukta. Tanduri is imported from Malda and other places in Bengal. Banaka is thinner and finer variety and is mostly used to weave soft fabrics such as turbans and handkerchiefs. Mukta is a coarse and durable silk used for kimkhabs, as fine silk would not withstand heavy gold patterns.

Refining Silk for Brocade Making

Raw silk is specially treated for brocades. It is first twisted (called 'silk throwing') after which the threads undergo reeling and checking for uniformity and roundness. When the yarn has been processed, it is bleached and "degummed", as raw silk has a gum-like substance (sericin) in its composition. This has to be removed in order to bring out the sheen and softness and to enable penetration of the dye. The task has to be done with great care as the fibers can weaken or get damaged. The silk is boiled in soap water for a certain duration and then sent for dyeing.

Importance of Colour

Colour plays a vital part in weaving a brocade. The charm and subtle beauty of the brocade depends upon colour synchronization. Colours are surcharged with nuances of mood and poetic association in fabrics and weaving as much as in painting.

- Red - the colour of love. The three tones of red evoke the three states of love.
- Yellow - is the colour of vasant (spring), of young blossoms, southern winds and swarms of bees.
- Nila (indigo) - the colour of Lord Krishna who is likened to a rain-filled cloud.
- Hari nila - the colour of water in which the sky is reflected.
- Gerwa (saffron) - the colour of the earth and of the yogi, the wandering minstrel, the seer, the poet who renounces the world.

Earlier, vegetable dyes were used during weaving. These produced fast colours, lasted for almost a generation, and remained as beautiful and vivid as ever. Nowadays aniline dyes have gained popularity as they are cheaper, less time-consuming and produce a larger variety of colours.

Making Nakshas (Designs) on Brocades

Making of *nakshas* (designs) forms an important part of brocade weaving. Banaras is the main center where the *nakshabandha* (designer) tradition prevails. The skill and imagination of *nakshabandha* plays a prominent part in making of designs. Designs are associated with legends and symbolism. The most popular motifs are drawn from nature.

In Banaras, it is said that *nakshabandha* families were brought to this country during the reign of Muhammed Tughlak (1325-1350 A.D.). They were supreme masters of the art of tying designs into the loom. Local artisans and weavers learned this art from these great craftsmen.

Some of these craftsmen were also great poets–perhaps they wove their poetry into their designs. One such renowned poet was Ghias-i-Naqsband, mentioned in Abul Fazl's '*Ain-i-Akbari*'.

The *nakshas* are first worked on paper. This part of the work is called *likhai* (writing). The *nakshabandha* then makes a little pattern of it in a framework of cotton threads like a graph. This pattern gives guidance to the working of that design into weaving.

Designs and motifs have undergone changes gradually and imperceptibly. These changes can be traced through paintings made during different periods. Ajanta and Bagh murals show the existence of different techniques of designs and textiles. During the Gupta period, popular designs were formal floral motifs or scrolls entwined with hansas or sinhas-bird and animal depictions.

In the 16th century, the old designs were replaced by Persian floral motifs. Akbari paintings show half-blooming flowers, the Jehangir period, full-blown blossom and the Shahjehan period, tiny blossoms with emphasis on the leaves. In the 19th century, with the advent of British rule, there was a drastic change in designs. Some brocades started depicting English wallpaper designs to suit the tastes of the British rulers.

Brocades are used by some for curtains and upholstery. Brocaded zari saris and lehengas are in demand for marriages, religious ceremonies and other auspicious and social occasions. Looking back a hundred years, one is amazed to find that in spite of rapid industrialization, most of the age-old centers of handloom textiles still continue to produce beautifully woven fabrics.

The main centers besides Banaras are Ahmedabad and Surat where saris of the finest silk, gauze and gold with lively colour schemes are woven. Murshidabad in Bengal was a reputed center for *kimkhab* during the 19th century. Paithan and Aurangabad are other centers of brocade manufacture. In the south, Triuchirapalli and Tanjore produce a variety of *kimkhabs* known as *gulbadan* in which gold wire is used profusely. Brocade weaving, a craft that was on the decline, is again showing a very promising trend. Most of the credit for this goes to the village handloom weavers, designers and dyers, who, with their combined efforts, have kept alive our tradition of weaving.

Shopping for Brocades

What to Look for

Besides the traditional Indian dresses like the sari, lehanga or ghagra, cholis (blouse), coats and jackets, a tourist can buy brocade bags, purses, cushion covers, and wall hangings. Brocade borders are also available. They can be used imaginatively to design clothes, cushions, scarves etc. Brocade is also sold by the yard. The heavier variety can be used for drapes and upholstery.

7) Indian Textile

The richness of colour and motifs in Indian textiles is overwhelming. Its use can be subtle or dramatic. A *tanchoi* brocade from Benaras will play on the contrast of one delicately differing shade against another in shadow and sun, while, a south Indian temple sari might have a body of shocking Indian pink and a border of parrot green with stylized elephants, tigers and peacocks running riot in gold on its trailing *palloo*!

Woven, waxed, tie and dyed, brocaded, embroidered, appliqued, block-printed, painted, stencilled, running the whole gamut from simple to splendid, a few rupees to a fortune, there is something for every season and ceremony, symbolic or merely spectacular.

Often seen abroad are block-printed Indian cottons and *Saurashtrian* mirrorwork, Indian silks and brocades, Quilts, Kashmiri carpets and shawls. Fascinating, though lesser known techniques, are the tie-and-dye *bandhni* saris and scarves of Rajasthan and Gujarat, in which fine cotton or silk is knotted into minute patterns with waxed string and dyed in successive deepening shades of different colours.

Similar to the *bandhani* technique is *ikat*. In case of the *patola*, *pochampalli*, *telia rumal* and *mashru* weaves of Gujarat, Andhra Pradesh and Orissa, the warp and weft threads are separately tie-dyed before being woven into intricate, stylized designs of flowering shrubs, birds, elephants and fish, set in geometric squares and stripes. Both *bandhni* and *patola* are associated with marriage and no bride's trousseau is complete without one or the other.

Amongst a myriad of stitches, two differing but equally exciting techniques, are the *phulkori* (flower-craft) of Punjab and the *chikkon* work of Lucknow in Uttar Pradesh. In its bold surface, satin stitch in vivid satin floss in oranges, pinks and flames, the *phulkari* reflects the vigour and vibrant energy of the Punjabi peasant, while the *chikkon* work's typical delicate white on white floral net and shadow work shows the subtlety and refinement of the Mughal court, where legend has it that Noorjehan, Queen Consort to the Emperor Jehangir, first devised the craft.

India has a diverse and rich textile tradition. The origin of Indian textiles can be traced to the Indus Valley Civilization. The people of this civilization used homespun cotton for weaving their garments. Excavations at Harappa and Mohenjodaro, have unearthed household items like needles made of bone and spindles made of wood, amply suggesting that homespun cotton was used to make garments. Fragments of woven cotton have also been found from these sites.

The first literary information about textiles in India can be found in the *Rigveda*, which refers to weaving. The ancient Indian epics–*Ramayana* and *Mahabharata*–also speak of a variety of fabrics of those times. The *Ramayana* refers to the rich styles worn by the aristocracy on one hand and the simple clothes worn by the commoners and ascetics. Ample evidence on the ancient textiles of India can also be obtained from the various sculptures belonging to Mauryan and Gupta age as well as from ancient Buddhist scripts and murals (Ajanta caves). Legend has it that when Amrapali, a courtesan from the kingdom of Vaishali met Gautam Buddha, she wore a richly woven semi-transparent sari, which speaks volumes of the technical achievement of the ancient Indian weaver.

India had numerous trade links with the outside world and Indian textiles were popular in the ancient world. Indian silk was popular in Rome in the early centuries of the Christian era. Hoards of fragments of cotton material originating from Gujarat have been found in the Egyptian tombs at Fostat, belonging to 5th century A.D. Cotton textiles were also exported to China during the heydays of the silk route. Silk fabrics from South India were exported to Indonesia during the 13th century. India also exported printed cotton fabrics or chintz to European countries and the Far East before the coming of the Europeans to India.

The British East India Company also traded in Indian cotton and silk fabrics, which included the famous Dacca muslins. Muslins from Bengal, Bihar and Orissa were also popular abroad. Chintz is cotton cloth, usually printed with flowery patterns, that has a slightly shiny appearance.

The past traditions of the textile and handlooms can still be seen amongst the motifs, patterns, designs, and the old techniques of weaving, still employed by the weavers.

Traditions

The textile tradition in India has been conditioned by a number of factors, like geography, climate, local culture, social customs, availability of raw materials, etc. A variety of raw material like silk, cotton, wool, jute, etc. is used in India for creating fabric. The geo-climatic and bio diversity of India has given birth to a myriad of textiles and weaving throughout India. Local, foreign markets, and export potential dictate the traditional textile scenario of today.

The hilly and alpine region of the country has a rich array of woolen textiles. The world famous pashmina and shahtoosh shawls of Kashmir are fine examples of the woolen textile of our country, so are the shawls and garments from Himachal Pradesh and the North-Eastern states. The textiles from the arid and semi-arid regions are bright and have rich embroidery on them. The people in the coastal areas of the south and eastern regions prefer garments made of white fabrics. Cotton and silk textiles are popular in these areas. Utilitarian items such as cushions, bed sheets, covers, table mats, napkins, curtains, etc. are produced throughout the country. Each state has its own unique contribution in making these utilitarian items.

Major Traditions & Style

Silk and cotton weaving predominate the weaving traditions in India. Silk weaving is common in most parts of the country, important centers being Mysore, Assam, Banaras, Murshidabad, Surat, Kanchipuram and Paithan, etc. There are numerous centers, which specialize in silk and cotton sari weaving. Some of the sari traditions which are popular are–Banarsi brocades, Maheshwari, Pochampalli, Kancheevaram, Patola, Paithani, Baluchari, etc. to name a few.

The mulberry silk which is largely produced in Assam is also a rare variety of silk used for making saree and traditional dress material. It's a traditional custom to wear mulberry silk outfit in the new year festival of Assam called bihu. This is a yellowish and brown coloured delicate material produced from the mulberry silk cocoon which survives on mulberry tree leaves.

The tradition of Appliqu and embroidery is well known to Indians since ancient times. Punjab is famous for its Phulkari work, which is a rich form of Appliqu. Appliqu work from Kutchh region of Gujarat is also very ornate and is done on bright fabrics. It is also famous amongst the tribals of Orissa, Rajasthan and Andhra Pradesh. The city of Lucknow is world famous for its Chikan style of embroidery, so is the crewelwork from Kashmir. Gujarat, Punjab, Karnataka, Rajasthan and West Bengal all have their distinct styles of embroidery.

Tie-and-dye, hand-printing and block-printing are common across the country and come in numerous styles, influenced by local factors. The tie-and-dye technique of printing, in particular, is popular in the arid and semi-arid regions of the country where people prefer brightly coloured clothes. The states of Rajasthan, Madhya Pradesh and Andhra Pradesh are main centers for block-printing.

The present day textile tradition of India is not only the reflection of our rich past but also caters to the modern day requirements of the common man. Though some of the traditional textiles cater only to the needs of the upper class of the society, there is a huge demand for utilitarian items such as bed covers, sheets, cushions, curtains, bags, table mats, furnishings, etc. There is a glut of such items in the domestic market.

The contemporary textile craft tradition of India is not only rural and traditional in ethos, but it is also capable of meeting the challenges of modern times. This craft tradition has achieved the status of a highly organized small and medium-scale industry.

8. Clay Craft and Pottery

Earthenware

Harappan pottery is generally plain with some black painted decoration. Large number of terracotta figurines have been found here. They were mainly used as toys or cult figures. A variety of birds, animals, and male and female figurines are also found.

In Hindu mythology it is said that Brahma, the creator of life made man from clay and put life into it. Brahma is also called Prajapati and it gave rise to the caste name of potter community as Prajapati.

In India simple earthenware and glazed pottery made with superior quality of clay or ceramic have been in use for centuries. The simple earthenware and utensils of daily use even today are made in almost every big village and towns in India. They are made with simple clay on traditional potter's wheel woking and are baked by them in their traditional ways.

The items commonly include pitchers and pots for storing water, vessels, earthen mugs, plates and cups for drinking and eating-objects for religious use and ritual purposes and pots for growing plants. There is a great variation in shapes and forms in different regions.

The figurines were made by hand. In some areas of Assam and Manipur, even shaping of the clay for a earthenware is done by hand without the help of the wheel. In some places, the size of vessel on wheel is amazingly large exhibiting the skills of the workmen. In Gujarat, pots, as high as five feet, are made.

The earthen pottery has for centuries been glazed through various indigenous methods. They are also made in bright colours. Especially, the figures of gods and goddesses are made in multi colours. The pots and utensils are also decorated with flowers, figures and geometrical patterns in bright colours.

Ceramic

Potteries made with porcelain and ceramic also have a large variety. Unlike earthenware, where all the stages of manufacture are performed purely by hand or traditional means, in ceramic pottery the help of machines is also taken.

In some cases, it is made with hand, painted and decorated by craftsmen, but finally baked in modern furnaces. In some cases, the shape is given through moulds but painting is done by hand and again baked in modem furnaces.

There are a number of famous centres of this sort of pottery. In Rajasthan, Jaipur is an important centre. Here, the pottery made with quartz has a blue colour. They are decorated with arabesque pattern and animals and birds. In U.P., Khurja is renowned for its glazed pottery with bright colours.

9. Stone Works

Stones have been worked upon for making articles of daily use, tools, houses, decorative objects, sculptures and even jewellery. In all parts of India, these objects arc made from a variety of stones found in specific regions. Use of stone building purposes and sculpture also dates back to thousands of years. The temples and Budhhist monasteries all over India boasts of stone sculptures dating back to almost two thousand five hundred years. Beautiful palaces, forts and other structures made from stone during the medieval period are part of rich Indian heritage.

Everyone's image of India is the Taj Mahal. Its exquisite marble mosaics and inlays and delicate trellises are still reproduced in Agra on beautiful boxes, tabletops, plates and bowls. The translucent white marble or alabaster is inlaid in Mughal flower designs in Mother of Pearl, Lapis and Cronelian.

Other stoneware to look out for in India is the statues of Mamallapuram (Mahabalipuram), which echo the vibrant, powerful themes of south Indian temple art, the green serpentine or rust Gaya stone, rock crystal and alabaster boxes, bowls and animal figures of Jaipur, Benaras and Bihar, the black chlorite utensils of Orissa and the wonderful red and buff sandstone pillars, balconies and windows of domestic and temple architecture of Rajasthan and Gujarat.

The large variety of stones available in Rajasthan makes it a prominent place for stone works. Presently, it is the most important place for marble statues. These are supplied to all parts of India. The grinding stones of all types are supplied to the whole of North India by Rajasthan. However, the most delicate and famous work done at Rajasthan is screen and lattice (jali) work (perforated screens). Beautiful screens in red sandstone and marble are cut here. The finest samples of these are available in various forts, palaces, and houses. Besides these, bowls, containers and stone boxes are also made.

In Tamil Nadu, Salem district is a centre of stone work. Here vessels, dishes, lamps and grinding stones are made in larg e numbers from soft grey and hard black stones. In Tamil Nadu, icons of stone are also made at Ramanathpuram and Tirunelveli. These are also polished.

Taj Mahal, with its magnificent decorative stone work, has inspired stone cutters in Agra for centuries. Here, mainly marble is used for making models of the Taj and other buildings, wall plates, jewellery boxes and other decorative pieces. Different coloured stones are inlaid in marble with a smooth finish. Floral patterns and geometrical designs are inlaid.

In Bihar, Gaya is the main centre of stone works. Besides statues of gods and goddesses in stone, a host of other articles like owls, asses and small boxes are made. Here, one can find a whole village of stone cutters (Patharkatti) dating back to almost four hundred years.

The stone cutters of Orissa also have a long history. Beautiful temples of Konark, Puri and Bhubaneshwar (there are many, but most outstanding is Lingaraja temple) are testimony of skills of stone workers. Sandstone and soap stone (a type of soft stone) are, the main varieties of stones used here. Models of temples, vessels, statues of gods and goddesses are the main articles.

Kathiawar region in Gujarat is another important centre of stone work. The stone-cutters here live in close knit structures. These craftsmen were also employed for reconstructing the famous temple of Somnath. Here again, vessels and statues are the main items. Kerala has a long tradition of granite stave works. Here grinding stones, ritual objects and decorative pieces are made.

In Kashmir, cups and plates of a stone called sang-inalwat are made. These are grey, yellow and cooking vessels, mugs, and lamps, etc. are also made. A variety of stone called serpentine was also use for making jugs and bowls which were quite popular.

In U.P. (Nizamabad and Chinhat), pottery with lustrous body is made. Nizamabad has a dark black pottery. These glazed potteries, have beautiful designs. Khurja is specialised in ceramic pottery with bright colours. In Gorakhpur, terracotta horses and elephants are a speciality. Here, figures of gods and goddesses are made for festivals.

For Durga Puja festival in Bengal, large figures of gods, goddesses, especially of goddess Durga are made. Wall panels and plaques in terracotta are features of this region.

Orissa and Madhya Pradesh have a rich tradition of terracotta roof tiles. In Madhya Pradesh, hand-moulded figures are also made.

In Kashmir, special glazed pottery is made in Srinagar. The use of deep green, blue and brown colours is prevalent here. Tableware of all shapes and uses has a large variety. In this region, other important centres are Ladakh and Jammu. Large storage jars of Jammu are famous. All articles of daily use, images and icons for Budhhist monasteries are made in bright colours in Ladakh.

In Gujarat, especially the Kutch region, is renowned for its earthenware. Toys, festival objects, ritual pots, and tieurcs are made here. The unique feature is the pale creamy colour and richness of decoration.

Maharashtra has a long tradition of making Ganesha, the main deity of this region, in all forms and shapes. Rajasthan has a special black coloured pottery. These are both polished and porous.

In Karnataka also, the black pottery is made. Here clay toys are a speciality. In Tamil Nadu, the images of deities are very popular. These are made in almost all parts. Vellore and Musilampatti are famous for using black and red colours. Kerala is famous for ritual pots made there.

In the North-East, Manipur is famous for its pottery. Here, the pottery is made mainly by women without the potter's wheel. Before baking, the pots are polished with stones.

The earthenware made at Goa have a rich red velvety surface.

10. Stone Craft

In interiors of India, stone craft is practiced through exquisite figures that are carved in relief with details engraved in fine lines. These objects are handmade artistic work made using hammer and chisels. In ancient times, stone carving was used for making small weapons like arrowheads, javelin points, hammer, etc. Excavations reveal carving of stone figures 3000 year old.

Rajasthan may be called the land of marble. The comparative scarcity of wood and the easy abundance of stone have led to concentration on the latter. Here, the silvats are stone - cutters who are especially engaged in making grinding stone. Makrana in Nagaur district is the major source of its marble. Jaisalmer city is a dream in stone, rising out of a desert, and Jaipur holds the pride of place for availability of marble articles. Known for marble idols in many temples in North-India, Khazane-walon-ka-rasta in Jaipur is the centre for this flourishing craft.

Carving is a major handicraft of Orissa. The art of stone carving in Orissa had reached dizzy heights of excellence perfected through centuries of disciplined efforts of artisans. The progeny of these artisans who built the magnificent temples of Parsurameswar, Mukteswar, Lingaraja, Puri and that wonder in stone viz. the Sun God at Konark, besides the beautiful stupas and monasteries of Lalitgiri, Ratnagiri and Udayagiri have kept alive the sculptural traditions of their forefathers.

Ancient tradition in stone carving in Bihar is proved by the magnificent sculpture of the Mauryan period. They had a technique of high polish which can still be seen in the Ashoka pillar at Sarnath, the beautiful black stone with a touch of green in it that surprises one with its lustre.

The temples at Belur and Halebid are the more exquisite specimens of Hoysala architecture and are unrivalled for their beauty. The 57 ft. Jain statue of Gomatesvara at Sravanabelgola, standing on the summit of a rocky hill which rises to 400 feet, is a remarkable example of Indian stone sculpture.

Jali work is quite distinctive. A significant variety is made with yellow limestone, others with coloured white marble. Some of the work is in filigreed, fretted marble or sandstone. Sculpting is a live art in Rajasthan and Hindu deities made in white marble and sometimes glided over are popular.

Balaghat in Madhya Pradesh has green soft stone from which the local carvers make a number of small items, animals, boxes, trays, etc. But the important products are the religious images.

Patharkatti in Gaya district is the most noted stone ware centre of Bihar. The place has the less expensive blue-black pot stone from which images and household articles like the pestle, the mortal kharal (medicine grinder), etc. are made. Buddhist icons are a specialty. Chandil and Karaikalla in Singhbum district and Dumka in Santhal parganas work in beautifully grained greenish black soap stone.

The temple carvings of South India are profusely strewn with their figures. In the famous Mahabalipuram carving, is arresting figure of Arjuna standing on the traditional penance pose an one leg. Then there is the comic figure of a stag scratching its nose with its hind leg. A buffalo chewing the kud is so alive as to seem the mouth is moving. So, even creatures like the pig, the duck, the monitor lizard, the fowl, the spider, all rub shoulders with the mighty elephant, the lion and horse.

The crafts person while working on the sajjar pathar first studies the natural design. The shaping is done thereafter very carefully with chisel and hammers. Water is sprinkled repeatedly to avoid heat generation. The stone is smoothened by rubbing with sand papers or file.

Dimensions of the figure to be manufactured are marked on a stone slab. Extra edges are removed from the slab by beating with a hammer. Big pieces of stone are cut vertically into smaller slabs, and rough sketches are made on it. The article is taken out from the slab with the aid of a saw. This slab is now converted in the form of the desired figure with a hammer and a chisel. Minor carvings are done by pointed chisel. Before carving, the stone is kept in boiling water overnight and treated chemically. This smoothens and whitens the surface of the stone. Polishing is done for the final finishing with sand or carborundum pieces. Several of the carved artifacts are painted.

In carving an image, the stone carver sketches a rough outline of the sculpture on the stone-block. The craftsmen sprinkle water on the stone during course of their work because the friction generated due to the constant chiselling away of the unwanted material results in the tools getting heated up. Finishing is accomplished in a variety of ways. An outline is drawn on hard or soft stone which is already cut to the appropriate size. Once the outline is incised indicating the shape, the final figure is brought out by removing the unwanted portions.

11. Wood Crafts

Woodcrafts of India are famous since ages and probably one of the most primitive arts. Woodcarving is an ancient craft that has been practised in India long before stone sculpture, which itself dates back to ancient times.

Indian wood worker designated as *sutradhar* has always held a high position in the society. Wood, which was used for fuel and making of tools in ancient times, can now be seen in every walk of life, from pillars, doors, windows to household articles.

Woodcraft is the artistic practice of shaping and decorating wooden objects into diverse forms. India is famous for wooden handicrafts. Wood has been crafted to form various utilitarian and decorative handicrafts items. Skilled craftsmen of each state create handicrafts using wood that is available locally.

Mainpuri in Uttar Pradesh is also known for its woodwork inlaid with brass wire on ebony or black sheesham. The states of Jamu & Kashmir, Uttar Pradesh, Gujarat, Karnataka and Kerala have developed distinctive styles of woodcarvings. Even Rajasthan is noted for its carved sandalwood and rosewood besides heavy ornamental furniture.

In the ancient times, goods of daily usable items, utensils, axes, toys and dolls for children were crafted with wood. Excavations at Indus Valley civilization have proved the existence of woodcrafts. From simple forms, basic shapes and crude utilitarian wares, Indian woodcrafts developed and spread its wings to become one of the most beautiful and arty handicrafts of the subcontinent.

Due to easy availability of varieties of wood, wood handicrafts could develop freely and gave a distinctive characteristic to the woodcrafts of each state.

The most common varieties used to make Indian handicrafts are teak, sal, oak, mango, ebony and mahogany. sandalwood, sheesham, rosewood and walnut which are fascinating and also expensive. These are used in producing fine pieces of furniture and decorative items. There has been a complete revival of the traditional and antique woodcraft, owning to its uniqueness. Indian artisans are experimenting with designs to create a blend of traditional and modern woodcraft.

Wooden boxes are chiseled out of exotic wood and finished with intricate carvings. Boxes are made from woods for different purposes, which are varied in designs. Wooden jewellery box has intricate carvings, brass inlay and hammered metal. These wooden jewellery boxes are hand crafted by master craftsmen.

The skills are reflected in the exotic woods that are veneered and inlaid with designs and attractive bandings. Available in finishes of Oak, Walnut, Mahogany, jewellery boxes have crushed velvet interior in red, green, purple, and blue colour. Wooden jewellery boxes are expertly finished and smooth to touch. These luxurious jewellery boxes not only protect your jewellery but are excellent gift items also.

Wooden gift box are excellent for packaging gift items meant for distance transportation. The wooden gift boxes are handcrafted and inlaid with design. Sometimes, the messages are also engraved in the boxes to mark special occasions.

Wooden Pen Boxes are crafted out of wood to hold pen. Engraved with designs, boxes are available in single and double units. Made out of variety of woods, handcrafted wooden pen boxes are available in many finishes. Wooden music boxes are enchanting collectibles, which are uniquely charming and wonderfully romantic.

With inlaid floral designs, imprinted with paintings and finished in lacquer, the wooden music boxes are meticulously handcrafted. Made of wood, the music boxes come in various shapes–round, heart-shaped, rectangular, and octagon and can also be used as jewellery boxes. The ornate collection of wooden decorative items like candle holders, napkin rings, picture frames, wall hangings, mirror frames, wooden coasters, ash trays, clocks, letters, name plates comprise of a variety of artifacts and decorative pieces that truly compliment the decor and impart an elegant look with their intricate carvings.

Scenes from the epics, particularly from the battlefield, forests and palaces are the themes for wood carving in India since ages. The tradition reached its excellence between 1420 and 1470, when king Zain-ul-Abadin built his capital, which testified to the richness of this heritage. The Kashmiri craftsman, however, rejoices in carving intricate and varied designs based on lively natural forms.

A variety of carved products bear recurrent motifs of rose, lotus, iris, bunches of grapes, or pears, and chinar leaves. Lhasa dragon motifs and pattans taken from Kani and embroidered shawls all find their place in wooden objects with deep relief carving.

Carved walnut woodwork is among the most important crafts of Kashmir. The wood is hard and durable, its close grain and even texture facilitating fine and detailed work. It also presents visually interesting effects with mere plain polished surfaces. Double-grooved battens hold thin sheets of wood together.

The wooden sheets are cut into geometric shapes using a template to ensure that the pieces can be interchanged. These modules are fitted into the grooves of the battens and a repeat pattern is built up.

Man, in his exuberance, seems to have devised further method of ornamenting wood by lacquering in which countless designs and colours can be executed. Udaipur in Rajasthan has a long tradition in lacquerware. The *kheradees* are the traditional wood workers, enjoying a respectable position in the community.

Plain lac ornamentation of wood creates the striped patterns in resplendent blending of colours. The designs are zig or dana work, atishi or fire, abri or cloud, nakashi, etc. The products made are usually tables, tea poys, lamps, decorative plates, chakla and belan, toys, pidis, small stools and so on.

Lac is heated to get its plastic form. Then, the colours are added with simultaneous hammering and kneading to be made into sticks. The wooden article on which the lac has to be applied is smoothened by rubbing it with fine pottery powder. After this, it is put on a lathe and rotated, while the lac stick is pressed against it. The friction softens the lac, which is then smeared all over.

To apply more than one colour, the spots are left blank where more rounds are taken to cover up each with a different tint. A lac turner spins out his designs in various colours with a sharp chisel. A marble polish is given by rubbing with a bamboo edge and then with an oil rag.

Ornamental lacquering involves zig-zig and dana work, atishi or fire abri or cloud, nakashi and etched nakashi, a painted decorative work. A number of layers, usually four, of lacquer in different shades, are made one over the other. On this, the craftsman works out the design using chisel, and then scraps out the colours. Two types of colours, opaque and translucent, are used.

Wood carving, one of Karnataka's oldest crafts embellished the doors and ceilings of temples and temple chariots. The most popular and noteworthy example of it, however, are the sandalwood carvings, which are a hereditary craft, going back several generations. It is mainly a household craft. An abundance of sandalwood in the forests of Karnataka provides an ideal medium for delicate craftsmanship to that class of artisans popularly known as the *Gudigars*.

Karnataka is famous for rosewood articles. It lends itself better to carving in the round than any other technique. Mostly modern furniture pieces and considerable variety of elephant figures, which are in great demand, are made in rosewood. It has superb example of structural carvings from ancient temples to modern palaces with massive aver-door frames, bracketed pillars and architecture in several styles that vary in treatment and technique.

The types of carving are in round, in relief, chip, incised and piercing. First, the object is totally detached from the background wood, therefore, carving in the round of a human or animal figure calls for the utmost skill as the figure viewed from any angle, must maintain its correct identity. In relief, the figure is etched and can be high when it stands out boldly or flat as in low relief. Chip consists of design being evolved by chipping the wood used mostly in ornamental and decorative work. Incising is done without groundwork, mainly for flower and creeper traceries.

Piercing is for effective ornamentation in which the wood is completely cut away leaving just the design and so calls for extra skill.

There are two varieties in sandalwood–srigandha, (close grained and yellowish brown in colour) and nagagandha (darkish brown) from which oil is extracted. Sometimes rosewood, and more often, yellow teak are used for minor parts like pedestals, backboards or border pieces, to keep costs down.

Things made with wood are widely used in day-to-day life. In India wood craft continues to be dominated by the expertise of craftsmen.

Varieties of Wood and Canework

The most widely used articles of wood are accessories of houses and household furnitures. The unique feature is beautiful carvings on these which are specific to diverse regions. The household furnitures have a large variety, shapes and decorative patterns throughout the country. Utensils, trays, cups, boxes, chests, etc. are made in a variety of ways. The decoration is done mainly through carving, polishing and inlay work with ivory, bone or metals. Wood and bamboo work is also prevalent throughout the length and breadth of the country.

Baskets, jars for storage, furnitures and other household items, toys, and decorative items are made.

Wood

In Gujarat, the use of wood is made to provide elegance to houses. Huge images of god and goddesses in wood adorn most of the houses. In temples and churches, ceilings, pillars, doors and windows have remarkable carvings, wall panelling, heavy doors studded with brass that are some unique features of these building.

Kashmir stands out as a prominent place for the works of wood. The walnut and deodar (a variety of pine) are most favourite woods in Kashmir. Bowls, wall plates and a host of decorative pieces made of walnut wood are prized items.

In the Rajouri region of Kashmir, a local variety of wood called *chikri* is used. This grain wood of cream colour is used to make combs, spoons and other small items. In Anantnag, fine quality of cooking spoons, sandals and toys of wood are made.

Saharanpur in U.P. is famous for wooden furniture, screens and decorative pieces. Here, the main wood used is shisham. Inlay of brass, bones and ivory (before the ban on it) in wood is a special feature of Saharanpur.

In South, availability of sandalwood in Karnataka has given rise to the wood craft. Beautiful carvings are done here. Large statues and elephants and a host of small pieces of art are made with this fragrant wood. Madurai is famous for the use of rosewood. Furniture and small decorative pieces with best samples of carvings are aplenty here. Rajasthan is also famous for bowls and plates made with rohida wood. These objects are paper thin. Here some folk figures and deities are also made.

Goa also has a good old tradition of rich use of wood in decorating houses and making elegant furniture.

The tribal regions in India also have their specific wood works. Spoons, bowls, smoking pipes and other household items are made in abundance. Nagaland is one of the prominent places where fine wood-work is done. Assam also has this craft widely practiced.

Another important skill in the area of wood craft is the wood lacquer work done in Bihar, Orissa and many parts of the South especially Karnataka.

In the North-East region of India, Assam is the biggest centre of cane furniture. Here, chairs, baskets, garden swings and household items arc made with cane. A variety of baskets with different types of cane are made. Mats of bamboo straps are quite common. In Mizoram, long baskets with broad tops and narrow tapering bottoms are made. Shitalpati mats are an exquisite variety of mats made in Assam. Bengal also makes good variety of mats. In Tripura, fine bamboo straps are woven in mats with the help of cotton threads.

In Kerala, a place called Pattamadai is famous for fine quality of mats. Here, thin strands of grass are woven with cotton thread. Another fine variety of mats in Kerala is made with the leaves of screwpine plant. Dining table mats and coasters in bright colours are also made here.

Baskets, hand fans and grain separators of sikki grass and bamboo are made in all parts of North India.

In Kashmir, bamboo reeds and a variety of willow are used fo making beautiful baskets and *kangris*. The town of Chirar-e-Sharif is the main centre of kangri-making. In Ladakh, conical-shaped baskets are made with willow and a local grass. In Himachal Pradesh also, various types of cane baskets are made.

Chairs and stools made of *sarkanda* variety of reeds are used in Delhi, Haryana, and U.P. These are locally called *moondhas*.

In Bihar, Mithila region is famous for a large variety of baskets, figures, mats, etc. made with a local grass called *sikki*.

Similar themes and patterns are echoed in wood. India was once called "the land that has no furniture," but wood was always extensively used, not only in architecture and sculpture but also for ceremonial carriages and palanquins, dowry chests, screens and myriad smaller articles, ornamental or utilitarian. Sandalwood is considered auspicious. Both in South as well as in North India, finely carved statuettes, fans, frames and boxes are made of this delicate, aromatic wood found there.

12. Metal Craft

There is evidence to suggest that moulds were used for casting many copper objects. Polishing is also evident on such objects.

Bronze is an alloy of copper and tin. The best example of bronze work is the statue of a dancing girl found at Mohenjodaro.

The tradition of metal crafts has continued through the historical times. More than two thousand years old, copper statue of Buddha from Sultanganj, is one of its own kind. Another example is the iron pillar at Delhi (near Qutub Minar). Except the manufacture of arms, all the traditions of metal crafts continue in Indian towns and villages.

Like other craft traditions, the metal crafts also have two aspects. The one is the making of the articles of every day use and the other is making of objects of art for decorative and other uses. The first category of metal works are prevalent in almost all towns and villages. Of these, the most common is ironsmith or *lohar* providing tools and implements to rural areas. The utensils for every day use such as *kadhais* and *tawa* are almost always made of iron. Cooking pans and storage vessels are made mostly with iron, copper, bronze or brass. Metals play a role in the religious life of people also. The idols of gods and goddesses and almost all the pots used for rituals and worship are made of metals of different types in different regions. Flower pots, statues, ornaments, decorative pieces and toys of different types are made in all parts of the country. Now the metals and their alloys are available to craftsmen in various sizes and shapes, although in some regions, even preparation of raw material is done by the artisans themselves.

The skills of craftsmen in their work on metals is of various types. In some cases, it consists of making of various articles of alloys with mixing metals in definite proportions to give them strength, particular hue and polished surface. In many cases, ritual objects, articles and statues were made with these alloys. The earliest alloys used in India were bronze and brass. The other two important alloys were panchadhatu and ashtudhatu. In case of panchadhatu, the metals used were copper, zinc, gold, silver and lead. The ashtadhatu had zinc, copper, gold, silver, iron, tin, lead and mercury.

Like other crafts, metalwork also has Kashmir and Ladakh as two of the important centres. Srinagar is the main centre in Kashmir where copper vessels and utensils for everyday use are made. They include cooking pots, flower pots, hubble-bubble (hukka) bases, water jugs, plates, basins and *lotas*. They are decorated with floral carvings and calligraphy. Besides being things of everyday use, these are highly ornamental and exhibit good craftsmanship. The copper objects made in Zanskar are great piece of art. Tea bowls, kettles, jugs and other articles of copper are decorated with floral patterns.

In Uttar Pradesh, Moradabad, Aligarh and Varanasi are the main centres of metal craft. Moradabad has a tradition of brasswork. Here flower pots, ashtrays, boxes, bowls, plates, *lotas*, candle stands and all sorts of decorative items are made. Presently, it is one of the major centres of export of brassware.

In Varanasi, articles of metal wire and ritual pots of brass and copper are made. Images of god and goddesses, not only in copper and brass, but in gold and silver, are also made.

Saurashtra region in Gujarat is also one of the major centres. Small containers of brass and copper in various shapes are also made here. The speciality of the region is embossing of figures of animals and floral designs on brass sheets which are used for making various articles. Among ritualistic items, temple bells are also made here.

In North-Eastern region, Assam and Manipur have a long tradition of making large plates, vessels and ritual pots.

Burdwan and Midnapur in Bengal are noted for their metal pots and pans. Neighbouring Orissa is also well known for its metal works mainly in silver.

The enamelling of metal has for long been practiced in Rajasthan (especially Jaipur). Enamelling is done with lac, paints, etc. The whole of South India has a very rich tradition in metalworks. In Tamil Nadu, the main items are images of gods and goddesses. The famous Nataraja in various dance poses is a favourite object. In Nachaiskoil in Tamil Nadu, domestic wares, images and lamps of various shapes and sizes are made.

Kerala specialises in the bell-metal. Making of ritual utensils and temple lamps of various sizes is peculiar to Kerala. Table lamps, at times five feet high, with mirror-like shine on bell-metal made in Aranmala on the bank of river Pamba are famous.

Bidar in Karnataka is famous for its *bidri* work. Bidri is a special method of ornamenting through damascening (art of encrusting one metal on another). In *bidri* work damascening is done with silver wire on the surface of iron or bronze. In this art form, decorative articles of various shapes made with bronze are dipped in copper sulphate solution to make them black. Following this, the floral pattern or designs are etched or engraved on the surface of these articles. Now the silver wire or small pieces of silver are finely inlaid. Finishing is done by smoothening the surface thereby fusing the silver in the articles giving them smooth finish and beautiful decoration in the process.

Various tribal groups in India have their specific metal craft traditions. In Chhota Nagpur region of Bihar and Orissa, iron and brass objects are made by tribals with their primitive techniques. In Bustar region of Madhya Pradesh, objects of daily use like, toys, images of deities, lamps and tools are made with iron and copper.

While in India, traditional craft-forms worth looking out for, are the engraved and enamelled *meenakari* brassware of Rajasthan and Uttar Pradesh has its main centre located at Jaipur and Moradabad. In Jaipur and Udaipur, you will also find exquisitely enamelled silver and gold ornaments and *objects d'art,* with precious stones embedded amongst the brilliant blues, greens and deep reds. Less well-known but stunningly subtle in its dramatic black and white is *bidri,* the silver damasque work which originated in the Old Hyderabad State. The stylized floral motifs or geometrical trell is a design borrowed from Mughal architecture. In Udaipur, Alwar and Jodhpur, you can still see beautiful daggers and shields made by descendants of the royal armour makers who now occasionally turn their hands to more domestically utilitarian objects–nutcrackers, scissors, and betelnut cutters.

Cire-perdue or the lost-wax technique of casting brass, bronze and bell metal objects, is also used all over India. Often cast using this technique, are the life-size bronzes of Hindu deities made at Swamimalai in Tamil Nadu, the austerely elegant ritual vessels of Kerala and the delightful *Dhokra* toy animals of Madhya Pradesh and Bengal.

Especially in Kashmir, walnut wood, black wood, mahogany, redwood and ebony are used, whereas in the South and the East, teak wood is carved and ornamented in a variety of ways.

The *sadeli* marquetry work of Surat in Gujarat, the *tarkashi* brass wire inlay of Rajasthan and Uttar Pradesh, ivory craft and mother-of-pearl inlay in South, the brass sheet inlay *pittara* dowry chests and doors of Saurashtra, the *kamangiri* figurative painted woodwork of Jodhpur and Jaipur, the brilliantly coloured lacquer work of Sankheda, Nirmal and Sawantwadi, the lattice lace of *jaali* screens from

Saharanpur and the flowers and foliage carved into the satin finish of Kashmiri walnut are unique in their own way.

13. Gold and Silver Works

Gold and silver have always been considered precious metals across the world.

In contemporary India, the silver and gold objects are made all over the country by goldsmiths. Kashmir provides good quality of silverware, especially, kettles, water vessels, cups, glasses and *hukkas* with deep cut ornamentation and motifs. Kettles, here, are made with copper while lid base and handles are of silver. The designs of Kashmir are exquisite. In U.P., some silverware is carried out in Moradabad, while Lucknow also had an old tradition of good silverware. The actual production is now diminishing here. Another important place in U.P. in this regard is Varanasi.

For centuries, gold and silver wire was made here and woven with sills to make fine sarees and dress material. The textiles thus made with scroll patterns, dots and stars in silver are called brocade. Trays and cups with delicate floral work from Ahmedabad are specially noteworthy while Kutch region specialises in decorative items with superior designs and deep carving.

This tradition continued during the 18th and 19th centuries. During this period European influence on ornament-making is also visible.

National Museum in Delhi has a very good collection of jewellery from Harappan period to the present (See Masterpieces from the National Museum Collection, ed. S.P. Gupta, National Museum, New Delhi, 1985). Victoria and Albert Museum has also brought out an excellent book on the jewellery collection in England–A Golden Treasury: Jewellery from the Indian subcontinent, Susang Stronge, Nina Smith and J.C. Harle, London, 1988.

As is the case with other crafts, jewellery is also made in almost every town, big or small. Goldsmiths are the craftsmen associated with making ornaments. Nowadays some artificial jewellery is made through machines also. Beads, gold and silver wire and chains are made with machines also which are shaped into jewellery by craftsmen. These goldsmiths fulfill the day-to-day needs of people in general. At Matheran and Western ghats in Maharashtra, are made grass ornaments. Necklaces, bracelets, armlets and girdles made in beautiful patterns are used mainly by the *thakurs* and *katharis* of western ghats. The tradition of these ornaments is hundreds of years old. Other specific ornaments of Maharashtra are *gathla* or *putalimal* (necklace consisting of gold coins) and *naths* (nose ornament) made in beautiful shapes. The Koli women in the region have their special jewellery. *Gathes* (earrings) and *kanthis* (multi-string necklaces) are of interest.

Gujarat and Rajasthan have a very rich tradition of jewellery. Gold and diamond ornaments dominate Ahmedabad and Surat jewellery. Kutchh region of Gujarat and Rajasthan specialises in silver jewellery which have a large variety. Use of colourful threads in jewellery is noticeable in Kutchh. Shekhawati in Rajasthan specialises in silver ornaments.

In Northern India, Kashmir has the most exquisite jewellery. Beads made by various types of stones are made into strings for neck. *Halqaband*, a necklace very popular in Kashmir, is made with gold or silver. They are studded with precious stones. Within Kashmir, Dogras and Ladakhis have their specific ornaments. Anklets of various types and *chaunkphool*, silver ornament worn on the head are the speciality of Jammu. *Kanavaji* are worn by rural women. Balti women wear beautiful half-moon shaped earrings made with silver wires and beeds of silver. In Ladakh, bendents and brooch with gold and turquoise are made. The most striking work of Ladakh is *perak,* an ornamental headdress. It is shaped like a serpent with a spread hood. It is made with a leather piece on which a cloth is fixed. On the cloth piece are stitched uncut turquoise stones along with corals, agate and carnelian. These are stitched and arranged in a number of rows. Silver or gold strips, and at times, a silver charm box, is also attached.

Awadh, Varanasi and parts of Western U.P. have gold-studded jewellery. Firozabad in U.P. has a rich tradition of glass bangles. The whole of India gets the supply of bangles from here. Garhwal and Kumaon hills in U.P. as also Himachal Pradesh have a rich tradition of silver ornaments. Kinnaur and Chamba in Himachal Pradesh have *kach* and *haurli* as neck ornaments, necklaces made with silver coins, large noserings and *chak*, a head ornament made in delicate and intricate style.

In the East, Bihar, Bengal, Orissa and Assam have their own style. The lac bangles made in these regions are colourful. In Bihar, Madhubani and Muzaffarpur are famous in this connection. In Orissa, Cuttack is famous for *filigree* work. Filigree is a process in which silver wires are pleated and flattened very thin and beaten into various sizes and shapes. These silver threads of varying thickness are used for making rings, necklaces, bracelets and earrings. The traditional craftsmen expert in filigree also use beautiful floral patterns to give shape to a number of objects. Gold and silver filigree work is done is small amounts in Bengal also.

In Assam, jewellery in gold, silver and stones set in metals is quite popular. A special bangle called *gamkharo* with a clasp to open it is popular. A special big type of ear rings called *sona* or *hona* are made here.

In South India, the ornaments are made mainly with pure solid gold with little or no stone work. Hyderabad in

Andhra Pradesh is an exception where stonework in gold is a specialised art.

Marriage necklace or *thali* is made in endless forms and shapes throughout South. More popular are gold beads, work or stamped sheet gold with appliques: wires and stamped motifs. Many of these are inscribed or decorated with figures of gods and goddesses of which Shiva, Parvati, Nandi snakes and mythological figures are quite favourite. Use of thick black thread to hold pieces together is common.

In Coorg region of Karnataka, gold necklaces with beads of stones are woven together. The necklaces with small gold pieces woven together are very common.

In Malabar and some other parts of Kerala, women wear *kammal* and *thoda*, a variety of large earrings. The nose stud in South also comes in many sires and various shapes.

Besides traditional South Indian jewellery, Hyderabad is home to *kundan* work. Kundan is setting of precious or semi-precious stones within a frame of gold. These stones are set in beautiful floral patterns. At times, the reverse side is ornamented with enamel work of bright colours. The *kundan* and *meenakari* work is done in Rajasthan also. Hyderabad also produces large amounts of glass bangles.

India has a large population of nomadic and pastoral tribes spread over the length and breadth of the country. These tribes have a rich tradition of ornaments. The materials used in most of the cases are silver, brass, bronze, bone, beads of stones and a large variety of sundry materials.

14. Ivory Craft

Ivory Craft is spread almost throughout India with each region having its own specialty. India, with its huge elephant population, has long been a centre of ivory work. Along with muslin and spices, ivory ranked among the topmost products sought from India by kings and courtiers of foreign countries in ancient times. The ivory carvers of Jaipur, Bengal and Delhi are known for their engraved models of 'ambari hathi' or processional elephant, bullock carts, sandals, caskets, book covers, and palanquins.

There is an Orissan tradition of offering ivory inlaid furniture to the Jagannath temple at Puri. Miniature shrines with delicate pillars and intricate relief floral work, caskets depicting scenes from myths and legends, and images of gods and goddesses have been a tradition in Kerala and Karnataka.

Nowadays, the list of ivory products in popular demand has spread to a number of commodities like chess sets, billiard balls and articles like perfume bottles, paper knives, trinket or pan boxes, and jewellery items like beads, bead necklaces, bangles and rings, made mostly in Delhi.

Rajasthan is famous for its ivory fans with attractive figures for handles and centre pieces for the dining table. The ivory work on the doors of the Amber Fort in Jaipur and the exquisite inlay in the Mysore Palace doors and the Golden Temple at Amritsar proclaim the role of ivory in architectural decoration.

Craftsmen of Gujarat carve exquisite human figures as also images of deities. Uttar Pradesh is famous for its ivory products of deities, dancing figures and decorative plaques.

Kerala has excelled in the field of painting on ivory. The state has plethora of temples with spectacular carvings that attest to superb workmanship. The scenes from the Ramayana and other epic stories and a statue of St. George on a giant charger, killing the dragon with his spear are some of the masterworks of ivory that prove their artistic achievement.

The superbly carved elephant in Delhi is an excellent example of the intricacy and delicacy of the ivory-carving tradition of Northern India. Ivory is a dense substance covered with an outer layer of rough bark which has to be removed first. The object to be carved is first sketched on the piece of ivory and a variety of chisels are used to carve the smallest of details. The tusk is dipped in milk to soften it for easy carving. Delicate carving is done using variety of files. The surface is first smoothened out by sandpaper and then dipped in methylated spirit with a brush if it is white, or if yellow, in water mixed with hydrogen peroxide, which whitens it. Carving entails systematic scrapping/scooping and chiselling of the materials from the core block.

Ivory is carved all over India, but chiefly at Amritsar and Patiala in Punjab; at Benares; Behrampore, and Murshi dabad in Bengal; at Surat, Ahmedabad, Daman, Balsar, and throughout Southern Gujarat; and at Sattara and other parts of Maharashtra; and also at Kerala, Vishakapatnam in South.

The subjects are richly caparisoned elephants, state gondolas in gala trim, tigers, cows, and peacocks, all carved as statuettes; and hunting, festive, and ceremonial scenes, and mythological subjects carved in relief. Ratlam, in Western India is known for its costly ivory bracelets.

Ivory consists of the tooth structure of elephant, walrus, hippopotamus, whale, etc. At one time, India had a flourishing craft in ivory. Presently, India has banned the practising of this craft, its trade and transaction in all forms. This has been done in view of protecting the elephants whose number is gradually declining.

In modern India, the state of this craft in 19th and 20th century has been recorded. Combs were one of the common articles made with ivory. These are available in various shapes and sizes in different museums. Hair pins, dices, chessmen, seals, buttons, decoration pieces and boxes for jewellery are various other items. Ornaments like, bangles earscrolls and rings were made.

The main centres of ivory craft were in Bengal, Mysore, Kerala, Rajasthan and Delhi.

In the South, Kerala had a rich tradition of making gods and goddesses. The craft was given special place in the state of Travancore. Here gods and goddesses, animals, birds, fishes, fruits, flowers, creepers, palanquins, thrones and engraving were most important. Another speciality of Kerala was the painting on ivory. Mysore produced figurines of gods and goddesses and inlay work on sandalwood objects.

In the North, Jaipur specialised in chess pieces,–Prince of Wales Museum (Bombay)—has a beautiful statue of musicians made at Jaipur. Other items made here were models of temples, jewellery, decorative pieces, birds and animals, etc.

In Gujarat, human figures, rose water sprinklers, elephants, camels, etc. were made with ivory.

Amritsar and Delhi also specialised in ivory work. Amritsar was famous for combs, floral and bird motifs and lattice (jali) work. The objects made at Delhi included chess sets, scent bottles, boxes, paper knives, salt pepper cellars, bookmarks, jewellery boxes, and items of ornaments like beeds, ear tops, bangles, broaches, rings pendants, etc.

In Bengal, decorative pieces and small objects were also made.

15. Gems and Precious Stones

A large variety of precious and semi-precious stones are found in different parts of India.

The diamond is the most precious of the stones found in India. The expertise of Indian craftsmen lies in cutting raw diamond in a specific style giving it the real glitter. The craft is practised in Gujarat. Here uncut diamonds are brought from different parts of the world and are cut by craftsmen.

Other precious and semi-precious stones extensively used in India for a long time are carnelian, steatite, agate, serpentine, jasper, amazonite, lapis lazuli, turquoise, amethyst, garnate, ruby, calcedony, rock crystal and emerald. Precious stones are widely used in jewellery all over our country. Besides, they are also used in decorating a variety of objects like small boxes, cups, glasses, costumes, statues, etc.

In Indian astronomy, and astrology, it is believed that different stones govern different planets and specific stones have been identified for specific planets. Similarly, people born under a particular zodiac sign are assigned stones favourable to that zodiac sign. These stones are generally worn in rings or as prescribed.

16. Azarak

One of the oldest printing technique used in India is the resist printed cotton–*azarak*. The finest azarak is produced in Sind (now in Pakistan). However, Dhamadhaka, Anjar and Khanda in Kutch are the chief centres of azarak printing in India. The printing of azarak involves several stages that continues for several days.

At first, white cotton cloth is immersed into water and soda, then bleached, and then again dipped into oil till it achieved beige colour. Then the first print (asul) is done with a mixture of gum, lime and water. The motif thus printed is white or pale red or red after dyeing it with alizarine. The second print (kot) is done with a solution of ferrous sulphate, thickened with earth, gum or grounded seeds. This print turns black after being dyed in alizarine: The third print (kher) is that of resist made of a mixture of earth, flour, khunr, aluminium sulphate and water. Sometimes molasses and gar are also added. This resist covers all the parts destined to receive a colour other than blue. Then its dyed in indigo. The cloth is now dyed in alizarine.

For printing, craftsmen use wood-blocks (pur). Several blocks are needed to complete the design. Craftsmen's tools are still primitive. Craftsmen use a straw, *tili*, for measuring the parts of the pattern and the distance between the points of the motifs. Copper pots are used for dyeing.

17. Kantha

Kantha, the patched cloth, was mainly made out of worn out and disused sarees and dhotis. Borders of these, used saris, etc. were cut, patched and embroidered. Women of all castes, but Brahman, including Muslim women do this embroidery. The stitches used are of simplest kind. The running stitch is the main. Red and blue colours are generally used. The design is mostly square or rectangle, with the centre space occupied by a lotus flower and its petals-which manifests ancient Indian symbol of universe. Four trees mark the corners symbolising four directions.

Thematically, its an enriched textile version of the art of the alpona (done on the floor). Themes from ancient mythology and legends are taken. In some kanthas, only the figures of animals are used. However, Muslim kanthas lack figures, etc. and use scroll instead.

The art of kantha died after the first quarter of the 20th century. It is not known when it began again; the new kantha, though same in technique, with widely spaced designs resembles more with certain types of paintings in Bihar and Bengal.

18. Chikan

It is done mainly in white cotton thread on white cotton. The embroidery is composed of large or small, simple or inverted satin-stitch, button-holing, darn-stitch, knot-stitch, netting and applique. The art developed at Lucknow under the patronage of the rulers of Avadh. Both, Hindu and Muslim craftsmen are skilled in the craft. At present, five different styles of cikap work are common: taipchi, khatwa, bakhia, murri and phanda, and jali.

19. Ari Bharat

It is a chain stitch embroidery done primarily by Gujarat women. In this, floral medallions and peacocks predominate. 'The Meghvals, Ahirs, Rabaris, Kathis, and Garasias use figurative motifs, local narratives and Puranic legends unlike their counterparts, the Islamic Banias.

20. Comb Works

Nagina in Uttar Pradesh is famous for its large variety of comb works with perforations and floral patterns on ebony wood. The art of comb-making and hairdressing is said to have existed at least 4,000 years ago. The designs on combs are same as jali designs of stone. Traditionally, the craft was restricted to Muslim community.

Combs are made in pairs, male and female. Male combs have teeth on one side and female combs have teeth on both sides. Male combs are called as Raja ka kangha, female combs are called as Rani ki kanghi.

A piece of the size and shape of the comb is cut from abnoos wood by a saw. The teeth are cut on the tapered side and design is on the thick side. The design is traced on it with a compass and is engraved with a drill machine. After the carving is done, it is smoothened and teeth are chiseled.

The piece is held in the left hand and the skill lies in holding the ari in right hand and cutting with the precise control of distance with the left thumb. The teeth are cut at a regular distance without any measurement. The piece has minimum thickness in the centre and tapers on both the sides.

A portion of horn is kept moist with coconut oil and heated before fire until it becomes almost as soft as wax. It is then worked or pressed into the required form, either with hands or by means of moulds made of hard wood. Then it is finished off with scraping tools and a small lathe. The whole body is then polished and ornamented with simple but graceful designs. The ornamentation is done in line with a fine, double-pointed steel graving tool. The tools used in this work are very simple. The various types of comb produced thus are jali comb with handle, double jali comb, juda comb, machli ki jali comb (fish jali), tel wala kangha (oil comb), marore ki kalsi ka kangha, kalsi ka kangha, double jali ka gol kangha, Raja-Rani ki kanghi.

21. Bidri

Carrying the rich cultural heritage, the creations of the artisans of India stand unique in maintaining the luxurious tradition of bidri in India. This is considered to be a unique kind of art form that defines the hard work and persistency by the artisans.

Exemplary of the traditional excellence, bidri in India has flourished in Andhra Pradesh. The history says that the art of bidri-silver inlay on a metal alloy flourished and reached perfection under the patronage of the Bahamans and Baridi dynasties. Bidar in Karnataka is the abode of this distinctive craft and also is named after the place though traditionally it originated in Persia about seven centuries ago. According to the history, this craft was introduced by the migrants in India and the craftsmen subsequently made it the art and craft identity of India. This art form is known for its lissome craftsmanship. The intricate metal work over the smooth and glossy surface of the artifacts is the most fascinating aspect of this world famous art.

Bidri in India is essentially the formation of brass alloy comprising of zinc, copper, lead, tin and traces of iron. This ancient craft, which originated as the older art of inlaying gold and silver on steel and copper, was practiced in Persia and Arabia. The usage of lustrous metals gives the created items of bidri work a sheen that is predominantly the distinctiveness of this particular art form. This craft is practiced in India hugely and the creations are well appreciated world wide for the stunning beauty of the items made from bidri. While the artisans create silver designs on a metalware, sometimes white silver is used to adorn the designs on black metal that give the items a proper ethnicity of the bidri culture. This craft not only deals with metals but exclusive designs are made on cloth to accelerate this craft a pace further. The embroiderers attempted to create embroidery with the same effect of bidri by creating silver embroidery on black cloth. The stitches and the elements needed for this embroidery work are same as Zardozi.

The basic material of bidri is an alloy of zinc and a small proportion of other non-ferrous metals. The original colour of the alloy is grey, but this turns jet black with the application of special clay or chemical. The dark background with an inlay of silver in intricate patterns is extremely pleasing. The designs, inlaid with pure silver, stand out dramatically against the black background. The designs are usually taken from the historical fort at Bidar and the frescoes in the Ajanta caves, though new designs have added.

The process of bidri is same everywhere in India, which includes moulding red clay and then pouring molten solution of copper and zinc over the created item. After casting, the surface of the cast article is smoothened very finely with sandpaper and then rubbed with a solution of copper sulphate. Rubbing makes the surface turn black and thus creates a suitable base for the process of designing and engraving. The engraving tools cut the intricate but delicate tapestry of design into the metalware. The most sensational work in the bidri craft is inlaying. Here the sheets or the wires of pure silver are hammered into the grooves of the design and the surface smoothened by the help of a buffing machine. After the inlay work, the surface is turned black by applying a paste of ammonium chloride, potassium nitrate, sodium chloride, copper sulphate and mud which darkens the body by producing a characteristic black patina, but without damaging the shining silver inlay. It is this contrast of black and silver that lends the work its beauty. At final stage, preferably coconut oil is rubbed on the piece to deepen the black matt coating.

The bidri in India has gained its recognition as the government has formulated several new policies to boost the artistic production of the traditional industries. The market scenario defines that bidri work has a great market potential in India as well as in the other parts of the world as far as the craftsmanship is concerned. The artistic pieces of bidri work are popular amongst the tourists.

Bidri in India has been extensively practised and the concept and creativity combined with the dexterity of the artisans have brought this unique craft to get a proper delineation. The most effervescent centers where this craft is hugely practiced are Bidar in Karnataka and Hyderabad in Andhra Pradesh. Among the few other centers, the names of Purnia in Bihar, Lucknow in Uttar Pradesh and Murshidabad in West Bengal are in the list. The artisans create designs which are primarily based on the nature and human life that ranges from creepers, flowers and sometimes human figures. The local craftsmen of a village near Purnia, in Bellori, who are known as 'Kansaris', are employed in molding and turning bidri vessels. The engraving and polishing are done by the 'sonars' or goldsmiths. Among the variants of the bidri craft, the artisans of these places also practise the 'gharki' style of bidri which is a less sophisticated variation of the bidri. Lucknow's Zar Buland is another form of bidri craft where the ornamental designs are raised above the surface.

The exclusively created bidri articles sometime serve the purpose of home decor that enhance the beauty of the houses and keep an aesthetic appeal as well.

22. Bell-Metal

Bell-metal is a hard alloy used for making bells. It is a form of bronze. Studies have revealed that metal alloys have been in use for workshop art in India from time immemorial, perhaps, as old as the temple building activity itself. Bell-metals are used to produce variety of items both for utility and aesthetic purposes. Indian bell-metal work is distinguished by ornate and sophisticated designs, finesse and finish. Bell-metal casting in Madhya Pradesh is essentially a tribal craft, practised by non-tribals in Bastar, Pranpur, Datia and Sagar, originally for the requirements of tribals alone. During the Gupta period, the Kurkihar centre for brass and bell-metal in Bihar was known throughout the world, and history records that two artists named Dhiman and Vithpal taught the craft to artisans from different countries of Asia.

Assam has special shapes and patterns of its own in metalware. The craftsman, called a *kahar* or *orja*, owns the tools and equipment in such establishments. Guwahati and Sarthebari are the important centres for bell-metal craft. Brasswork is an important Assamesse cottage industry with the highest concentration being in Hajo in Kamrup district.

Old references date the bell-metal craft of Manipur to the late 17th or early 18th century. It is a cottage industry and is virtually confined to two areas of the valley, viz. Heirangkhoithong (at Chinga Makha) and Aheibam Eikai (at Khongnang Pheidekpi). Both are about four miles south of Imphal and are three miles apart.

The antiquity of the use of iron in India is proved by its reference in earliest literature, the Vedas. Brass and bell-metal articles required by the people are partly produced in Assam and Tripura. The craft is practised in Agartala, Narshinggarh, Soonamura and Kailasahar.

The main feature of cire-perdue (lost wax) process is that the clay core is retained within the metal covering lending weight and strength to the product inspite of the thinness of the metal inlay. The religious objects made in bell-metal are mainly figures of tribal deities. Votive lamps, anklets, and *turai* (tribal bugles) are also made by the lost wax process.

Kerala is the home of the bell-metal craft. The cooking vessels wide open with flat or curbed rims called *urlis*, are classic in line and dignified in their simplicity. Huge cauldrons called *varpu* are made for use in temples. It has also a great tradition of wide range of tumblers in many sizes, very elegantly shaped. There is a special jug, the lower part rounded in convolutions and a long spout jutting out at the side. In the ornamental line, there are a variety of jewel boxes, oval or square, one with eight sides, fastened in front by a big bold ornamented chain, pan boxes, lime jars, each with a different artistic finish and floral or creeper design.

Two distinct types of products made in brassware and bell-metal these days are cast pots and bowls with the lower half black or a natural dark colour. Dhokra articles, mostly figures of riders and elephants, candle stands, the fish type sindhur clan (vermilion box), etc., were made by the cire-perdue or lost wax process. The flexible brass and silver fish is a special item, made by a goldsmith community concentrated at Haveli Kharagpur in Monghyr district.

A shallow bowl on a stand is a typical item in both brass and bell-metal and is called *horsy*. It has delicate motifs on the sides or sometimes on the cover. *Donari* (looks like pendants) is essential at weddings, to be given with dowry.

Krishna Kand is a dish in the shape of a large bowl, with a broad encircling rim at the neck,resting on a small pedestal. *Senga* is a lidded betelnut container, which looks like a ritualistic lamp. An article with very chaste lines is a large bell with Garuda at the top. Similar patterns are made with dots, line and circles with a hammer to form attractive ornamentation both on the borders, as well as over the surface.

Bell-metal is most attractive with its soft surface and the old gold tint. It is used in making cooking dishes and eating plates as it does not tarnish and needs no tinning like copper. Bell-metal articles are cast by the cire-perdue process. The core of the figure is roughly shaped in clay. Instead of laying on the wax in an even thickness, thin wax threads are first made. These are arranged over the core so as to form a network or are placed in parallel lines or diagonally, according to the form of the figure. The head, arms and feet are modelled in the ordinary way. The wax threads are made by means of a bamboo tube into the end of which a moveable brass plate is fitted. The wax made is softened by heat. It is then pressed through the perforation at the end of tube and comes out in the form of long threads, which must be used by the workmen before they become hard and brittle.

The shaping of an object is done either by beating with a hammer the ergot or sheet metal to the approximate shape while heating, or by pouring the molten metal into a vessel made of clay for ordinary ware, and wax for more delicate objects. The beating process is often preferred for bell metal and copper to make the object more durable. It can also be subjected to further tempering for strengthening, by heating the article red hot and suddenly dipping in cold water. If it turns black in the process, it is rectified by light hammering. There is also the turning process done on the lathe, often worked by a string. The part of the article to be turned is fixed to the outer end of the lathe by gum. As the lathe rotates, the chisel is applied to the part requiring turning. It not only cuts away the unwanted bulk but also smoothens the article by scraping and brushing. Soldering is done by using a metal alloy which the artisan himself prepares where articles are manufactured in several pieces which have to be joined together to form a composite whole. After this, polishing is done by vigorous rubbing, either by hand, or if it is plate, by feet, using a rag.

A mould made of clay mixed with husk is made of the object to be cast, which is then dried and polished, wrapped in a cover of fragile melted bee-wax wires. When the wax is finally melted as also a pouring channel for the molten metal, it pre-empt the vacated space in the final casting. Several coatings of clay are applied and dried until the clay mould gets leather hard, after which the wax is melted out. The molten metal is then poured into the voided replica chamber while the mould is kept red hot. The article is then ready.

Bihar artisans use a mixture of wax and resin and also pitch from coal tar. They mix two kilograms of pitch with 250 grams of resin, melt the two items and strain them separately. Then they mix the two and heat the mixture over fire, stirring it all the while. This process of mixing takes two hours or sometimes more. The mixture is strained again before using. The manner of use of this mixture is identical with that of resin. These artisans are very precise in their work and follow their technique meticulously.

Some of the articles employing this technique are figures of tribal deities, votive lamps, *turai* (tribal bugles), peacocks, chameleons, cobras, deer, horses, human beings, musicians, ornament boxes, rice-measure bowls, animals figurines, utensils, jewel boxes, ornamental chain, lime jars, lamps, floor stands, various shallow bowls of hemispherical shape.

Figures of riders and elephant, candle stands, fish-type *sindhur don* (vermilion box), *kalash* (water pot), *sarai* (a platter or tray with or without cover), tray, *tau* (a kind of vessel for cooking), *lota*, *kahi* (a dish), *tai* (musical instrument), bells, shields, swords, daggers, swords, hilts, pan boxes, sengabetel container, krishna kanti dish, etc. are some other objects that are usually made using this technique.

23. Tarakashi

Orissa, the land rooted in customs, traditions and folklore, is a home to many handicrafts and art forms such as patachitra, applique work, terracotta, brasswork and not the least among them is the silver filigree work of Cuttack, popularly known as *tarakashi.*

The art is ancient, and dates back to the dawn of early history. A tinkling of anklets, a glimmer of silvery light, a shimmering artifact with a sheen of purity, this delicate craft is especially renowned for its unparalleled intricacy.

The works in tarakashi are a combination of beauty and utility. Like all other crafts, tarakashi is gloriously alive to and caters to modern tastes while retaining all essential traditional past. Forms of animals, birds, flowers and even miniature handbags and other souvenirs are made. The Konark Chakra and temple are great favorites as mementos. Scenes from the Mahabharata, depicting the chariot of Arjuna driven by Lord Krishna, are quite popular.

The artists work with an alloy of 90% or more pure silver. Silver is beaten and then drawn into fine wires and foils. The wires are then made finer by drawing silver through a series of consecutively smaller holes to produce finer strands. Then the wires are twisted into various shapes by binding them into different designs and soldering them with pincers and scissors specially made for the purpose. The end results are articles and ornaments of eternal beauty.

Techniques such as granulation, snow glazing and casting are also used innovatively to heighten the effect. Platinum polishing is done to give a more lasting shine whereas fusion of silver and brass or other materials is done to create some rather interesting effects.

The filigree jewelery is particularly rich in patterns. The arm jewellery, necklaces, toe rings and especially anklets are popular among the people. Various kinds of intricate anklets, combining use of semi-precious stones are greatly preferred. Vermillion boxes, brooches, pendants, earrings are also in great demand among the people.

24. Sholapitha

Sholapitha is derived from a 'reed' that is available in the marshy wetlands of Andhra Pradesh, West Bengal, Tamil Nadu and Assam. This craft is popularly known as *shoalpith* in West Bengal and *netti* in Tamil Nadu. The core of this reed is white in colour and is exposed when the outer layer of the stalk is shaved. The core — light, porous, soft, and pliable — can be shaped to suit the imagination of the artisans.

The artisans shape this reed into many objects like scaled down models of churches, temples and mosques, carved images of Maa Durga during Dussehra in Bengal, marriage headgear, flowers and garlands, and toys and mobiles. Flowers of a large variety are made from *shola*. The crown of the deities is made in paper pulp with the paper decoration fixed on it. It is one of the most impressive forms of ornamentation.

The sholapitha plant is recognised by the shallow layer of leaves that float on the marshy water. These are then dried thoroughly. Good quality pith is pure white and smooth with a soft bark and no nodes. *Kath*, the knife, is used to shave the outer cover of the stalk, so that the white core is exposed. The stalk is cut into cylindrical pieces, so that the white core is left after the outer layer is peeled off. Then it is pared and turned into a sheet. Dozen of such sheets are rolled within the other and the consolidated roll is tied tightly at both ends, into two and on the cut side v-shaped indentations are made with a sharp knife. These sides are dipped in colour solutions and dried. From the roll, the worker tears out pieces, an inch in length, by holding the uncoloured end between the thumb and the index finger, twisting the pith piece into a flower. Once the flat sheets are made, a dozen of these can be tied tight at one end and cut into pieces to create various shapes, both geometrical and floral.

Craftspersons spend months on a piece, carefully carving out the details. No part of the sholapitha is wasted and leftover bits are used for making various designs of flowers, birds, and animal figures. Several flowers are made, like jasmine, rose, chrysanthemum, etc. These are strung on a thin wire to make crescent shaped *veni* (stringled flowers) with a wire fastener to go round the bun of hair. Slit tin foils are used for extra decoration, which is cut into different sizes and pasted to the pith pieces. Glass beads are also used for this process. Sometimes thin gold and silver threads are strung into the pith flowers to embellish them.

The colouring on the finished product is done with bright coloured paint. Sholapith items form an integral part of the major religious rituals in West Bengal. The finest examples of the skill can be seen during the Durga Puja celebrations. Traditionally, the artisans have also crafted ritual and decorative items like garlands, conical topors, or the head-dress worn by young boys during their naming ceremony and by bridegrooms, and the *mukut* worn by the bride.

In Tamil Nadu, the craft flourishes in pockets of Thanjavur, Karaikkal, Tiruchirapalli, Nagapattinam, Pudukottai and in the Union Territory of Pondicherry. Entire families in these areas are engaged in the craft. Artisans from Tamil Nadu even make model townships and replicas of temples, churches, and mosques, along with other architecturally significant buildings, complete to the smallest detail.

An interesting feature of the shola is that it was the material used during British times for the production of the Sola Topi which was a necessary article of headgear as protection from the hot mid-day sun.

25. Glass Crafts

Glass craft has its ramification that spread from items of home decoration to the household items, glass bangles, to glass painting and mosaic. The ancient scriptures prove the existence of glass items during that period though they were not used hugely as it is used in recent times.

The glass craft, as an art form, was introduced in Europe, and during the Middle Ages, the Chinese artisans mastered the craft from Europe. According to the ancient history, the collaboration of East India Company and China was responsible to introduce the art in India.

During the initiation period, the dwellers of India would paint pictures related to ancient scriptures, popular stories, epic themes, portraits, and icons. That was just the beginning and since then there was no looking back. Even today, glass craft is loved for its simplicity, gaudy appearance and indeed for its artistic elegance.

The gorgeous bangles made of glass are hugely in demand in many places of India and are an example of the craftsmanship of Indian glass craft. They come in different colours, shapes, styles and trend.

The glass bangles are inexpensive and adorable for their look. Glass bangles are often studded with glass gems, spirals of base-metal wire, foil and spangles amid a wavy striping of other colours. Glass also produces jewellery like necklaces that are made out of intricately cut glasses of incandescent colours deftly polished which gives the shimmer of elegance.

The art of painting has got a new dimension in glass painting and with the introduction of glass painting the art of glass craft gained a whole new facet. Glass painting, as an expression of glass craft, got its exposure in India in the late eighteenth century and early nineteenth century. Glass painting requires glass of superior quality, which is imported from Britain and Belgium for exclusive glass painting.

Glass craft engages the manufacturing of showpieces of different sizes and shapes. Various decorative glass bottles of stained glass, decorative glass decanter are admired for interior decoration. Exquisitely decorated crystal flower vase, glass bottles, glass decanters are available in wide variety and come in various tint.

Glass lamps are decently designed with eye-catching hues and designs in the recent days and stands as a logo of the artistry of glass craft. The lamps are available in traditional and modern outlook. They vary from hanging lamps, ceiling hanging lamps, hanging candle lamps, beaded hanging lamps to hanging lamp shades.

Chandeliers are a variation of glass craft that serve the purpose of enhancing the grandeur of decor. Variety comes in different forms like chandelier lampshades, beaded chandelier, crystal chandelier, and so on. Glass candleholder, votives, tableware and lantern are found in enormous variety. A large variety of Christmas decors are offered like glass ball, glass animals, Christmas decoration hanging, etc. for decoration.

Another kind of glass craft is the craft of ceramic, which are very popular as one of the Indian crafts. Regional differences reason the variations of ceramic craft. Though the ceramic craft requires the involvement of hand for making the items, but due to the huge demand of the items, machines are involved to create things of identical quality and standard. The ceramic items are made durable by adding stone to the mould. Some ceramic items are candleholders, lamps, show pieces, sculptures and statues.

26. Coconut Crafts

Coconut crafts in India has grown with each passing year with tremendous innovativeness and care. Coconut palm tree produces one of the diversified fruits where every bit is utilised in a variety of ways. However, the shell and inner core of the coconut in most cases is thrown away or used as firewood for cooking.

Coconut crafts are mainly manufactured in South Indian states that feature the majority of coconut plants. Indian states like Kerala, Tamil Nadu and other coastal states have abundance of skilled artisans for making coconut crafts.

The coconut shell, which enclose the renel and a very beautiful and hardy object, seems to have simply offered itself to man to make what he could of it. One can create different items by using a little creativity and ingenuity. The process of coconut crafts involves sketching, cutting, sanding, and buffing to create the finished product.

The shell of the coconut of the required size is selected. Its outer surface rubbed by a steel tool while the inner part is smoothened with a chisel. A circular base and a handle separately made with shell are attached to the cup by fixing screws. First, boot polish is applied and then a final coating of French polish is given for high class finishing. It also involves the casting of whole bell-metal article. Bees wax and charcoal are mixed and melted, filtered through a coconut shell craft piece of cloth and deposited in cold water, heated again and pressed on a small square piece of lead with a variety of designs. This is then pressed against wooden model of article under preparation. When this model has been completely covered by wax, it is removed and the wax mould is given three coatings of a mixture of clay and chalk powder. Sometimes, paddy tusk is also added and it is then dried in the sun.

After it gets heated, the wax comes out through the opening provided for the purpose. The mould is then placed over a crucible in which copper and zinc are melted, and the positions of the two are interchanged so that the liquid fills the cavity left by the melting of the wax. When the metal cools, the mould is removed and the surface smoothened. Then, the coconut shell is fixed inside the frame with gum and a paste prepared by boiling sealing wax in water.

There are variety of coconut crafts like bowls, vases, roses, rose-water sprinklers, teapots and others are made from coconuts. Nowadays, coconut shells are carved into useful and decorative articles such as fruit-dishes, wine cups, finger-bowls, ice-cream cusps, lamp stands, vases, pen and pencil stands, cups and saucers. Articles like hukkas, larger vases and lampshades are also made of coconut shells with brass bindings. The coconut crafts like table lamps, jewellery, finger bowls and other objects have become quite popular.

Lamp stands encased in brass and smaller coconut shell articles are made in Thiruvanthapuram, Attingal and Neyyatinkara, while larger items are made in quilandy in Kozhikode district in North Kerala. Combining coconut shells with brass bindings also makes often hookas and large vases. Coconut fibre is cleaned, smoothened and made into various dolls and toys with beads and coloured threads to give it a decorative appearance.

The most wanted coconut crafts include bowls, vases, roses, teapots, wine cups, finger-bowls, ice-cream cups, saucers, pen and pencil stands, hukkas, lampshades, fruit dishes, table lamps, finger-bowls, roses, jewellery, vases and teapots.

27. Sikki Grass

The *sikki* grass articles made by the women of North Bihar are entirely different. Sikki seems to grow almost anywhere in this region even by the roadside. It is most attractive for its tall and lush and with a lovely golden shade. It is out only once after the rains and the cut pieces are stored for use throughout the year.

Sikki grass dyed in red, blue, black and gold is imaginatively wrought into a variety of articles such as baskets and boxes, human figures, replicas of gods and goddesses, toys, animals, birds and models of chariots and temples. The desired forms are generally shaped with ordinary grass called *khar* which is coiled and encased in the softened *sikki*, while many of the motifs are derived from the local tantric traditions.

Sikki is obtained from the dried stems of a succulent plant. The upper portion of the stem, which contains flowers, is discarded and the remaining portion cut into small pieces and preserved for making attractive sikki ware. The golden-yellow sikki is used to create lovely dolls, toys, and baskets using the coiling technique. Before being woven, the grass is dyed in bright translucent colours and the shimmering golden grass, glowing through the paint, gives the articles their characteristic luminosity.

The coiling technique, which is the oldest, is used in sikki. The common long grass is coiled and stitched together with the sikki, dyed in several different shades using a thick needle called *takua*. Especially, in constructing the sculpturesque forms, the whole build-up is made by the coils. These forms are completely folk, and in a style, all their own.

28. Phulkari

It is a form of embroidery of Punjab done in darn-stitch over counted threads by using floss-silk thread on a coarse madder red or indigo blue homespun cotton. It is traditionally done by Hindu Jat women on odhnis, skirts and blouses. Nowadays, besides the traditional *phulkari* (in which pattern is sparsely spread), '*bagh*' (garden) technique, in which dense silk embroidery is used with patterns in which only edges are covered; sisader or mirror work embroidery are also common.

Phulkari, literally meaning flowerworking, is an embroidery technique from the Punjab. Simple and sparsely embroidered oddnis and shawls, made for everyday use, are called *phulkaris*, whereas garments that cover the entire body are made for special and ceremonial occasions and are known as *baghs* (garden). Phulkaris and baghs were worn by women all over Punjab during marriage occasions and other festivals. This handicraft did not arise out of any pure artistic motive, but mainly to satisfy domestic necessity. The inborn talent and spontaneous approach of the uneducated village women, her deft hand, and resourcefulness have raised such works out of the realm of necessity into the domain of art, pleasing in colour and designs as they are.

There is a custom that phulkaris and baghs are given to brides at the time of marriages. Some best phulkaris and baghs are known to have been made in Hazara and Chakwal, areas of Northern Punjab. There is a belief that the art of phulkari came from Iran where it is known as "gulkari". There is reference of phulkari in Vedas, Mahabharata, Guru Granth Sahib and folk songs of Punjab. The main characteristics of phulkari embroidery are use of darn stitch on the wrong side of coarse cotton cloth with coloured silken thread.

Phulkari is an art of decorating shawls, dupattas with embroidered floral motifs. The smaller the stitch, finer is the quality of the embroidery. The silk threads in golden yellow, crimson, red, orange, green and pink are usually used for the embroidery. It is worthy to note that a single strand was used at a time, each part worked in one colour and the varied colour effect is obtained by clever use of horizontal, vertical or diagonal stitches. Many folk songs on phulkari are part of Punjab culture.

The phulkaris of Punjab are of two types, one carrying a regular row of stylized motifs either of flowers, fruits or birds, and other carrying a rich repertoire of the folklore and motifs taken from everyday life. The centre often carries a stylized lotus form, the two cross borders at the ends carry rows of stylized lotus form, of stylized animals and bird forms, or flowers. The remaining surface is covered with a variety of motifs such as a train on wheels carrying human forms, birds and animals rushing across the horizon, while peacocks move across the surface and strange mythical birds and animals mingle together in harmony.

The Punjab phulkari is of a spectacular nature. The word means flowering and it creates a flowery surface. The phulkari stitch derives its richness from the use of darning stitch placed in different directions–vertical, horizontal and diagonal. Embroidery is done from the wrong side. The pattern is controlled by counting of thread, but quite often the outline of pattern is embroidered on the cloth in green thread. The needle picks up only one thread at a time, so that the background of pattern is delineated with single lines of colour in extremely fine stitches. In the front, the stitch ranges from A½ to A¼ cms in size.

The stitching is done with silk thread, though occasionally cotton threads in white and green are used, and sometimes even woollen. A peculiarity of phulkari is that the fabric itself is used geometrically as an inner decoration, so that the medallions and diamonds, etc are not just patterns sewn on but become an integrated combination of colours, yellow and madder brown. This is only possible where absolute accuracy in thread counting is observed.

In *bagh* work, the stitch is so refined that the embroidery becomes the fabric itself. The quality of the workmanship is measured by the smoothness at the back that can only result from the evenness of the stitches.

29. Sitalpati

Sitalpati, literally means cool mats that are very popular and aesthetic in design. These mats are luxurious in their feel and more expensive than other mats. Sitalpati mats are crafted from the marantra dichotoma or mutra reed. The finest sitalpati is used in Assam to sleep on, as it is cool for summer nights.

The *patikars* (makers of mats) of Cachar and Dhubri districts of Assam make the sitalpati, an extremely fine floor. A relatively new design development has been the use of sitalpati mat cuttings as an embellishment on bags of all varieties, on pen stands, and other table top items. It is used in plenty as a floor mat, as a prayer mat, and also as a wall hanging.

The production of sitalpati is a household industry in Assam. Generally, men prepare the cane slips, while women do the weaving work. People, mainly from Kacchhar district of Assam, are involved in this craft. The mat makers mostly belong to the Muslim community. The villages famous for the production of sitalpati in Cachhar district are Katakhal, Kaliganj, Basigram, Karimpur, and Sridurgapur.

Sitalpati are lovely mats and very much expressive of their quality and are made from green cane slips. The usual motifs are creepers, trees, animals, birds, geometrical designs and stylish human forms. Each design is enclosed in a square made up of lines. Sometimes, different animals made in a single mat are also found. Circles are mostly repeated but with different decorations. *Chowpat*, a design of four squares with four empty squares are also made. Procedure of making sitalpati is as follows.

The manufacture of 'sitalpati' involves many complicated processes. Sitalpati is made from a marshy reed indigenously named as *mohtra* reed. Unlike reeds of the 'khag' variety, it has no joints. Like other reeds, it grows on marshy and waterlogged areas and is found in abundance in choked up tanks and damp hill slopes.

The reeds are washed in soda and dried. Then they are split to clean out the soft stuff inside and sized to make all the pieces in equal width. These pieces are then boiled in water for three to four hours and dried. Colouring of the splits is done by indigenous methods. White (ivory) colour is obtained by boiling the splits in water, wherein other ingredients, such as boiled rice juice, hibiscus safdariffa and tamarind leaves are mixed. For black colour, the splits packed into bundles are wrapped up with mango barks and kept under the mud for about 7 days.

In order to obtain red colour, the cane splits are boiled in water mixed with 'mezenta' (a kind of chemical dye-stuff).

After that, they are stiffened with starch (boiled rice water) and dyed if necessary. The splits are then woven in a closed weave and designs are made by using dyed slips. Generally the warp is of one colour and the weft of another. Some times two styles are worked together to produce a number of designs.

The sittalpatti designs produced by the 'patikars' of Assam are *fulpata* (flower leaves with creepeers), *dalani*, cup-plate, Taj Mahal, trees, birds, etc.

30. Bamboo Crafts

Bamboo crafts in India are very popular due to their eco-friendly attributes. Since ancient times, bamboo crafts have been occupying a significant position as India produces a huge amount of bamboo and cane. The bamboo craft, associated with cane and bamboo, had been a part of Indian crafts since long giving rise to the expression of tribal art and provided them with livelihood.

As India is blessed with skilled artistry, these types of craft developed in this country very soon and with the changing style and trend, the craft has developed its designs and deftly blended tradition with fashion.

The Indian artisans are dexterous in creating bamboo crafts and arrays of bamboo items are famous in Indian as well as in abroad. Basically, the artisans create variations in their creations. The craftsmen create different items with the help of different bamboos and canes that are locally known as 'sundi', 'barjali', 'harua', 'golla', etc. which are required for making furniture and baskets.

It is observed that, generally, three species of cane are exploited in commercial quantities- Jati (Calamus tenuis), Tita (Calamus leptesadix) and Lejai (Calamus floribundus). Some less important qualities like Sundi (Calamus garuba) and Raidang (Calamus flagellum) are also extracted for creating superb designs.

Generally, the products of bamboo are of two types, namely articles required for day-to-day use, and of medium quality, that are more suited to local requirements; another type is articles of finer quality, both decorative and functional, to meet the requirements and tastes of more sophisticated markets. Items like baskets, chalani, crossbows, kula, khorahi, dukula or tukuri, dala dukula or tali, doon or kathi, bamboo mats, etc. are some of articles made from this grass.

Some of the Indian States are famous for creating beautiful bamboo items like mugs for rice beer, hukkas, musical instruments, floor mats, fishing devices and handles. In this respect, the name of Assam, Tripura and West Bengal can be mentioned. This traditional craft has received greet success in making winnowing baskets, special pitaras, oval boxes, oblong caskets, and flower baskets. Assam, a state with abundant raw materials, has a large variety of beautiful products. Some of the well known bamboo and cane crafts are baskets, chalani, dolls, toys, etc. which are made in different sizes and fine designs. One the most interesting and colourful item of bamboo is leaf-headgear for tea garden workers and farmers. Umbrella handles made of bamboo are a speciality of the North-East.

A number of designs like leaves, plants and creepers are etched on these articles. A variety of these furniture items are made to suit the modern homes. Apart from all these, bamboo mats are extensively used for construction of temporary walls and sheds, big pandals, roofing of country boats, dwelling houses, etc.

Caning is also a famous craft in India. Cane is used to make trays, baskets, and many utilitarian objects. The core central portion of the cane stick and the strips are used to create beautiful fancy articles. Walajapet in Vellore district is famous for cane articles. Moreover, stylish furniture is created by bamboos that are apt for fashionable houses.

Bamboo and cane crafts have been getting more admiration from all over India and the government is thinking to promote this type of ancient and tribal craft to capture the international market. The bamboo and cane crafts have remained the backbone of the rural economy of the country. The government is planning to promote these crafts by providing aid.

31. Chindi Durries

Chindi Durries are available in beautiful patterns. The patterns are of traditional and modern types. History of durrie weaving goes back to ancient times, when the concept of weaving had taken shape. This item of floor furnishing was manufactured in the villages and towns both for the household consumption and selling in the local market.

Large floor and tent durries in solid colours and bold red/blue stripes and borders were made in cotton warp and unspun cotton owing to the varying sizes. The durries were woven on the horizontal devices, placed on the floor. The width of the device could be changed as per the size of durrie. Chindi durrie weaving is mainly practiced in Maharashtra and Uttar Pradesh.

Today, this industry is a major revenue earning resource. Chindi durries are most commonly used item in ones living room and bedroom and their very important use is seen in the prayer room.

Over past few decades, chindi durries have been impressively influenced by the designers intervention and a new range of concept in terms of sizes, colours, designs and forms opened the new vistas in the export market for these durries.

The designs may be unicolour, multi-colour in cut shuttle technique. Craftsmen are more keen on working on geometric designs as their favourite. The patterns are complimented with beautiful borders having all the possible colours. Block printing is also seen on the borders which is an ancient art.

The scrap cotton fabrics or leather are picked up in bulk and are shredded into small strips on *hasia* generally by women. These strips act as the wefts during weaving. Dyeing may sometimes be carried out of the cotton warp chindis. The horizontal ground loom, consisting of two wooden beams, to which the warp threads are attached, is used for making chindi durries.

The designs are followed on the loom as per the graph. Chindis dyed in different colours are kept in different piles. Since the chindis have a restricted length, each chindi is picked and inserted in the warp with fingers. If the same colour is repeated, another chindi is inserted. At least two/ three warps have double chindi to avoid any holes in weaving. *Panja* is used repeatedly to set the chindis. Chindis are rotated round the warp bundle of three or four warps on the two corners at the beginning and at the end of each row. A little trimming is done here and there. These are then washed and finished.

32. Lac Craft

Lac handicraft in India is quite an old art. Lac work is applied to furniture and other decorative items. Lac is manufactured in many parts of Bengal, Elambazaar in Beerbhum, Lohardugga district of Chhota Nagpur and along the banks of the Parulia, between Jhalda and Ranchi in the Manbhum district. Stick lac is also manufactured in Chhota Nagpur, Raipur and Sambalpur. The making of multicoloured lac marbles, lacquered walking sticks, lac mats, lac bangles and lacquered toys are carried on almost everywhere.

Multicoloured balls and sticks are made by twisting coloured melted sealing-wax round the stick or ball from top to bottom in alternate bands. Thereafter, the stick or ball is held before the fire, and with a needle or pin, short lines are drawn perpendicularly through the bands of sealing-wax, drawing the different colours into each other, when the stick or ball is rapidly rolled on a cool, smooth surface. The netted mats are made by allowing the thread of sealing wax twisted round a stick to cool and then drawing off the whole coil. This is then broken into sections of three or four turns each, which are linked together into "mats".

Lac bracelets and ornamental beads are manufactured at Delhi and other places in the Punjab. The lac bracelets tinfoil is mixed with silver with half its weight of dry glue and these are pounded together. The mass breaks into pieces when it is thrown into water. This is stirred and the water is poured out. When the solution becomes pure, it is boiled, and allowed to cool. Silvery glue is seen on it that is spread with a brush on the lac and polished when dry by rubbing with a set of glass beads. Lac bracelets are ornamented, with little glass beads and bits of tin or copper foil stuck along the edge.

Lac bracelets are also manufactured in the district of the Panch Mahal in Madhya Pradesh. Lac is collected by the Bhils in the neighbouring forests of Ali Rajpur, and Devgad Bariya and sold to grain dealers which are again sold to the town lac manufacturers. The bangles are separately formed. They are slipped over the oily conical head of a rice pounder. When it is about half-covered with rings, they are heated so that without melting they stick to each-other. Thereafter, a pattern is printed on the cylinder of bracelets. Two ounces of thin tin and a small lump of glue are pounded together till they form a dull grey metallic paste.

Next day, it is boiled in a copper vessel. The cotton stamp is taken, dipped in the tin water and it prints its pattern on them. Once a day for three days, a varnish is applied that turns all the white dots of the tin pattern into a beautiful golden colour. The pattern is completed by fastening the bracelet with drops of tin water made red with vermilion, white with chalk.

Yellow and red striped armlets also know as *golias* are worn between the elbow and shoulder. The industry gives employment to the families at Dohad and Jhalod. Lacquered wooden bracelets and wooden toys are also made at Ahmedabad and Surat and in Mysore and Harpanhalli. Lac ornaments are made at Ellichpur in Berar. The Rajputana boxes have a dull background, decorated with conventional, geometric, flower forms, of two colours arranged in the alternate rhythmical manner. The lacquered paper mache work of cashmere is the choicest in India. It is used for native pen cases and boxes which are painted throughout with the shawl pattern in many colours.

Jhunjuna and *Chusni* for babies, tops, bats, balls, models of aeroplanes, rail engines, telephone sets, jumping sets, tea sets, caravans of camels and elephants, sets of musicians and sadhus of India, models of carts and animal figures, furniture items; bed posts, cradles; utility articles like *sindoor* boxes, flower vases, powder boxes are other example of things made out thus.

Coloured lacquerware is made in Sheopur, Rewa Budhi, Bhopal, Gwalior, Ratlam and Sabalgarh. Etikoppaka in Andhra Pradesh is one of the most important centres of this craft. The lacquerware of Savantvadi, once a princely state, is a traditional craft. The traditional craftsmen are known as Chittorees, picture makers. The production now is mainly centred on lacquered imitation fruits and vegetables. Chennapatna holds an honoured place in the lacquerware world.

Navrangpur has a distinct type of lacquering with its own designs and colour schemes. Their speciality is a box made generally of bamboo, sometimes of papier mache, brightly lacquered and highly decorated with folk motifs, animals, flowers, birds traditionally used for exchanging gifts.

Making lac bangles is another popular craft in Mithila and is one of the important folk art. The bangles have numerous types such as lahathi simple bangles, tisiphula bangles of marriage, chagotava vsukhapuri thin, mathapa, mobya, bijulichata, phulavari, sahana, etc. Beautiful designs are made on each of these types of bangles. Each area specialises in different designs. The designs of bangles of sursand in Muzaffarpur district of Darbhanga division retain the traditional colouring and pattern.

Lac combs are used by tribals as hair ornamentation. The comb itself is made of a soft local wood and the decorative motifs on it are done with jungle-lac. Navrangapur of Koraput district is the most well-known centre for jungle-lac craft.

The main industry for lac is in Bihar. In northern Bihar, about one hundred tons of refuse lac which remains in the sack after squeezing, is used for bangle cores and the better quality lac is used for decoration. Lac bangles are worn by married women of the aboriginal tribal people of Bihar including Bhumij, Mo, Munda, Oraon and Santhal tribes.

Lac jewellery, especially bangles, is worn on all auspicious occasions in Rajasthan as they are considered a sign of good omen. The bangles are either plain or studded with glass pieces, bright stones — sometimes precious ones — and beads. They are extremely beautiful. The plain bangles have lahariya (wavy) or zig-zag designs. The ornamental ones are in several varieties, like path and phooldar (floral). They are also set with salma and patri.

Lac jewellery set with glass chatons is also a popular item in Rajasthan. Jaipur city is the biggest centre of this activity.

33. Screw Pine

The screw-pine mats have an old romantic history. Screw pine weaving of mats is one of the oldest crafts practised by women in Kerala. The leaves for this mat are taken from the sword-shaped thorny screw-pine plant. The Mats were once the favourite of sailors who used to employ them as sails for ships. There is a place near Quilon called Kadalpai sail mat which indicates that this was once a centre for producing the sail mats popular at the time even with the foreign ships.

There are two varieties of screw pines used in the making of mats. The short variety is used for a number of items as it can be both bleached and dyed. The entire process is laborious as the leaf has sharp thorns growing in both direction on its ribs. A long and thick coconut fibre is used to remove the thorny edges on the midrib of the leaves, followed by the splitting which is done with thinner coconut fibre.

The finer varieties of mats need narrower splits and as they need to be extra silky, so they are boiled in milk. The strips can be dyed in a multitude of colours for ornamental designs. The weaving is done crosswise; and interlacing continues as new strips are added. On completion, the edges are hemmed with narrow screw-pine strips. Superfine mats made of very fine screw-pine leaf splints placed about 10 per inch are woven by the experienced craftsmen.

But in the coarser variety of mats, the edges are woven simultaneously and the weaving starts with two strips, while at the edges, it is continued with a single strip. Embroidery in the form of decorative stitching adds to the attractiveness of the products. A two-ply mat consists of a fine upper layer and a coarse bottom one stitched at the edges. The coarser variety of maps is commonly used as a sleeping mat, while the large and rough mats are used for drying grass.

34. Patachitra

The patachitra, the folk painting of Orissa, has a history of great antiquity. The 'Patachitra' paintings exhibit the use of strong line and brilliant colours. These are religious paintings which covers themes and events from Indian mythology and Puranas and are mainly made on silk or on old cotton glued with paper.

Patachitras are painted in a regular series, like Dashavatar of Vishnu and activities of Lord Rama & Krishna, etc. The Patachitra paintings have a basic resemblance to the old murals of Kalinga region dating back to 5th century B C. The best Patachitra paintings are found in and around Puri, especially in the village of Raghurajpur. The artists colony, known as Chitrakar Sahi, is in the vicinity of the local temple.

Apart from the mythological stories, there are figures like a dancing girl or mother and child. The most popular patachitra paintings are the figures of Jagannath, the crowned God of Puri with Brother Balaram and Devi Subhadra. Many scenes are however from the life of Krishna, the fountain head of inexhaustible anecdotes of colour and excitement that people never tired of. Krishna's dancing with gopis and playing of various pranks on his playmates charging the environment with an air of mischief are favourites.

The eternal idol of Radha and Krishna set in a riot of exhilarating colours assail our eyes with vivid red, orange, yellow for the background and lapis lazuli for the sky, dark green for dense brooding trees, parrot green for the grass. Against this glowing background is blue figure of Krishna, and in pink purple, wheat and brown and a whole host of shades are Krishna's playmates, touched off by gold and silver brushing. For an important occasion, there will be sumptuous elephants surrounded by mangal ghats (sacred vessels), gaily painted with trees, creepers, leaves, flowers, animals etc.

The folk paintings or patachitras have painting done on cloth which the artists prepare themselves by coating it with a mixture of chalk and gum made from tamarind seeds to give the surface a leather-like texture on which the artists paint with earth and stone colours.

In Patachitra, painting is done by brushes with a mixture of clay and powder from a stone rich in iron-oxide, or by incising and cutting a pattern on the raw pottery using comb-like and knife-like tools.

Paintings depict gods of the Hindu pantheon i.e. Radha & Krishna, legends and Jagannath.

35. Cotton Fabrics

Cotton fabrics are said to be the pearl of Indian weaving. It were as though these craftsmen were magicians and waved wands to produce what seemed like dreams. The weightlessness of these fabrics has been sung by many poets, comparing them to the moonlight on the tulip or a dewdrop on the rose.

Indians have known weaving of material from cotton since 5000 years. Cotton is woven universally all over India and one can take note of only a few places for their distinctive weave.

The conventional cotton weaving revolves around 'khadi' which is woven by hand using handspun yarn. In India, 23 different varieties of cotton are found. Cotton is used in producing a wide range of items like: summer wear, saree, bedsheets, napkins, shirts, tablemats, etc.

Cotton fabric is very popular in India as the soft twist imparted by the hand, maintains the hairiness of the yarn to an extent which gives maximum comfort. Indian states have their own traditional weaving tradition.

Beautiful sarees are produced from cotton. The elegant varieties of saris from Andhra pradesh, Orissa, Madhya Pradesh, Gujarat and Uttar Pradesh are popular for their intricate designs.

36. Tande

Toda tribal embroidery is one of the most famous embroidery forms in India. When the sun is warm, the Toda women sit outside their house embroidering the handsome pudukulis, which protect both men and women from severe cold.

37. Shell Crafts

Sea shells and conch shells have for centuries been used for making a variety of objects. Conch shells have religious and social significance also. These are used through out the country for blowing on religious occasions. The statues of goddess Durga show her holding a conch in one hand.

In a number of coastal areas, these shell items are made in present day India. In Vishakhapatnam, tortoise shell is used for making trinklet boxes with designs in geometrical patterns and floral designs, etc. In Bengal, different types of bangles are made. Children's bangles called ginibala are beautiful with various patterns on them. In Neyyatinkera near Trivandrum (Kerala), small items of daily use are made. Here whole conch shells are shaped in to various forms. Small shells or cowries are also used for making a variety of items like necklaces for animal strings with large, coloured beads, as troppings especially for horses, camels and cows, etc. Cowries are also used for decoration as trinklet boxes, bags, stalls and shawls, etc.

Shell crafts are in great demand in India. It has religious and social significance. The ornaments made out of shells are favourite with people from all stratas of society. Shells are the most colourful and fascinating objects known to man other than gems since time immemorial. They served as money, ornaments, and musical instruments, drinking cups, were used in magic and in the making of fine porcelains.

They were also the symbols in rituals and religious observances. Shells such as giant clam, green mussel and oyster support edible shell fishery, a few like scallop, clam and cockle are burnt in kiln to produce edible lime.

The conch shell is considered especially sacred since time immemorial. It is one of the pre-requisites in religious performances and the blowing of the conch has been regarded as auspicious at religious as well as social functions. Its sound is said to symbolize that of the cosmic universe. Conch ornaments in the olden days were very popular.

The ancient city of Korkai, on the Indian shore of the Gulf of Manar, was made sub-capital of the Pandyan king because of the heavy revenues it brought from the selling of conch shell. Excavations have revealed numerous conch shell products, including some inlay work requiring great skill, with even buildings decorated with conch pieces. Bangles and other kinds of ornaments are also made from conches. Shell horn is the whole conch intact used for religious purposes. On this, beautiful ritualistic designs are made, mostly floral, sometimes those of figures, the most popular one being the lotus, which is also symbolic.

The process of working on the conch is as follows:

- The apex, tip and edges are first cut off with a hammer and the inner dust is cleaned.
- Next, tightly wedged between two bamboo stakes, the shell is placed between the right heel and left toe of the artisan.

- With the aid of saw, the base is cut and from the remaining portion, the ring shapes are sliced by a curved saw.

For finishing, holes are sealed with wax and five coloured drops are painted on the joint. The bangles are then put in nitric acid solution and finally polished with a dry cloth. In order to utilize the broken pieces, they are joined together to make them into coloured bangles. The pieces are tied together by an extremely thin tin coil and then coloured. Bangles, bracelets spoons, forks, lockets, costume jewellery, decorative measuring bowls, and armlets are made out of it.

The tortoise shell has a very limited use. A large number of shell workers are organized as private units. Their products extend from cleaned and polished decorative shells to table lamps, ashtrays, jewellery and buttons. A number of finer objects can be made from the polished shells with their pearly shine. Small boxes, round and square, as well as bangles, are made of tortoise shell.

The tortoise shell has very limited use. It is used along with ivory. The shell surface of the box is overlaid by net as it were of intricate patterns of ivory fretwork so that only through this perforated lacy surface, one get the orange glow of shell.

The design consists of fine geometrical patterns or epic figures, or animals fringed by floral edging. The best-known product of shell is a beautiful octagonal jewel box with the ivory net cover. Bangles, bracelets, spoons, forks, lockets, costume jewellery, decorative measuring bowls, armlets, small boxes, bangles, jewellery, decorative items, table lamps, ashtrays, buttons, etc. are made out of them.

The abundance of small and large varieties of shells being along the Indian coast, the seashell craft is being practised by coastal people. Seashells have been known to please every person's eyes with their majestic shapes and colours since ages.

The shells are used to produce a variety of products, starting from attractively designed animals to human figures depicting ethnic costumes of various sizes. We can trace existence of this craft since Portuguese rule in Goa which is the centre of craft activities in India. In Portuguese architectures of Goa, one can see doors and windows decorated with seashells. In that sense, it can be said that the seashell is one of the original crafts of Goa.

The seashell products of Goa are known throughout the length and breadth of our country. The items produced by the craftpersons are both utility and decorative. The items include posters, curtains, chandeliers, pot hangers, table lamps and mirror frames, etc.

The seashells are to be picked up and collected along the sea beaches. The shell is generally defiled and some times buried deep in the sand and hence undergoes process of cleaning. The shells are cut to desired sizes and shapes and then washed in water. Further cleaning is done with chemicals so as to give the shells, a sparkling and ornamental look. The shells after cleaning are used in making of various products as per the designs and shapes of the items, e.g. posters, chandeliers, curtains, pot hangers, table lamps, table mats, clock and mirror frames, etc.

38. Ikat

The most ingenious method used for patterning during the weave is *ikat*. It can be differentiated on the basis of whether only warp, or weft, or both are tie-dyed. In the patola of Patan and Orissa both warp and weft are so resist-dyed that when woven, the patterns on the warp and weft mesh to create the desired inclines of figure/pattern. It is called the double mat.

In the ikat of Patan, sharp grain of patterns emerged due to the matching of the elements of the motifs used in the resist-dyed warp and weft; while ikat of Orissa grain is often not sharp, but in half-tone because here also, though the warp weft are resist-dyed, the designs of the two threads do cover each other. Besides, in some cases pallav and two borders are created by not using ikat alone, but by weaving, very often with extra weft.

The term 'ikat' steams from the Malay-Indonesian expression mangikat, meaning to bind, knot or wind around. Ikat known as tie-and-dye textile design, is known around the world. Some experts are of the opinion that the technology came from far eastern countries but actually the name was given to the technique by Indonesians. But, study reveals that it started and developed in India also, at least, in certain clusters like Orissa, Gujarat and Andhra Pradesh and upto certain extent in North, East and North-Eastern India. *Ikat* is equivalent of the Indian *bandhana.*

Orissa has a patola style of its own. The designs usually are in floral patterns, with animals, and certain traditional motifs, like fish conch. The cotton ikats in Orissa are fabulous with firm accent on the geometrical patterns in heavy waves.

One of the most popular motifs used in the fabrics is the Gaja (elephant) particularly in Khandua (odhni) used by brides at marriage time. Large and small stars, elephant, deer, parrot, *nabagunjara*, lotus and other flowers, creepers, kumbha (small triangles), danti (tooth-like) patterns have been used in silk and cotton fabrics.

In principle, ikat or resist dying involves the sequence of typing (or wrapping) and dyeing sections of bundles yarn to a predetermined colour scheme prior to weaving. Thus, the dye penetrates into the exposed sections, while the tied sections remain undyed. The patterns formed by this process on the yarn are then woven into fabrics.

In ikat technique, the designs in various colours are formed on a fabrics either by warp threads or weft threads (single ikat) or by both (double ikat).

In single ikat fabrics, the warp or weft threads which are tied and dyed as per design are to be positioned accurately in proper sequence in weaving as required by the design and colour scheme.

In case of double ikat fabrics, not only warp and weft threads, which are tied and dyed as per design should be individually positioned in proper sequence, but the relative position of each warp threads and weft thread forming the design should be accurately ensured. In these textiles, forms are deliberately feathered so that their edges appear hazy and fragile.

This effect is achieved by the use of very fine count yarn, tied and dyed in very small sets. In tie-and-dye process, increased number of colours used in bringing out figures increases the number of tying and dyeing. If the designs are all over and connected with each other in some way, by tie-and-dye links, all the picks in fabric may have to be tied and dyed.

Ikat, the technique by which the warp or weft or both can be tie-dyed in such a way that when woven, the 'programmed' pattern appears in the finished fabric. Of resist-dye techniques, the use of clay or wax-resist has long been known to Indian textile printers and painters, who would stamp or delineate the fabric with resist and then immerse and re-immerse in dye.

To reserve areas of the warp or weft or both, before the process of weaving with tied threads, and then to dye the yarn, is a more interesting process that requires greater skill. And this seems to be more closely aligned to processes of tie-resist and warp-resist after weaving, than to the application of impression of a resist to the surface of a fabric.

Up to the beginning of this century, Chirala in Andhra Pradesh was renowned for an exquisite type of cotton sari, lungi, rumal and yardage in a range of Ikat techniques. One of the products of this place is known as telia rumal, a many-purpose cloth used as lungi, loin-cloth, shoulder-cloth and turban-cloth which was a popular import item in many Islamic countries.

Due to the heavy use of tel (oil), in the process of preparing the yarn for weaving, this variety of textile has deserved the name telia, meaning 'oily'. The techniques and designs of telia rumal have been adapted to make saris, spreads, and yardage material.

39. Himroo

Himroo is one of the oldest fabric used as dress material by nobility. The word 'Himroo' is derived from the Persian word Hum-ruh which means 'similar'. Himroo is the replica of the rich kum-khwab which was woven by the pure golden and silver threads in olden days. It has its origin in the ancient style of weaving known as jamawar in Kashmir and was introduced to the south (in cotton) by the Mughals for the warmer climate.

Himroo was brought to Aurangabad in the period of emperor Mohammad Tughlaq, when he had shifted his capital from Delhi to Daulatabad. Aurangabad himroo was used by the royal families. Himroo from Aurangabad is much in demand for their unique style and design.

Himroo, the fascinating fabric from Maharashtra, is an extra-weft, figured fabric with a solid ground of satin or twill, decorated with figurative motifs and manufactured ordinarily from cotton and viscose rayon yarn on a cotton ground. It is also woven from silk yarn and gold thread on a silk ground.

This special cotton brocade is woven on a throw-shuttle loom and has an art-silk or silk mix. It has a complicated technique of weaving. The design has to be decided at the outset since two kinds of threads are mixed. The designs are geometrical and floral. Intricate creeper designs are more popular in himroo.

A luxurious extra-weft figured fabric with a cotton base and a silk or art silk weave, himroo is ideal for rich stoles and furnishing material. The design are geometrical-like circles, octagons, ovals, diamonds, hexagons and of fruits like pomegranate, almonds, pineapple; and of flowers like rose, lotus, jasmine, birds and animals; designs of flowering creepers, running designs formed with leaves and stems which interlock sometimes to form intricate patterns. This material is used for coats, cloaks, and shawls, as also for furnishings.

Himroo is a kind of a brocaded material woven on a simple throw-shuttle loom on the principle of the extra-weft figuring with cotton used in the warp and art silk in the weft. In this preparation, the *jala* or design is most important. This is where initially the entire design is worked out, and prescribes where the extra-weft silk yarn is to pass through some of the warp threads, which is the most complicated job. The *jala* consists of a bunch of threads, the number determined by the design, suspended from the ceiling. The threads being tied each to the threads below in a horizontal position by wooden supports. Twin loops hang to receive the warp threads on their way to the heads. When ready, it is attached vertically to the loom. The weaving consists in interlacing of the weft yarn with the warp at right angles.

About himroo shawls, the great adventurer Marco Polo once wrote of the fabric that was given to him in the Deccan region, "It is as fine as a spider's web and kings and queens of any country will take pride in wearing it!"

40. Dhokra

Dhokra art is one of the earliest known methods of non-ferrous metal casting known to human civilization. The oldest form of metal casting 'dhokra' is popular because of its primitive simplicity. This art style is speciality of semi-tribal communities of Central India located in Madhya Pradesh,West Bengal, Orissa and parts of Vindhya range. It is a very important handicraft because of its, more or less, exclusive folk character. The dhokras of Bihar, Orissa, and West Bengal are distant cousins of the Madhya Pradesh. They all, perhaps, belong to a tribal group of that area.

Made by tribals, dhokra is notable for its strength and shapeliness of design. Its motifs are mostly drawn from folk culture. While among the animals, the elephant is most popular, other motifs, include human heads, kings, manas or miniature replica of measures, containers with lids, with or without locking devices, images of deities like Ganesh and Durga, lamps and lamp stands. The last being made in several intricate designs in shape of trees and branches with as many as hundred lamps in one stand. Of late, some utilitarian articles like candle stands, ash trays and pen stands are also being made keeping the essential folk design intact.

The dhokras use lost-wax process to cast hollow brass objects and images. The essence of the process is to model the object in wax, each one individually, around a hardened clay core which has approximately the shape of object to be cast. Layers of soft, refractory material are laid over wax model and hardened into a mould.

The wax between core and mould is lost or burnt out as mould is heated. Then molten metal takes its place and hardens between the core and inner surface of mould which holds a negative impression of the wax model in all its detail. The outer surface of hardened metal, therefore, reproduces the shape and details of original wax model, with the core producing hollow interior. The hard core and mould become spongy and soft on firing and are easily removed.

The most famous Dhokra artifacts are: images of Ganesh, Durga, lamps, lamp stands, candlestands, ashtrays, penstands.

41. Leather Crafts

The Indus valley civilization mentions the history where several references were found regarding the leather craft of India. The concept of leather craft came into existence when men realized the usage of animal skin for their clothing. The people of lower classes and rural areas initially practised the craft of leather in India.

In recent times, leather craft has lots of things to offer varying from caps, to clothing, to footwares, to decorative items. Leather craft has occupied a large industry that trades not only in India but also the overseas. Utilitarian items from leather like shoes, jackets, lampshades, pouches, bags, to belts, wallets, stuffed toys, etc. are found in umpteen amounts and maintain an indigenous quality.

Different cities and regions have their speciality in different items. Exclusively designed lamps and lampshades made from leather carry an eye-catching effect. Leather shoes, jutties, bags, mushks, embroidered leather items and items designed with geometric pattern are found in different places according to demand. Some regions of India reflect tradition of leather products that are painted with epic and mythological pictures in gold and silver.

Toys and puppets made of leather were used by the puppet masters in India since ages and are still reckoned as one of the finest examples of leather craft. Split-ply camel girths of Rajasthan are generally made manually by hand without involving any sort of loom. Goat hair or cotton cord is woven into yarn on the spindle that is then doubled to make it two-ply and so on. A four-ply yarn is used for girth, with each ply being two-ply, black-and-white yarn.

Pre-leather items such as shoes, gloves, coats and suitcases are specialized leather craft items of a particular locale. Zari works with gold and silver threads in leather items like *jooties* and *chappals* proves the artistry and enhances elegance to the embroidered products.

Leather jooties are sometimes decorated with silk, beads; sometimes applique work is done to add magnificence to the item. Knuckle pad is an embroidered leather craft that is vividly colourful and has an elegant look. The leather is embroidered, studded, sequined, and stitched in a variety of attractive traditional designs. Sometimes, the "jutis" are intricately decorated with gold and multicoloured threads to give them gaudy look. The leather items include footwear and ladies handbags, other items like ornaments, diary folders, leather seats, puffs and 'pidis' are also of great demand and found in polished attractive hues. The leather craft of Shantiniketan encompasses the art of 'batik' and embroidery.

Mojris footwear is a leather craft that is well admired for its craftsmanship and variations of designs. "Kashidakari" is an art that is done on the 'jootis' with silk or metal or beads or done in applique with thin leather pieces of different colours.

'Peshwari' is another kind of jooti that is worn by both men and women. 'Nagra' is a jooti that is admired in all places of India and those are embroidered with Mughal motifs in gold and brightly coloured threads with intricate and brilliant designs.

'Kolhapuri' chappals are crafted indigenously as its origin lies in Kolhapur in India and well admired by all over India and abroad.

Leather is hugely used for manufacturing jackets, gloves, coats, etc. as they are in demand and goes with the recent trend. Leather sofa sets, cushion covers, etc. are made keeping in mind the recent fashion and trend of interior decoration.

42. Paper Craft

The tradition of the paper craft in India is fairly old. The paper industry was located mainly in Patna, Delhi, Rajgir, Avadh, Ahemdabad, Gaya and Shahzadpur (near Allahabad). Since the paper is one of the easily perishable materials, the traditions of the paper craft have been left unrecorded. The earliest records available are in the form of the large number of beautiful manuscripts, the royal farmans and account-keeping by prosperous merchants in the Mughal period.

The industry was, however, indigenous and on a small scale so as to cater to the local needs. Men engaged in paper making could be found on the outskirts of the provincial capitals or of big towns. Their locality was known as the kagazi mohalla (kagaz-paper; mohalla-area or locality).

Paper craft is a seasonal activity. The paper with its various varieties and wide range of colours offers a very colourful choice to the craftsmen. The combination of various kinds of papers in different forms and styles makes paper craft one of the best crafts of India.

The paper craft in India has widely been used in different types of decorations. The decorations may be in forms of flowers, kandeels, kites and effigies. Rituals of Muslims and Hindus associated with general decoration and entertainment composed the majority of this craft.

Khamp (a thin bamboo strip) is used to give skeletal support to any paper product. Depending on the size, the number of bamboo strips may change. Kites are generally made by fixing a square paper on diagonal bamboo strip and a curved strip covers the upper part of the diagonal.

Tazia-making involves construction of huge bamboo minarets which are covered with paper. The effigies and other fire works made during Dusshera festival are meticulously filled with the explosives giving sparkle, sound and light.

Some of the paper artifacts are: kites, masks, bowls, paper puppet, and decorative birds, kandeels (lamp shades), guldasta (flowers), pankhe (fans).

43. Sanganeri Prints

Rajasthan is famous in India for its dyeing, printing and embroidery cloth since centuries. Floral, geometrical or animal motifs are major designs of printing. Sanganer near Jaipur is the center for block and screen-printed cotton cloth. The fascinating range of block-printed fabric in bold colours may be further embellished by embroidery.

The Sanganeri block prints usually consist of floral motifs. Basic colours are scarlet, black and brown. But now, with increasing technology and use of synthetic dyes, unusual combinations of scarlet and pink, purple and orange, turquoise and green are gaining market demand. The Sanganer prints are always on a white background famous for its artistry and intricacy of design.

Various floral designs, geometrical and God figures are included in its prints. Folk designs are also found as they retain the basic Sanganeri printing style. Nowadays, besides traditional prints, modern designs are also found on block-printed cloth. Instead of hand-block printing, these days, screen printing is getting popular.

The traditional *ghagras* of Rajasthan carry these block prints in a very artistic manner. These ghagras with added style has a place in the fashion world.

Block-printing is done with the help of wooden blocks, known as chhapas or buntis found in different shapes and sizes. Blocks are made of seasoned teak wood with design on the underside of the block. These blocks are dipped into dye to print the pattern on the cloth. These wooden blocks have different floral motif carved on them. These blocks are the main tools of the printer.

The blocks are designed in such a way that it allows release of excess printing dye. The new blocks are soaked in oil for 10-15 days to soften the grains in the timber. The printing table is long enough so that good number of fabric could be printed altogether. The fabric to be printed is pinned over the table and printed block-by-block.

Cloth is bleached and then folded into two or four layers depending on the thickness of the cloth, before printing. The design or the layout of the pattern is made using wooden blocks dipped in *geru*, a burnt sienna colour mixed with water.

In the traditional Sanganeri prints, the ground is in white or pastel shades with floral cones and sprays scattered with in symmetrical borders. The chhipas of Bagru produce a variety of fabrics printed in motifs of the gulab or rose, neem leaf, gobi or cauliflower, mirchi or Chili, mukut (crown), dhaniya ki bel (coriander sprig or creeper). Kota was traditionally known for its blue-black saris. Jodhpur prints were often masked by dense bands running the length of the fabric in scarlet or brick-red, orange and lemon on moss - green or indigo-blue.

The jarribhat sari which is the wedding dress of the local people has an interesting design worked from squares. Chittorgarh, an important erstwhile principality of the Ranas of Mewar, had a large number of printers who print fabric for ghagras with stylished mirch buta distributed over an Indian red background. Block-printing has become popular because of the simple process which can create such amazing prints and that too in bold and vibrant colours.

The printing table is covered with sand sprinkled with water which is then covered by a wet cloth. A special block with raised surface and deep grooves is dipped in liquid wax and pressed over the cloth and when it comes into contact with the cool surface, it solidifies the wax.

The whole material is next dyed in dark red colour and dipped in hot water to melt the wax. The piece presents interesting tonal effects.

44. Shawl

Naga Shawl

Situated in the north-eastern part of the country, Nagaland is an important part of the colourful culture of India. A Naga shawl is the most important part of the dress and is woven with cotton and staple fibre, though some wool is used. Shawls vary from simple white ones to elaborately designed ones with symbols and colours. The tsung kotepsu has a white woven band stitched along the centre of the shawl and is woven over with figures of elephants, tigers, mithuns, cocks, and circles, representing human heads. It has horizontal black, red, or white stripes.

A rich and brave man's acquisitions and achievements are picturised on it. The lotha naga shawl is woven in nine parts and stitched together. Many traditions and beliefs are associated with the weaving and wearing of the traditional dress. When a Konyak woman gets married, she wears a shatni shawl which is preserved and used only to wrap her dead body. Convention demands that a rongtu shawl be worn only if the mithun sacrifice has been conducted over three generations.

The Naga shawl is the most important part of their dress. Each tribe has its own patterns with simple clean lines, stripes, squares and bands being the most traditional design motifs. Naga fabrics retain their original attractive patterns, yet, external influences on colour and design are also evident.

The looms used are mostly narrow loin looms. Technically, Naga loom consists of a simple back-strap with a continuous horizontal warp consisting of six sticks serving as the warp beam, lease rod, heald stick, beating sword and extra warp beam. Loin loom products, mainly shawls, are woven with a rayon weft.

The Naga shawl weaving is done mostly with cotton, the staple fibre though some wool is used. The centre of the shawl is woven over with figures of elephants, tigers, mithun, cocks and circles, representing human heads. The fabrics are dyed in indigenous colours.

Uttarakhand Shawls Blanket

Weaving without ornamentation is an age-old tradition in Uttarakhand hills. The pure-wool shawls blanket from hilly areas of Uttarakhand specially Almora and Nainital are reputed for their warmth, softness and subtle beauty.

Sheep with thick fleece are raised in the higher mountains of Uttarakhand. The wool is spun by men and women in long winter seasons. This provides both warmth and softness. Panki is used as a wrap around with fur touching the body. The pashmina weaving is not as fine as in Kashmir but has it own softness, warmth and grace. Panki is heavy shawl with hair on one side. Thulma has hair on left sides.

Twill weave and plain weave techniques are used for weaving. Traditionally, soothing natural vegetable colours were used in shades of yellow, orange, brown and grey. Currently, synthetic colours are also used. They are woven using 2 to 4 ply hand spun yarns in 10 sq./13 sq. count with plain, twill or diamond weaves and simple geometrical designs.

The softness of the end product is achieved through the hand-finishing processes without use of any mechanised equipment.

Kashmir Shawls

Many speculations have been made by historians about the origin of Kashmir shawls. The local tradition held so far is that the founder of the shawl industry was Zain-ul-Abidin (1421-72). He is said to have introduced the twill tapestry technique with the help of Turkistan weavers.

It is also said that Mirza Haidar Tughlat was the originator of Kashmiri shawls. Mughal emperors also encouraged the shawl industry.

Woollen shawls are popular because of the embroidery worked on them which is special to Kashmir. Wool woven in Kashmir is known as raffel and is always 100 per cent pure. Many kinds of embroidery are worked on shawls. Sozni or needle work is generally done in a panel along the sides of the shawls. Motifs, usually abstract designs or stylized paisleys and flowers are worked in one or two, occasionally three colour, all subdued.

The fineness of the workmanship and the amount of embroidery determines the value of the shawl. Sozni is often done so skillfully that the motif appears on both sides of the shawl each side having a different colour.

Another type of needle embroidery is popularly known as Ari work because of the design and the style in which it is executed. This is done either in broad panels on either side of the breadth of a shawl, or covering the entire surface of a stole. Flowers and leaves are worked in stem stitch in bright colours.

A third type of embroidery is hook embroidery motifs better known as flower design finely worked in concentric rings of chain stitch. It is on pashmina shawls that Kashmir's most exquisite embroidery is worked, sometimes covering the entire surface, earning it the name of Jamavar. A Jamavar shawl can, by virtue of the embroidery, increase the value of a shawls three-fold. Shahtoosh, the legendary rung shawl is incredible for its tightness, softness and warmth.

Pattern drawing is the most important job, which is transferred to a graph by a highly skilled craftsman. The colouring is however, done by the colour caller with a black and white drawing before him, beginning at the bottom and working upwards calling out each colour, and the number of warps along which it is required to extend until the pattern is covered.

All these designs are then transcribed into a coded pattern that the weavers can decipher and guide others by calling out aloud the number of warp ends to be covered in a particular coloured weft. A second weaver sits on the loom to accelerate the process and the chief weaver recites the weft repeatedly for him to follow. In some shawls, there are two-sided weaves, usually of the same design, but sometimes in different colour schemes known as do-rookha.

The most popular types of shawls are: pashmina shawls, ring shawls, shahtoosh shawls, kani shawls, jamavar shawls, amli shawls.

45. Brassware

Indian brassware is popular all over the world. Sheets of brass are transformed into marvelous objects of art. Metal engraving is an ancient craft, which finds reference in the Vedas. Archeological findings of the copper tools of 300 B.C. at pre-Harappan sites of Baluchistan and Kali Bangan in Rajasthan, reveal the existence of metalware in Indian sub-continent.

The antiquity of use of iron in India is proved by its reference in our earliest literature, the Vedas, as also instructions on tempering it to make steel. The iron beams of Konarak Sun Temple in Orissa and the iron pillar at Qutab Minar in Delhi are two, out of numerous examples of the durability, of the old iron works in this country.

Brassware items cover a wide range and include vases, perforated lamps, tabletops, fruit bowls, planters, jewellery boxes, and picture frames. They are embellished with various kinds of engraved motifs - flowers, landscapes, jungle scenes and geometric patterns.

Brass casting is done by the Kansaris and items produced include icons mainly Radha Krishna, Laxmi, pot bellied Ganesha, Vishnu and crawling Krishna called Gurundi Gopal, bells or ghanti, lamp stand or rukha and lamps or dipa.

The major items manufactured in the beating process are plates or thali, deep round containers called kansa, small containers called 'gina' (tumbers), water containers called gara and buckets or baltis, large cooking utensils and storage vessels called handi, various types of pots and pans, ladles or chatu, perforated flat cooking spoons, etc.

There are also a number of items used for puja or worship. Of these, the important are, the ghanta or the gong and thali for offering of the food to the deities.

A thin coating of lac is applied on the article, for the engraved wares. A design is traced out on a metal ware. A pattern is traced on the part of the object to be engraved, with the aid of a pencil. Engraving is done by controlled strokes with the thapi on the chisel, which touch the surface of the designed part.

The engraving is done in three styles, viz, chikan, a motif of bold flower decoration which stands out against the chased and lacquered surface, marori, minute lacquered patterns covering the entire surface, and bidri, minute leaves and flowers in an all-over design on a chased and lacquered surface.

The process consists of preparation of the material by melting the required material in the crucible and then placing the molten metal into an earthenware container. After molten metal sets, it is taken out and after repeated hammering and beating, the desired shape is given. Sometimes, for making a single item two or three pieces are separately made and joined mostly with rivets.

In few places, the surface of the items are also engraved with various designs including floral and geometric patterns besides human and animals figures and occasionally they are also painted with enamel paints. The items produced by the beating process are many and the designs also vary from place to place.

The popular brassware are: vases, perforated lamps, table tops, fruit bowls, planters, jewellery boxes, picture frames, animal figures, toys, hukkas, wine jugs, water-bottles, surahis. Thali, plates, kansa, tumbers, water containers, buckets, utensils, handi storage vessels, various types of pots and pans, ladles or chatu, perforated flat cooking spoons, ghanta, gong etc., are some other brasswares.

46. Horn Craft

Horn craft is the rich cultural heritage of the artisans of Paralakhemundi, Gajapati district of Orissa. Originally carpenters by birth and trade, they took to horn craft during the reign of Sri Krushna Chandra Gajapati Narayan Deb, the Maharaja of Paralakhemundi.

A variety of small objects from animal horns are made in different parts of India. Horn of rhinoceros was used for some medicinal purposes and making charms. This has now been completely banned to protect the species. Horns of other animals are used for making combs, pins, small animals, birds, toys, buttons, small trays, cigarette cases, boxes, ashtrays, pen stands and lamps, etc.

It is impossible to tell precisely when or how this handicraft was born. It is believed that K.V. Appa Rao is the father of horn craft in its present form. The maharaja patronized him for his fireworks, for one particular variety of which the hollow part of a horn was used as a container. When the king came across an exquisitely carved wooden crane, he was inspired to get a similar one made of horn. The work of the art carved by him from the solid part, a horn, highly pleased the Maharaja. Appa Rao with his innate business acumen assessed the potentiality of the craft and set up a workshop.

Efforts were also made to introduce new designs and more sophisticated tools. The very word Paralakhemundi became synonymous with horn-craft.

Horn articles of Paralakhemundi are mystical and are blended with a superb fashion design. They make stylized birds and animals which seem so alive, cranes for instance, look as though if they opened their beaks, they could talk; or the birds appear to be twittering; or the tiger seems just about to jump on you. Little touches of silver filigree are added to the horn article to give it an unusual look, also to items like bangles, perfume jars.

In Cuttack horn and filigree work are combined to produce decorative jewels, bangles, etc. The other important centers include Sarai Tarin in Uttar Pradesh, Honawar in Karnataka and Thiruvananthapuram in Kerala. The craftsmen of Thiruvananthapuram are famous for making different kinds of crane birds in horn.

Cow horns, buffalo horns, stag antlers and tusks are used in horn craft. The desired object is carved from the solid part of a horn after soaking it in water. If shaping is necessary, then the carved piece is heated to a specific temperature and shaped. After that, its surface is smoothed down with the help of a rough file, flat file or half round file and a sharp stainless steel blade respectively. Necessary bores are made to fix appendages.

In the past, eyes were made of the stag antler stick at the center of which a bore was drilled and stuffed with lacquer burnt in a luminous flame. After drilling bores, light incisions and grooves are made in the required places on the body of the horn work. At this stage, it is handed over to the women for polishing. They rub the articles first with an eighty-count sand paper and then with wet khrshana leaves on surface which is rough.

The polishing is contained till the horn work is smooth and shiny. Then, it is thoroughly cleaned with water and dried in open air. After drying, it is further polishing with cow dung ash or charcoal ash and the various parts are assembled. Applying either limestone paste or white varnish, highlights the desired areas. Finally, coconut oil is smeared all over to give the horn work a beautiful sheen.

Pen stands, table lamps, paper weights, lamp shades, snuff boxes, walking sticks, vermilion container are some of the most common products. Fish and fowl, flora and fauna, men and women, in fact, the entire gamut of creation is rendered in a naturalistic manner.

The list remains incomplete without a mention of the horn deities, especially Lord Jagannath. In keeping with changing times, inspiration for decorative pieces is being drawn from modern art as well.

47. Bone Craft

In Orissa, bone carvings of animals and mithuna figures are common. Carved combs of bones and horns are a specialty. The most important centers include Sarai Tarin in Uttar Pradesh, Honawar in Karnataka and Thiruvananthapuram in Kerala.

The design on the bone carving is floral and figurative based on the inspirations from the Mughal architecture and foliage. Initially, ornaments were made out of the natural bones, but for the past many years, bone is treated with many attractive colours of natural stones like feroza, topaz, quartz, etc.

Procedure of making Bone product

Raw bone of dead animals is cut into pieces of desired size and immersed in water for 12 hours. This process softens the bone. Later, these pieces are scrapped and cleaned. Then they are shaped to a desired object on a lathe. Carving is done with the aid of a file drill. Carving entails systematic scrapping/scooping and chiseling of the materials from the core block. The crafts made from ivory and shell are also very famous.

The important horn and bone artifacts are: jewellery, ornate table lamps, chess-sets, cigarette holders, napkin rings, salt and pepper sets, laughing Buddha, table-lamps, chess sets, animal figures, decorative plaques, bridges of animals, paper cutters, the emblem of India, napkin rings, salt and pepper sets, tooth picks, hair pins, bangles, lockets, necklaces, figures depicting Indian dances.

48. Masks

Mask is basically an important part of theatre craft that has been connected with the rituals and Indian history since antiquity. India is the place where such theatre crafts are in huge demand because of the fact that India is the centres of theatre and drama. Masks of different cultures and times connote that masks existed since the ancient times.

The word 'mask' has a foreign origin. It is, perhaps, derived from the French term 'masque' or the Italian word 'maschera' or the Spanish term 'maiscara'. The word is also considered to have its origins in the Latin words 'mascus' and 'masca' which connote ghost. Even Arabic term 'maskharah' which is another originator of the term 'mask' implies jester or man in masquerade. The history says that masks have been used since antiquity for both ceremonial and practical purposes in India.

Masks are made in India in several states and this is particularly the art of the tribal people. Sometimes, the people of different states make masks to earn their livelihood. There are different kinds of masks like bhuta masks of South India, painted mask bastar of Madhya Pradesh, Hanuman masks of Orissa, papier mache tiger masks of Himachal Pradesh, wooden masks of Nepal.

Apart from these masks, Karnataka is the centre of a particular mask, especially, headgears called 'kiritams' which are used by the artists performing Kathakali dance. There are variations in the headgears as different headgears are made to represent different characters. The headgears of religious figures, strong, gentle, devoted, and loyal differs from the headgears of vicious and destructive characters.

Among the other masks made in India, the wooden masks of West Bengal are an important component for the social and cultural activities. The craftsmen of this state, mainly from Purulia, make wooden mask for the 'chhou' dancers. In Malda, the masks are used by the 'Gambhira' dancers.

The tradition of Darjeeling and Tibet also incorporate the use of masks in their devil dances and other religious festivals. 'Chhou' masks are discernible as they are the representation of the gods, goddesses and characters from the mythology and history of India. The artisans associated with 'chhou' masks are mostly located in and around Charida and Bagmundi of Purulia district in West Bengal.

The artistry of hilly areas allows the wood carving on wooden masks which are painted vividly with exclusive tint representing the evil spirits of the mountains and the demons.

Masks are used for their expressive power as a feature of masked performance, both ritually and in various theatre traditions. The ritual and theatrical definitions of mask usage frequently overlie and merge but still provide a useful basis for categorisation.

The image of juxtaposed comedy and tragedy masks are widely used to represent the performing arts, specifically, drama. Ritual masks are used all over the world. They are highly distinctive in forms and many more forms have developed by the progression of theatre craft and time.

The function of the masks may be magical or religious; they may appear in rites of passage or as a make-up for a form of theatre.

Masks share an aesthetic value with the carved images of monstrous heads that dominate the facades of Hindu and Buddhist temples. These faces or kirtimukhas, 'Visages of Glory' are intended to ward off evil and are associated with the animal world as well as the divinity.

Ramlila performances which are done annually nine days before celebration of Dussehra in various part of Uttar Pradesh gives an ample scope for making masks related to this performance. Generally, costumes and jewellery are cheap ostentations with bold motifs and designs.

Ample use of zardozi embroidery is done to decorate the costumes and the *mukuts* (head gears) of the performers. Mathura is known for making the *mukuts*. Large masks depicting animals and human models are made at Ram Nagar.

Masks play the role of familiar and vivid element in many folk and traditional pageants, ceremonies, rituals and festivals which are often of an ancient origin. Having a traditional value, it is important to the religious and social life of the community as a whole or a particular group within some community.

There are some communities in India, who live on creating this particular item of theatre craft. The artisans follow some ways to give each mask a distinct look. These masks play a key part within world theatre traditions, particularly non-western theatre forms. They also continue to be a vital force within contemporary theatre, and their usage takes a variety of forms.

In many cultural traditions, the masked performer is a central concept and is highly valued.

There are different types of masks. The masks made for the kathakali dancers, 'kiritams' made for the 'rishis', hunters and religious figures. These particular masks look different from each-other as each 'kiritam' represent separate persona. To make these masks, wood used is decorated with closely knit silver beads on a red scarlet base.

In order to beautify the masks, further decoration is done with fixing glass pieces on aluminium foils while large glass flower petals and small silver beads are in the centre. Various other decorations are done with pieces of jewellery, vines of golden stems and leaves, green buds, grapes with peacock feather stems, and a golden circle of foils converging on a round piece of glass in the centre and represents a fully blossomed flower.

At first, the fabric to be embroidered is fixed on a wooden frame and stretched tightly. Design is traced on it and with the aid of a needle, zari, stones, salma, sitara, etc. are embedded on to it. In case the fabric is to be printed, then it is done with various colours by a brush.

The tradition of masks depicts its existence in India since the antiquity. Even in recent times, the contemporary theatre tradition values the use of the different forms of masks to suit the persona of different characters in dramas and theatres.

In some states of India, the culture of folk tradition plays a vital role. In this nineteenth century, the artisans are trying to reconstruct the art of making masks by adding modern arts into them.

49. Patola

Patola is one of the finest dyed fabrics produced anywhere in the world and seen at its best in the silk wedding saris of Kathiawar and Gujarat.

Patolas are one of the most beautiful products of the Indian handloom and among the most colourful of ancient Indian textiles.

The famous Patola weaving of Patan is known for its colourful and strikingly beautiful patterns. It is characterised by tie-and-dye work. Some of the important designs are rattan chowk, in which diamonds cross with diamonds as they are interspersed around walnut, narikunja, dancing girl, parrot and elephant, chhabri is a basket made up by four elephants, waghkunjar, tiger-elephant.

Also, there is a variety of leaf and flower and geometrical patterns. The colours are vivid and pleasantly harmonised.

In making patolas, silk is always used as a yarn. The warp colours are dyed in the lightest colour to be used in the pattern, then the portions which are to be next darker in shade are traced on a bundle of threads either by charcoal or pencil.

After completion of dyeing work of warps & wefts, the threads of the warp of different repeats of a pattern are put together in a sequence on the loom so that the design becomes visible. The threads of wefts are wound on to bobbins and kept in the bamboo shuttle for weaving process.

The threads with in the pattern are then tightly tied with a cotton thread where the marks are made. The formula continued with threads that are to bear the next shades of the pattern until the darkest shades are reached. The weft is treated in the same way so that while weaving it crosses the warp, each of its colours synchronise with the same warp. In the weaving, the weft is woven properly into the warp with extreme dexterity and precision.

Thus, the desired figures are obtained by juxtaposition of similarly dyed shades on equal lengths of warp and weft, and interlacing them.

The patola is woven on a primitive hand-operated harness loom made out of rosewood and bamboo strips. The loom lies at a slant, with the left side being lower than the right side. The bamboo shuttle is made to move to-and-fro through warp shades. Each weft thread is thoroughly examined and matched with each part of the warp design pattern while weaving.

50. Tillajutis

Leather tanning seems to have reached a high stage by 3000 B.C. which paved the way for a wider use of this wonderful material that man sought.

The earliest skins were used to sit on like mats and highly prized were of the tiger, but equally valued were those of the deer, particularly of the dark variety.

Tillajuttis of Haryana are sewn out of locally cured leather and the ornamented with silk. Men embroider, beads, and designs dom in applique, with thin leather pieces of different colours.

The designs are extremely delicate and the colours used are vivid ones. An equally colourful item is the embroidered knuckle pad.

Pattern of the shoe or chappal is drawn on a thick paper. This tracing is kept on the leather, which is cut accordingly by sharp edged knife. To the edges of the leather for sewing, weight and thickness by the side is considered. If a heavier weight skin is sewn, inner edges to be joined are carefully thinned.

Once skived, heavy leathers are handled like light and medium weights. Stitch gauge is used to mark the seams for stitch holes. Lighter the leather, smaller the spaces between the stitches. To give a firm support, glue is applied to the flesh or inner side of seam.

51. Meenakari

Meenakari is basically an ancient form of art in India that has been praised since its introduction for the superb designs and combination of colours. From the prime age of this craft, the artisans were named as 'meenakar' who were involved in creating different meenakari items.

In some work, the entire object, such as pendant, is covered with this exclusive technique. On a typical pair of 'kara' bangles with three-dimensional 'makara', elephant, lion or bird head terminals, additionally decorated with diamonds, rubies, and emeralds, as they often were, is a dazzlingly opulent object that embodies a galaxy of goldsmith arts.

A special type is 'ek rang khula mina', in which single-colour transparent enamel fills all engraved area, leaving gold outlines exposed around figural details. 'Pachrangi mina' (five-colour enamel) is a special multicoloured style of enamelling. The five colours used are 'safed' (opaque white), 'fakhtai' (opaque light blue) 'fakhta' (a dove), 'khula nila' (transparent dark blue), 'khula sabz' (transparent green), 'khula lal' (transparent red).

Meenakari is the art of decorating metal with enamelling. It was introduced by the Mughals though originated in Persia. Raja Man Singh of Amber brought this art to Rajasthan. He invited skilful meenakars from the Mughal palace at Lahore and established them in Jaipur which became the centre of Meenakari later on in India.

Meenakari design needs a high degree of skill and techniques. Colours like red, green and white, dominate this art of enamelling. Nathdwara, Bikaner and Udaipur are the famous centres for silver meenakari. Pratapgarh is known for glass enamelling. Delhi and Varanasi are also important centres for exclusive meenakari designs. In India, Meenakari work has developed in the places like Punjab and Lucknow including the other meenakari centres of India.

The design for the meenakari in India is made on the metal surface by the craftsmen called 'chitras'. The design is engraved by the 'gharias' such that depressions are created. Sometimes, the meenakari is combined with the art of 'kundan' to make the created articles an amalgamation of enamelling and stone carving. After the design is created the enameller applies different colours with brushes on the engraved design.

The base is first covered by white or pink enamel, upon which different colours are applied in order of their hardness. It is then heated to enhance the richness of the colours. 'Gulabi mina' (pink enamel) is derived from 'gulab' (rose) which has been popularly associated with the Varanasi enamelling style. It includes areas of painted enamel, generally flowers, executed in translucent pink on an opaque white ground.

All other enamelled areas on the object are created in the 'champleve' style, which makes this a mixed style of enamelling. The technique requires at least five separate enamel applications.

When a single transparent coloured enamel is used to fill the ground around an opaque figure, various colours of ground like 'lal zamin' (transparent red ground), 'sabz zamin' (transparent green ground), 'nil zamin' (transparent blue ground) are chosen to contrast with and set off that of the subject. 'Bandh mina khaka' (opaque cartouche or outline) is a technique in which the figure in transparent colour is surrounded by an opaque enamel cartouche. The object when ready is polished and cleaned. Generally, hand burnishes are used to cover any exposed metal.

Besides jewellery, other items which were known for their meenakari work were various shaped *huqqas*, *paandaans*, flasks, sprinklers and a lot more.

Huqqas were a favourite item for the meenakari artists. Various hues and ambitious designs were used in the meenakari art which was part of the huqqas. Different shaped huqqas with the engraved meenakri work were made during the Mughal period.

Paandaan is another piece of art work which sees profuse use of meenakari work. Paandaans of the Mughal era are found in all the three metals namely gold, silver and copper.

In conclusion, it can be said that both silver and gold metals are used as the base for Meenakari work in India. At present time, Meenakari is done in the metals like silver and copper to suit the need and style of the modern people. In addition to the jewelleries and other items, the Meenakars create exclusive items that serve the decorative purpose.

The items that are created with amazing artistry include meenakari bowl set, chowki set, hand-casted meenakari chowki with white alloy metal, meenakari arm chair, meenakari almirah, meenakari Roman chair, meenakari gun box-cum-seater, utility box thrones, dining set, decorative frames, key holder, photo frames, ash trays, pen holder, etc.

51. Durrie weaving in India

Durrie weaving in India has been a cottage industry for many centuries, historically in many small villages and towns of Uttar Pradesh. Apart from this, during late 19th and early 20th centuries, the prisoners in Indian jails worked arduously on this cottage craft creating spectacular narrative curries. These curries would have sceneries depicting village activities, natural flora and fauna. A large number of landless weavers were sustaining themselves on durrie weaving.

Floor coverings have always been an important part of the interior of home in India, the use of furniture being very limited. Weaving of curries in various designs, especially by the young Punjabi girls has been a long tradition in Punjab. This handicraft still has an undoubted importance in Punjabi art.

The art of carpet weaving was brought into the Indian subcontinent by the great Mughal emperor Akbar in the middle of the 16th century. As one of the oldest and major industries, Indian carpets are known world over for their design, colour and craftsmanship.

Haryana has today emerged as a major carpet producing center, as a result of long years of research and practice. The tools that the weaver uses are simple and these have remained unchanged with time.

The kinds of patterns created in curries are varied. The striped durrie is the quintessential Indian feature over rug. Blue and white striped durries were known by their literal translation such as nili chithi meaning blue spot and nili pattidar meaning the simple blue stripped durrie. Uniformly repeated geometric motifs framed by simple borders as well as pictorial designs, with a woven narrative including images of flowers, birds, reptiles and people were woven in Mugal karkhanas (work shops).

Farshi or floor durries were large, striped and geometric, used by ordinary people, affluent traders and merchants. Tent curries carpeted outdoor marriage pavilions and large ones were often laid on the floor beneath pile carpets spread in the darbar halls of Maharajas. The largest curries are still commissioned for palace decoration and may extend over eighty feet in length and twenty-five feet in width.

The colours used in durries were very bright hues earlier, but have now changed to subtle colours due to market demand. Durrie is a handy substitute to carpets made of velvet cotton material and displays a multitudenal array of colours to suit all tastes from the very chic to the very casual.

Durries are familiar objects in almost every home in the villages of Haryana. Mostly hand woven in cotton and cotton/wool mixtures, in bright basic colours such as yellow, red green and blue, they are made in Panipat, Ambala and Kurri (Hissar). Punja durries with floral, geometric, bird and animal motifs are especially attractive.

They are used on floors, beds and divans. Durrie fabric is also used to make colourful, practical shoulder bags. Panipat carpets are woven in wool, on traditional looms, in designs which have come down from generation to generation, with some old Persian design still being used.

The technique of durrie weaving can be seen in its most primitive form in the villages of Rajasthan, Punjab and Haryana where girls are normally put to the task at an early age so that they can prepare rugs that will form part of their trousseau.

In contrast, girls in Navalgund, a village in Karnataka that produces a small number of unusual durries, are never taught the craft lest they spread the skill outside the family after marriage. Durries come in numerous designs although the most common are stripes of different colours and geometrical designs. Sometimes, animal and bird motifs are also used. Fine curries in brilliant colours made of cotton and silk have become a speciality of Salem (Tamil Nadu) while those made of jute fibre are woven in West Bengal.

53. Papier Mache

Papier Mache is one of the unique craft that developed during the Mughal era and is still being practiced by a lot of craftsmen all over India.

The articles made out with papier mache are used as a house-hold activities and decorative items. Successful experiments have been made with replicas of famous temples, forts and gates in papier mache. Important centres for this craft are Gwalior, Ujjain, Indore and Harda.

The Shantiniketan school of artists did some pioneering work in introducing this craft in West Bengal. Today, quite a number of craftsmen in and around Calcutta have taken up the craft and their products have found a market for their beauty in designs and excellence in craftsmanship.

The products include animals and birds particularly cocks, parrots and pigeons papier mache folk products especially bowls are pleasing. Gold and silver leaves are also used on larger articles, figures and objects like the houseboat are depicted. Landscaping is also done on wall plaques, trays, large bowls, screens, writing sets, etc. The craftsmen of Purulia make a variety of masks, mythological in character, that are used during folk festivals by the chau dancers of Orissa.

The technique of papier mache craft involves two steps. The first is making the object from the raw material called sakhtasazi. The second stage is painting and decorating the object called naqashi.

The raw material is produced by grinding paper, cloth, rice straw and copper sulphate in a pulp. This raw material is made into various shapes with the help of moulds of clay, wood or metal. After drying, the shapes are cut and separated from moulds. These pieces are again joined with a special glue made from gypsum and glue. The object is rubed to get a smooth surface.

Papier mache articles are made of waste paper applied in layers and pressed together on wooden modules. Waste paper is soaked in water for about 10-15 days, and beaten up with a hammer. Gum is mixed thoroughly to this pulp. Multani mitti is added and kneaded to get a pulp paste. This pulp is beaten so that a roller can roll it.

These sheets are pressed on to the required mould many times by an invert of a broken pitcher and dried for some time. The mould is separated after drying and the object is taken out.

This object is in a raw form and is finished, polished and coloured. File is used to smoothen it. Also, a thin mixture of white clay is applied for further softening. Imagination

runs wild as craftsmen breath life into this mould, bringing out a variety of expressions on masks.

For painting and decorating gold, white, black and red colours are commonly used. The artists prefer their own colours by mixing various herbal and chemical substances. The articles are hand painted with beautiful designs and floral patterns, scenes with human figures and animals, etc.

Papier mache in Kashmir is never fully pulped. It is softened by water and the desired thickness obtained by pasting on the mould layer over layer. The object under preparation is kept covered in a wet cotton cloth and while in a moist state, is covered with a thin layer of plaster of paris mixed with glue, and then smoothened and burnished to a fine finish with a wet stone after which, the ground colour, zamin as it is called, is applied.

The ground may be in colour or gold or tin foil; it is burnished with a piece of agate after drying; then fine verdigris powder is applied to lend a subtle greenish tint to the metallic background, or with a lac preparation, where a red tint is needed. On coloured grounds, black, blue, rose, green, violet, brown, almond and dark olive are generally used.

The most popular articles are pen stands, trays, jewellery chests, bowls, table tops, small and big boxes, candle stands, decoration pieces and eggs of various sizes and shapes.

CHAPTER-6

HANDICRAFTS OF DIFFERENT STATES OF INDIA

Handicrafts of Kashmir

Jammu and Kashmir is not only home to the vast cultural and ethnic diversity but also the myriad arts and crafts that have been carefully nurtured for the past centuries. A variety of motifs, techniques and crafts flourished in the land as the people from different regions flocked through this beautiful place and many of the skilled craftsmen decided to settle amidst its charming abundance of natural beauty. With time, these arts have gained even more distinctiveness and today Kashmir is known for woolen textiles, Pashmina shawls, embroidered suits, Kashmir silk saris, papier mache, woodcarving, hand knotted carpets and lots of other traditional crafts.

Carpet

Kashmiri carpets are world renowned for two things - they are handmade and they are always knotted, never tufted. The yarn used normally is silk, wool or silk and wool. Woolen carpets always have a cotton base while silk usually has cotton base. Sometimes, however, if the base is also in silk then the cost increases proportionately.

Occasionally, carpets are made on a cotton base, mainly of woolen pile with silk yarn used as highlights on certain motifs. The soothing blend of colours makes the Kashmiri carpet a prized possession.

Carpet weaving in Kashmir was not originally indigenous but is thought to have come in by way of Persia. Till today, most designs are distinctly Persian with local variations. One example, however, of a typical Kashmiri design is the tree of life.

The colours of Kashmiri carpets are more subtle and muted than elsewhere in the country. The knotting of the carpet is the most important aspect, determining its durability and value, in addition to its design. Basically, the more knots per square inch, the greater its value and durability. Also, there are single and double-knotted carpets. A single knotted carpet is fluffier and more resistant to touch.

Namdas

Far less expensive are these colourful floor coverings made from woolen and cotton fiber, which has been manually pressed into shape. Prices vary with the percentage of wool - a namda containing 80% wool being more expensive than one containing 20% wool. Chain stitch embroidery in woolen and cotton thread is worked on these rugs.

Papier Mache

To make papier mache, first paper is soaked in water till it disintegrates. It is then pounded, mixed with an adhesive solution, shaped over moulds, and allowed to dry and set before being painted and varnished. Paper that has been pounded to pulp has the smoothest finish in the final product.

The designs painted on objects of papier mache are brightly coloured. They vary in artistry and the choices of colours. Gold is used on most objects, either as the only colour, or as the highlight for certain motifs, and besides the finish of the product, it is the quality of the gold used which determines the price.

Pure gold leaf, which has the unmistakable luster, is far more expensive than bronze dust or gold poster paint but also has much longer life and will never fade or tarnish. Varnish, which is applied to the finished product, imparts a high gloss and smoothness, which increases with every coat.

Cardboard, usually indistinguishable from papier mache, gives in slightly when pressed firmly.

Shawls

There are three fibers from which the Kashmiri shawls are made - wool, pashmina and shahtoosh. Woolen shawls being the cheapest while the Shahtoosh are the most expensive ones.

Woolen shawls are popular because of the embroidery worked on them, which is a specialty to Kashmir. Both embroidery and the type of wool used causes differences in price.

Many kinds of embroidery are worked on shawls - 'sozni' or needlework is generally done in a panel along the sides of the shawl. Motifs, usually abstract designs or stylized paisleys and flowers are worked in one or two, occasionally three colours, all subdued.

Another type of needle embroidery is popularly known as papier mache work because of the design and the style in which it is executed. This is done either in broad panels on either side of the breadth of a shawl, or covering the entire surface of a shawl.

Ari or hook embroidery motifs are well known flower designs finely worked in concentric rings of chain stitch.

Pashmina shawls are unmistakably soft and its yarn is spun from the hair of the ibex found at 14,000 ft above the sea level. Although pure Pashmina is expensive, sometimes blending it with rabbit fur or with wool brings down the cost.

Shahtoosh is the legendary 'ring shawl', renowned for its lightness, softness and warmth. The astronomical price it commands in the market is due to the scarcity of raw material. High in the plateaux of Tibet and the eastern part of Ladakh, at an altitude of above 5,000 meters, roam Pantholops Hodgosoni or Tibetan antelope. During grazing, a few strands of the downy hair from the throat are shed and it is these, which are painstakingly collected until there are enough for a shawl.

Yarn is spun either from shahtoosh alone, or with pashmina to bring down the cost. In the case of pure shahtoosh too, there are many qualities–the yarn can be spun so skillfully as to resemble a strand of silk.

Not only are shawls made from such fine yarn extremely expensive, they can only be loosely woven and are too flimsy for embroidery to be done on them.

Unlike woolen or pashmina shawls, shahtoosh is seldom dyed. Its natural colour is mousy brown, and it is, at the most, sparsely embroidered.

Chain Stitch and Crewel Furnishings

Chain stitch, be it in wool, silk or cotton, is done by hook rather than any needle. Because of the high quality of embroidery done on wall hangings and rugs, Kashmiri crewelwork is in great demand all over the world.

All the embroidery is executed on white cotton fabric, pre-shrunk by the manufacturers. The intrinsic worth of each piece lies in the size of the stitches and the yarn used.

Saffron, Walnuts, Almonds, Honey

Pampore, outside Srinagar, is the only place in the world besides Spain, where saffron is grown. It is the most expensive spice in the world. The climate of Kashmir is ideal for walnut and almond trees, which grow here in abundance.

Natural honey too, is a produce of the apiaries, which abound in the state.

Silks, Tweeds

Tweed is woven in Kashmir with pure, never blended, wool. The resultant fabric competes favorably with the best fabric in the world. Sericulture is another important industry of the state. The cocoon reared in Kashmir is of the superior quality, yielding an extremely fine fiber, and any silk woven from this thread becomes known.

The fineness of the yarn lends itself particularly well to the weaves known as 'chinon' and 'crepe de chine', in addition to the universally recognized silk weave.

Pherans

This garment seems to be fusion of a coat and a cloak and is loose enough to admit the inevitable brazier of live coals, which is carried around in much the same way as a hot water bottle.

Men's pherans are always made of tweed or coarse wool while women's pherans, somewhat more stylized, are most commonly made of raffel with splashes of ari or hook embroidery at the throat, cuffs and edges.

The quality of embroidery and thickness of the raffel determines the price.

Basketry

Willow rushes that grow profusely in marshes and lakes of Kashmir are used to make charmingly attractive objects such as shopping baskets, lampshades, tables and chairs and are generally inexpensive.

To increase their life span, unvarnished products should be chiseled and frequently sprayed with water, particularly in hot, dry climates, to prevent them from being brittle.

Walnut Wood

Kashmir is the only part of India where the walnut tree grows. Its colour, grains and inherent sheen are unique and unmistakable, and the carving and fret work that is done on this wood is of a very superior quality.

There are two types of walnut trees - the fruit bearing species whose wood is so well known, and one that bears no fruit and is locally known as 'zangul'. Zangul has none of the beauty of walnut wood, being much less strong and possessing no grain while the walnut wood is almost black and its grains are much more pronounced than the wood of the trunk, which is lighter in colour. The branches have the lightest colour, being almost blonde and have no noticeable grain.

The intrinsic worth of the wood from each part of the tree differs–that from the root being the most expensive and the branches having the lowest price.

A cheaper product is liable to warp, or in case it is taken to warmer climes, will crack or shrink. Knots are usually concealed skillfully in the sawing, as it is difficult, though not impossible, to mask them while carving.

Carving is the demonstration of the carver's skill, and walnut is eminently suitable for this, being one of the strongest varieties of wood.

There are several varieties of carving–deep carving usually with dragon or lotus flower motifs, two inches deep or more; shallow carving, half an inch deep done all over the flat surface; open or lattice work, usually depicting the Chinar motif; and most popularly, semi carving, which is a thin panel along the rim of a surface, with perhaps a centre motif.

The advantage of the semi-carving is that it allows the grain of wood to be displayed, together with the carver's skill. Naturally deep carving with all the skill and labour required is the most expensive.

Copper and Silverware

Shops in local market of the old city abound with objects of copper lining the walls, the floor and even the ceiling. One can see craftsmen engraving objects of household utility like samovars, bowls, plates and trays.

There are floral, stylized, geometric, leaf and even calligraphic motifs that are engraved or embossed on copper, and occasionally silver, to cover the entire surface with intricate designs which are then oxidized, the better to stand out from the background.

The work known as 'naqash' determines the price of the object, as does the weight.

Handicrafts of Uttar Pradesh

Handicrafts of Uttar Pradesh have a distinct style and have been patronized by the royalty in the past. They speak of the rich tradition of craftsmanship that has developed over years in the state. Therefore, Uttar Pradesh has evolved as an important center of craft in the country.

Handicrafts are integrally related with the lives of the people so much so that each city here specializes in some handicraft or the other.

The arts and crafts in Uttar Pradesh are not famous only in India but all over the world. Right from the silken saris to the earthen pottery, carpets weaving to chikankari embroidery, Uttar Pradesh is always on the forefront in artifacts.

Specific region deals with the specific art or craft such as Varanasi for its silken saris, Mirzapur and Bhadoi for their carpets, Agra and Kanpur for their leather craft, Moradbad for its metalware, Lucknow for its cloth work and embroidery, and the entire state for its pottery.

Chikankari of Lucknow

Lucknow, the capital of Uttar Pradesh, is known for fine embroidery called chikankari. Chikankari is intricate embroidery done on saris, kurtis and veils, which are in practice in the city for thousands of years.

The delicate art of embroidery has its origin in the city of nawabs. Its name has been derived from the Persian word 'chikan' meaning cloth wrought by needlework. Earlier, it emerged as the court craft but with the keen efforts of the art lovers, this craft was publicized and became the important commercial activity.

The various patterns of the chikankari are muree, lerchi, keelkangan and bakhia. The charm of this craft lies in the minuteness, evenness and sheer excellence of craft as well as the use of white embroidery on white cloth.

The motifs of chikankari range from mughal architectural design of buildings to vine themes and from birds to animals. The chikankari work is usually done on the sari and kurta pyjama and is most suitable for summers.

The taste of nawabs in each perspective is appreciated in what your say is about their clothing and its embriodery.

Varanasi Brocade or Kinkab

The beautiful and gorgeous Benarasi sarees, which are worn by the Bengali brides, have their origin in Varanasi. The

Benarasi sarees exemplify the unique craftsmanship of the handicrafts people where gold and silver thread is used on fine silk.

This handicraft has a rich tradition in the state and the Benarasi sarees is one of the most expensive sarees in India. Mubarakpur is an important silk center in the state, where various silk sarees are produced.

There is no match to the rich Varanasi brocades created on the fine silk or cotton fabrics with the use of golden and silver thread on the 'pallas' and the field of sari. The gold thread with the silver background defines the grandeur and the geometric patterns in the 'butidar' and 'jaal' style just adds to its beauty.

It has become a trend among Indian brides to have a few benarasi saris, especially, the deep red golden zari sari among its wedding attire. The design motifs of these brocades are intricate floral and foliage patterns, kalga and bel, and in sari pallas and dupattas, a string of upright leaves called jhalar. The designs of the motifs vary according to the durability of cloth.

Jewelley

The most significant and renowned craft in the state is the handicraft of zardozi or silver and gold embroidery. In Varanasi, Agra, Lucknow, Rampur, Bareilly and Farrukhabad, zardozi or zari work is an age-old profession. Here exquisite zari embroidered bridal outfits and salwar kameezes are produced which have a huge market all over the country.

An Indian woman is incomplete without jewellery, which is never inexpensive anywhere in the world. Indian jewellery craftsmen are highly skilled and are able to create any design and set loose stones into any pattern, just by following a picture. The cost of the gold is the chief component because craftsmanship in India is less expensive than in any other country.

Jewellery making is also an old and popular handicraft of Uttar Pradesh. Hastshilpi of Uttar Pradesh specialize in making lightweight gold and silver ornaments with emphasis on filigree and open work

Stonecraft

The hub of the stone craft in India is Agra, the supreme example of which is Taj Mahal. The art of carving the thin marble slabs to make the fine lattice windows is the most difficult for the craftsmen.

The other marble products available in Agra are mirror frames with lace like fringes, fretwork balustrades, bowls, garden furniture, etc. Another specialty of the Agra is the inlay work on marble with the colourful and precious stones to form a multitude of mosaics. The tourists purchase some artifact to remind them the trip and it will also be used as a decoration piece in room back at home.

Carpets

Uttar Pradesh is known for weaving carpets, which have developed as a small-scale industry. Shahjahanpur, Mirzapur, Bhadohi are the hub of carpets in the state. They have their own distinct designs, which have various names like kethariwala jal, jamabaz, kandhari, etc.

After the Persian and Arabian carpets, it comes the turn of the local carpets prepared at Bhadoi, Shahjahanpur and Mirzapur. The majority of population in these areas are affiliated with the profession of carpet weaving.

With the exotic designs of flora and fauna, Taj Mahal, "Kethariwala Jal", "Jamabaz", "Kandhari", etc., the industry has succeeded in attracting the national market.

Art Metal Brassware

In Uttar Pradesh, Moradabad produces the large quantities of art metalware. It is especially famous for its colour enameling and intricate engraving.

There are two types of engravings. One is called nakshi which is done on the tinned surface while the other is known as khudai which is done on lac-coated unpolished brass.

Pointed steel pencil is used to make design in khudai type. The metal brassware consists of the traditional vases, Ganeshas, laughing Buddhas, stools, trays and contemporary beautiful bowls. Natraja is the most beautiful article in the brassware to be gifted and kept as a decorative item.

Glassware

Fearozbad has become synonymous with the name of glassware. Earlier only glass bangles where produced but with the help of sophisticated machines, full-fledged glassware is produced. The entire populace is involved in this industry.

Varanasi specializes in making the glass beads and exports most of the production. Similarly, thin glass plates are produced which after cutting into pieces called tikklu are used by women to decorate their fabrics.

In Saharanpur, intriguing glass toys are filled with the coloured liquid called rachkora and the mouth piece of hukka are produced.

Glass bangles with multitude of colours matching with every dress are the most used ornament in the state.

Pottery

In Uttar Pradesh, Khurja has evolved its own style in the earthenware. By adding colour to the dull and unattractive pottery, Khurja gave a lease of life to it. The shades and the designs in contrast to its background can attract the attention of any person with the aesthetic sense.

Apart from Khurja, Rampur surahis along with the water containers from Meerut and Hapur are famous all around the nation for their shapes , designs, colours and their ability to keep the water cold even during harsh summer days. Its attractiveness calls every one and purchasing a mug for coffee is not a bad idea at all.

In brief, the hands of the legendary artisians and the master craftsmen have the magic to turn the ravage into gold. The silken touch with the masterly style produces the best sketches, designs, patterns and structure that are unique in their own nature captivating the hearts of every one who have a glance of it.

The state's articulate craftsmanship is the intimate part of the tradition, the Banarasi silken saris, glass bangles from Ferozabad, chikankari suits from Lucknow are the important artifacts that enchant its every visitor. If you want to feel their charm, attend any fair and you will get clean bowled by the first sight of these masterpieces that not only looks fabulous but allures the visitor to own every item.

HANDICRAFTS OF UTTARAKHAND

Uttarakhand, cradled in the lap of the lofty Himalayas, boasts of snow-crapled peaks, stealthy glaciers, meandering rivers, mist-laden valleys and exotic species of flora and fauna.

Inspired by this flawless natural splendor, the people of Uttarakhand have created and nurtured variour forms of arts and crafts since ages. Crafts, usually utility items like doors, windows, rugs, carpets, baskets, copper utensils, or the folk art Aipan made by Uttarakhandis, have a unique touch of nature in their designs.

Owing to the stiff competition faced by these arts and the crafts from the modern and cheap machine-made products, the Government of Uttarakhand felt the need to take concrete steps for their revival and promotion in order to prevent this precious creativity from fading away.

With this vision, the Uttarakhand Handlooms & Handicrafts Development Council (UHHDC) was constituted. UHHDC acts as the apex body for the overall development and promotion of handlooms and handicrafts in the state. It aims at generating sustainable employment opportunities in these sectors by promoting specialized products for commercialization.

Aipan–Folk Art

Aipan, the main component of Kumaoni folk art is more commonly known as alpana making in various parts of the country. This art has its origin in the ritualistic pratices of the Kumaonis and has been passed through generations as a part of tradition.

Aipan expresses the sancity of the creative imagination of these people.

The motifs of aipan are used in shawls & stoles, wall hangings, bookmarks, photo frames, coasters, tablemats, cards, stickers etc.

Ringaal Handicrafts

Found in abundance all over the Himalayas, ringaal is a species of bamboo used for making various types of baskets, kitchen utility items, mats (moshtas), furniture, etc. Unlike the tropical variety of bamboos, which grows at lower heights and in wet climates, ringaal is temperate species found in higher and colder regions.

The farmers of Kumaon are experts in making beautiful crafts from ringaal. However, they practise this craft more as a tradition than as a means of earning livelihood.

Rambaans Handicrafts

Adding a new look to the traditional crafts made from jute and hemp, the rambaans crafts have created good market demand in a surprisingly short period. As many as 300 species of rambaans plants, generally known as sisal, are found in abundance all over these hills. Some of these species yield fibers, which can be used to weave various decorative and utility items like bags, purses, wall hangings and show pieces.

Coperwares

Copper is deeply integrated with the Himalayan culture from as old a period as the 12th century, when a number of craftsmen from the plains migrated and came here. The art of copperware, which took birth then, has kept evolving with time.

The coppersmiths make gagars or coper pots, water tillers, drinking glasses, musical instruments, masks and other utility items used in houses and temples.

Wooden Crafts

Exquisite woodwork has been the specialty of Uttarakhand since times immemorial. Abundance of timber, the suitable temperature for insulation of wood, availability of local skilled labour, prevalence of family tradition has contributed to the growth of this craft in this region.

Historical evidences also support the presence of intricate wooden carvings in Uttarakhand. Entire woodworks of 'chaukhats' and 'tibaaris' found here are now on display in the National Museum of Delhi. Some of the carvings in the Gunjyal village are as old as 600 years.

Utility and decorative items like walking sticks, animal figures, miniature models of famous temples, idols of Gods, etc. made by Uttarkhand craftsmen have acquired special place.

Apart from that, products made of driftwood and pine bark carvings are some other beautiful pieces produced by these craftsmen.

Owing to its altitudinal placement, Uttarakhand provides climatic conditions most appropriate for animals like sheep, angora rabbits and pashmina goats. This has given it the scope to extract some of the finest quality of wool from these animals. Thus, woolen products are a dominant craft in this area.

Traditionally, woolen crafts were produced in these regions mainly for local consumption. In the rural and border areas, wool extracted from animals like sheep is used to make products like kaaleen, pankhi, thulma (thick blanket), chutka, etc.

The designs and techniques used are influenced by the neighbouring Tibet. Johar-Munisiyari in Pithoragarh district are famous for producing woolen carpets and thulma.

Almora has been producing its famous tweeds, woolen carpets and artistic woolen shawls. The other places where this craft has been practiced are Bageshwar, Nainital, Dehradun, Chamoli, Rudraprayag and Uttarkashi.

Handicrafts of Rajasthan

Rajasthani handicrafts are richest in India. The state is well known for its exquisite handicrafts. Depicting the rich culture & tradition of the state, beautiful handicrafts of Rajasthan keep their exclusivity.

Handicrafts of Rajasthan is an add-on of attractions of the state. Travellers and tourists love to see and purchase exquisite handicrafts while on Rajasthan tours. Exquisite handicrafts of the state proudly depict the masterpiece creativity of the Rajasthan people.

One of the most colourful regions in India, Rajasthan is a land which is endowed with invincible forts, splendid palaces, waves of sand dunes and serene lakes.

One can observe an unusual diversity in the state of Rajasthan in its all forms – life style of people, culture, traditions, customs, costumes, cuisine, dialects and music. But, Rajasthan is famous not only for its magnificent monuments but also for handicrafts.

Popularity of Rajasthani handicrafts is not only in India but also all over the world. The handicrafts of Rajasthan are famous for its variety, the use of lively colours, exceptional artistic work all of which show the tradition and culture of Rajasthan. Some of important Rajasthani handicrafts are following.

Textile

Rajasthan is popular for its die technique. Dyed and block printed fabrics of Rajasthan are very popular.

Exquisite Rajasthani textiles (Bandhani or Bandhej textiles) are an excellent example of Rajasthani rich form. Tie and die techniques are used to make bandhej textiles. bandhej kurtis, bandhej sarees, etc. are popular among people.

Blue Pottery

Rajasthan is famous for blue pottery articles. Blue pottery is an art which has its origins in Persia. Some blue pottery articles are flower vase, surahis, pots and jars, lampstands, doorknobs and other household items.

Blue potteries of Rajasthan are popular form of exquisite Rajasthani handicrafts. Jaipur is perhaps the most known place for blue pottery in Rajasthan. To create blue potteries, blue, green and white are the colours mainly used.

Metal Crafts

Rajasthan is also famous for metal crafts. During one's tour of Rajasthan, one can see and purchase various type of beautiful metal craft items such as figurines, pill boxes, brass enameled swords & shields and other useful items.

Jewellery

The desert land of Rajasthan is rich in jewellery. Every region of Rajasthan has its own unique style of wearing ornaments. In the state of Rajasthan men are also very fond of ornaments just as the women. While touring this state, one can see and purchase traditional Rajasthani jewellery.

Handmade Jewellery

Handmade jewelleries of Rajasthan are rakhi, bala, bajuband, gokhru, timamyan, etc. Meenakari is one of the most popular jewellery works of Rajasthan. Meenakari is enameled gold and silver jewellery.

Carpets & Durries

Woolen carpets of Bikaner, Jaipur and Tonk are popular. These carpets are hand-knotted with stunning designs based on Persian styles. Cotton durries of Jodhpur and Jaipur are very popular. The geographical motifs and pastel shades make these durries beautiful.

Wooden Handcrafted Furniture

Rajasthan is famous for wooden handcrafted furniture. Specially, Barmer and Jodhpur are famous for the craft of wooden furniture. Kishangarh and Shekhawati have their own style of ornate furniture.

When we talk about crafts of Rajasthan, we can not forget to discuss about the exquisite designs of Rajasthani wooden furniture. In different part of Rajasthan, one can see carved wooden furniture having different styles and designs. Exquisite motif and design works on wooden furniture are eye-catching.

The most famous work on wooden furniture in Rajasthan is the latticework. Jodhpur and Kishangarh are known places where from one can purchase carved casket, screens, doors, chairs, tables, shelf, etc.

Leatherware

Rajasthan is famous for designer jooties with embroidered uppers, designer leather handbags and other leather items.

Miniature paintings

Rajasthan is also famous for its exotic paintings. The paintings of Rajasthan are lively and multi-hued.

Gujarat Handicrafts

Gujarat is blessed with rich and vibrant tradition of handicrafts. It is widely differing in proportions of its patterns to the element of wonderful exquisite artifacts in various forms. It stands unique with diverse arts and crafts – a mixed combination with aesthetic appeal.

Gujarat has an ancient history and a glorious cultural heritage. The age old crafts of the place have survived till date. The art and crafts are preserved and are even practised widely across the state.

The handicrafts of Gujarat are famous for their colour scheme, detail and intricate work and artistic appearance. These handicrafts are a product of skilled craftsmanship of India. There is a wide variety available in handicrafts. One can choose from silver jewellery, embroidery, furniture, clay items, handmade durries (carpets), stone crafts and other materials.

Needlework / Embroidery

Needlework of Gujarat is famous world over for its elegance and accuracy. Embroidery is Gujarat's quintessential handicraft. Ari bharat, appliqué works are unique with their traditional skills.

Embroidery is one of the most delicate handicrafts practised in Gujarat. The art of embroidery is primarily practised by the wives of herdsmen, nomads and agriculturists, as a secondary source of income. The patterns vary with the community and region.

There is a wide variety to choose from, like bavalia embroidery, banni embroidery, rabari embroidery, as well as the embroidery done by the communities of Ahir, Jats, Sodha Rajputs, Mutwa and Mukka. Apart from the usual embroidery work, the state is also famous for gold embroidery done on fabrics.

Toran is the most common embroidered doorway decoration with hanging flaps, which is supposed to ventilate good luck. Pachhitpatis (embroidered frieze) are hanged from the corners as a welcome symbol to the visitors. Chaklas (embroidered square pieces) are used as furniture covers while bhitiya is an impressive wall hanging. Abhala (mirror inset embroidery) has now become a part of the ethnic chic fashion world, where small mirror discs are fixed with closely worked silken thread.

Usually the mirror work is done on a dark background with motifs like flowers, creepers, petals, etc. The motifs are inspired by daily life, ancient beliefs and rituals, but they vary from place to place and are passed down over the centuries.

Tie-and-dye–Bandhani

The tie-dyed fabrics of Gujarat are the best produced in India and are demanded all over the world. Bandhani (the tie-and-dye fabric) is famous for its intricate designs and patterns. Used as wedding outfit called as 'gharchola odhni' and sarees, they grace every Gujarati family women.

The bandhinis are also brocaded with fine thread zari work. Also known as 'bandhej', it is produced on superfine cotton 'mulmul' (muslin) sometimes combined with gold checks and motifs worked in the 'jamdani' technique. Bandani of Jamnagar, Mandvi and Bhuj are famous all over the world.

Dyeing is a hereditary art here. In the past, cloth was dyed in colours extracted from trees and flowers. The Sarkhei suburb of Ahmedabad was one of the indigo manufacturing and exporting centres.

Brass and Iron Items

One of the popular craft of the region is items in brass and iron. These items are best found at former princely state of Saurashtra and Kutch. The items available here are fine betel nut crackers, copper-coated iron bells, knives and cutlery.

These are made by descendents of the erstwhile court sword smiths and jewelers. Brass items are also manufactured at a large scale here. The brass industry of Jamnagar is one of the largest in India.

The items offered here are brass and iron utensils, cutlery, knives and scissors. One of the best places to buy such stuff is Anjar.

Beadwork

Beadwork is another Gujarati specialty from Khambhat and Saurashtra. Motifs and patterns are dictated by the technique of putting two and three beads together. Beadwork objects are used in wall decorations, potholders, etc.

The best beadwork is produced by the 'kathis' (tribals). Worked mostly on a white background, they use colours that are vibrant with very distinct patterns. Beadwork 'torans' are usually placed over doorways.

Pottery

Pottery is one of the oldest handicrafts of the state and is being practiced since the ancient times. The creativity of the potter in moulding the clay in a well proportioned utensil is just amazing. Later, these utensils are painted with vibrant colours to make them attractive.

Pottery from Gujarat is popular as it achieves excellence with traditional crafts. Village potters turn wonders of clay into artifact pieces that attracts.

Clay utensils are made which are used by village homes even today. Terracotta toys are another craft of the potters of Kachchh, but it is in the Aravallis and Chhota Udepur tribal lands that potters make the famous long-necked terracotta figurines of the Gora Dev (tribal horse God), said to protect crops, villages and families from evil spirits, evil intentions and natural calamities.

Potter communities also specialise in mud wall paintings, and you could get plaques, inset with mirrors, made for your house or garden decor from Kutchh.

Woodwork

The lacquered furniture of Sankheda near Vadodara, another important handicraft industry, has become synonymous with Southern Gujarat. The furniture and woodcrafts of Surat, Kutchh and Saurashtra are also popular. Minakari furniture from Rajkot is as attractive as Sankheda furniture.

Woodcarving is an ancient art of the state which has attained a very high standard of technical skill. Some of the best examples of woodcarvings are found in temples and houses in many parts of Gujarat. Saurashtra and Sankhed in the Vadodara district are also known for their lacquer work.

Furniture

The art of making wooden furniture is practiced primarily in southern Gujarat. Sankheda, near Vadodara, is known for its lacquered wooden furniture. The craft of making wooden items includes rounding the wood with tools.

This is followed by painting it with floral and abstract designs in bright shades of gold, silver, maroon, green, vermilion, and brown. This is done with the help of sticks dipped in a coloured mixture of dyes, powdered zinc, lac and resin. Mahuva, Surat and Kutch are also famous for making lacquered furniture similar to that of Sankheda.

Apart from this, the artisans at Surat, Kutch and Saurashtra are skilled at making beautiful designs and intricate filigreed appearance of lace on wood. Rajkot is famous for its minakari furniture and offers attractive low slung chairs, Indian style sofa sets, chairs, centre tables and settees.

Woodwork is also practiced at places like Jetpur, Kutch and Pethapur village of Gandhinagar district. Here, you can buy old wooden blocks used for printing fabrics which can be joined into a table top, decorative screen or a partition or used as door knobs, ornamental pieces or paper weights.

Textile culture

Gujarat has a unique dress culture which evolves the Textile culture with its extravagant quality with traditional and modern design patterns. The rogan, zari, tye-and-dye and exclusive patolas are the state's graceful textile culture patterns. Peacock motifs, geometrical patterns, ikat weaving, akrakh work are some of the excellent influence with traditional and modern designs.

Furnishings

Gujarat offers a wide range of furnishings from simple and elegant cushion covers to quilts and bedcovers in a wide range of styles. Pleasantly embroidered and with micro mirrors, they have geometrical or animal motifs, patch worked, etc. Quilts are another popular handicraft item. They come in a variety of styles from simple geometric designs to more complex patterns. Other utility items are woven and kalamkari table covers, tablemats, and block-printed bed land and table linen. The traditional floorspread 'namdas' and 'durries' from Kutch, is woven with camel and goat hair and even wool and cotton.

Patola

It is one of the finest handwoven sarees from Gujarat. The famous patola of Patan is known for its colourful geometrical pattern which are strikingly beautiful. The unique tie-and-weave method of patola results in identical patterns on both the sides of the fabric.

Zari

Gold embroidery is an ancient craft, practised since ancient times. The zari work (gold embroidery) of Gujarat dates back to the Mughal period. Surat is the biggest and the most significant zari manufacturing centers of India. The zari work is practised mainly in gold and silver threads. It is a detailed and meticulous process. The items available in the market range from decorative boarders, shoe uppers and evening bags to accessories. One of the most popular items here is kinkhab, which is woven using gold and silver threads.

The zari industry of Surat is one of the oldest handicrafts whose origin can be traced to the Mughal period. The history of 'zari' (gold embroidery) industry of Surat dates back to the Mughal period. Surat is one of the biggest and most significant zari manufacturing centres in India.

The principal types of products are real gold and silver threads, imitation gold and silver threads, embroideries such as 'chalak', 'salama', 'kangari', 'tiki'–mainly the ring and the 'katori'–for modifying in the kinkhab (cloth of gold) and the zari border weaving, embroidery, laces, caps, turbans, saris, and blouse pieces. Gold and silver threads are commonly used for weaving the 'kinkhab'. The Gharchola and panetar (dresses worn during weddings) are exceptional pieces with zari work.

Durries

Durries, carpets, blankets and rugs are still woven on primitive pit looms in the villages of Kutch. The artisans weave the designs with their hands and work on the machines operated by foot pedals. These carpets are known for their beautiful patterns, contrasting colour schemes and intricate weaving. The durries available here are made from wool, goat hair, and cotton. As a result, handloom weaving is an important occupation in villages, situated on the Ahmedabad - Bhavnagar highway.

Jewellery

The art of making jewellery and precious stone-cutting and processing is a traditional handicraft of Gujarat. The folk jewellery of excellent designs, characteristic of each village and each community is a typical art of Gujarat. Gold, silver, iron and brass works are antiquity of Gujarat.

Silver Jewellery

Silver jewellery is the specialty of the state of Gujarat. The premier centers of silver ornaments are Rajkot and

Ahmedabad. Other than this, Kutch is also known for silver engravings and ornaments. One can also pick tribal jewellery in silver from Poshina.

Some good quality daggers and knives with beautiful sheaths and hilts can also be bought from here. Khambhat (Cambay) is known for the ancient craft of stone cutting and bead making. Many precious and semi-precious stones are cut and polished here along with agate. It is mined in the hills along the Gulf of Khambhat. They are finally converted into polished ornaments and utensils.

Temple culture

The excavations at the Harappan sites in Gujarat at Lothal, Rangpur, Rozdi, etc. have brought to light some of the very ancient handicraft articles. Temple curtains have Goddess Durga riding tiger as well as other illustrations from Puranic legends. It is heavily decorated and embroidered decoration hung over the entrance and is considered a symbol of warm welcome.

Handicrafts of Madhya Pradesh and Chhatisgarh

In the heartland of India, lies its largest State, Madhya Pradesh. Filled with lush forests, magnificent monuments, exuberant festivity and blissful solitude. In this land of wonderful and contrasting variety, handicrafts lend a touch of mystique–a charm unique to Madhya Pradesh. They radiate an aura, exhibit hereditary skills, whisper painstaking craftsmanship and evoke an urgent desire to learn more about the land and its colourful people.

Be it a deftly woven silk or a cotton blended saree or block-printed fabrics, stuffed leather toys, floor coverings or for that matter, folk paintings, bamboo, cane or jute woodcraft, stonecraft, ironcraft, metalcraft, terracotta, papier mache, zari work (gold thread embroidery), ornaments, dolls...each hand-crafted product of Madhya Pradesh is charming enough to sweep you off your feet.

Bamboo & Cane Works

Bamboo & Cane occupy an important place in rural life: utility articles such as agricultural implements, fishing traps, hunting tools and baskets are made of bamboo.

In Madhya Pradesh, these are generally made by a community called Basor or Basod, who sell them in weekly markets. Shahdol, Balaghat, Mandla and Seoni regions of Madhya Pradesh are main bamboo producing centres apart from Chhattisgarh and Bastar.

Here, the artisans have skillfully harmonized their age old knowledge and techniques with new designs, to meet modern market demands. The Gond, Baiga and Korku tribal communities are highly skilled in the craft of bamboo.

Chances are when you visit MP, you'll actually find 'the houses with bamboo door. Bamboo thickets are a common sight in the state and the tribals are experts at putting it to use.

Crafting bamboo articles for daily as well as decorative use is a popular pastime of the Gond, Baiga, Korku and Basor or Basod communities. You can buy anything from agricultural implements, fishing traps, hunting tools to baskets at local weekly markets. Apart from Chhattisgarh and Bastar, the main bamboo producing centres are Shahdol, Balaghat, Mandla and Seoni.

Dolls & Toys

There exist here cute, colourful little dolls to give bland old Barbie a run for her money. These dolls are made out of small cloth pieces and are produced in Gwalior, Bhopal and Jhabua. Battobai's (a craftswoman from Gwalior) dolls are known the world over and are exported in large numbers. The dolls made here are interesting pieces of work, influenced by different cultures and traditions of India mirroring the diversity and uniqueness of the country.

Floor coverings

(a) Durries

The floor coverings of Madhya Pradesh consist mainly of durries (flat-woven carpets) in a rich variety of designs. A durrie, essentially a thick cotton woven fabric, is made near Sironj.

The technique of making these durries is quite primitive, but the colours and patterns more than make up for what they lack in finish. Durrie weaving is the domain of women in the rural homes of Sironj, Jhabua, Raigarh and Jabalpur.

Especially in demand are the cotton and woollen punja durries, handwoven in various colours, with patterns based on kiln designs, geometric traditional motifs, and animal and human figures.

A durrie, essentially a thick cotton woven fabric, is meant for spreading on the floor, and is made all over Madhya Pradesh, especially near Sironj. The basic technique of weaving a durrie in its most primitive form, can be seen in rural areas. The more universal durries are made by women in their homes, in the 'Punja' technique. They are usually in bold patterns and bright colours with folk designs.

Apart from Sironj, Jhabua, Raigarh, Jabalpur and Shahdol are leading centres of durrie weaving in Madhya Pradesh. Cotton and woollen punja durries, handwoven in various colours are designed to suit traditional as well as modern home decor. Patterns are generally based on kiln designs, geometric traditional motifs, and animal and human figures.

(b) Carpet Weaving

Though MP never took centrestage in the chequered history of India, it could not remain entirely untouched by the happenings around it. Along with the Rajputs, Marathas and the British, the mighty Mughals too left their stamp on this vast state.

Carpet-weaving, which came to India from Persia, was a craft very dear to the Mughals. Thanks to their encouragement and patronage, Gwalior developed into a carpet-weaving centre.

Pattern is an integral part of knotted carpets and traditional patterns have continued with varying combinations since the last 200 years. The weavers here are undisputed masters of not only weaving but dyeing too.

The colouring was earlier done by means of natural dyes, but presently it is being done with synthetic dyes as well. Alas, as elsewhere in India, colouring here is now done more with synthetic colours instead of eco-friendly natural dyes. Woollen carpets in vibrant colours with both floral and geometric designs are a good buy.

Since the Mughal times, Gwalior in Madhya Pradesh has carved a niche for itself in the weaving of carpets. Later on, weaving also began in the Shahdol & Mandla belt.

The weavers have used their ingenuity to transform traditional motifs into modern designs; drawing from the treasury of ancestral motifs–trees and flowers in carefully blended colours.

Paintings

The art of painting in India goes back to prehistoric times. Evidence of this is rampant in the astounding cave paintings found in Madhya Pradesh.

Drawings on walls of caves and rock shelters served a twofold purpose: decorating homes and appeasing deities. While the adivasis (tribals) of yore traced simple, very basic forms to ward off evil spirits and disease, more sophisticated art survives in the Buddhist rock-carved monasteries of the middle of the first millennium AD, such as Ajanta in Maharashtra and Bagh in MP.

Another form of art, widely practiced in MP is the mandana. Auspicious diagrams are drawn on the floor with rice paste, coloured powder, flower petals or grains of rice, often with symbolic motifs set within floral and geometric patterns. These are meant to attract cosmic powers for the well being of the household in which it is done.

Mughal miniature paintings also figure as a footnote in MP because the Persians of the court of Malwa were enthusiastic patrons.

Folk Paintings

Throughout different periods of history, we find a definite established tradition of painting on various objects, particularly on intimate objects of everyday use, floors and walls; and in almost every instance, the depiction being associated with some ritual.

Folk paintings of Madhya Pradesh, especially the wall paintings of Bundelkhand, Chhattisgarh, Gondwana, Nimar and Malwa, are living expressions of people, intrinsically linked with the socio-cultural ambience of the area. They are not mere decorations but also spontaneous outpourings of religious devotions.

The paintings, based on local festivals like Karwa Chauth, Deepawali, Ahoi Ashtami, Nag Panchmi, Sanjhi etc. are usually done by women using simple home-made colours.

In Bundelkhand, painting is usually done by a caste of professional painters called chiteras. In the paintings of

Chhattisgarh, mud plaster base is used, over which linear patterns are etched with fingers: the process is called 'lipai'. The women of the Rajwar community are specialists in 'lipai', whereas Pando & Satnami communities make linear designs similar to a woven fabric.

Chhatisgarh is also the home of the art of tattoo which is done by women of Badi community. The tattoo patterns are complex and beautiful and have immense potential of being further modified and incorporated into designer prints.

The Rathwa Bhils of MP and eastern Gujarat commonly install a deity in the form of a ritual wall painting within the home. Outside the sacred enclosure, other paintings depict incidents from daily life, usually featuring horses.

The Bhils and Bhilala tribes of Madhya Pradesh paint myths related to creation called Pithora paintings. Horses, elephants, tigers, birds, gods, men and objects of daily life are painted in bright multicoloured hues. In the Gondwana region, unmatched creative vision has been shown by the Gond and the Pardhan tribes who have impressed audiences at exhibitions in Japan, France, Australia and other countries.

The Malwa, Nimar and Tanwarghar regions of Madhya Pradesh are known for their Mandana wall and floor painting traditions. Red clay and cow dung mixture is used as base material to plaster the surface against which white drawings stand out in contrast. Peacocks, cats, lions, *goojari*, *bawari*, swastik and *chowk* are some motifs of this style.

Iron Craft

The tradition of iron craft in Madhya Pradesh has been passed down from generation to generation and stands unmatched in skill and creativity. In the interiors of Madhya Pradesh's villages, the craftspersons practise traditional skills and techniques to craft iron in myriad inimitable forms.

Iron crafting begins with obtaining iron ore from local mines which the ironsmiths mould into various shapes and forms. Gond, Muria, Bhatra, Dhruva tribals, practise the tradition of offering horses, swings, tridents, etc. made out of iron, to gods on fulfillment of their wishes.

There is also a custom of gifting to daughters exquisitely carved "deeyas" on their wedding. Keeping pace with changing times and tastes of buyers, today craftspersons produce various objects such as birds, carved deeyas, candle stands, lattice, furniture, lamps and decorative items, each piece as an object 'd' art enabling the craft to reach its zenith.

Tribal statues have come to occupy a very special place in modern day interior decoration and tribal artisans have won the recognition they so rightly deserve.

Jute

Next to cotton, jute is the cheapest and most important of all textile fibers. It is used extensively in manufacturing different types of packaging material for agricultural and industrial products. Its coarse character has a unique charm while natural colour, heavy texture and twilly kind of body typify its earthiness.

Jute handicrafts are available at Bhopal, Raipur, Indore and Gwalior. The items include hanging lamps, baskets, flower vases, swings, hammocks, purses, table mats, footwear, etc.

Metalcraft

You'll hear the ironsmith's hammer going clang-clang in every little hamlet of India, but what makes the metalwork of Madhya Pradesh unique is the creativity and spontaneity that the tribals breathe into it.

The Gadhavs of Bastar, in their simplicity and isolation from the world of progress and modern civilization, bring forth their own unique view of life, nature and the Gods through age-old processes of metalwork.

The Gond, Muria, Bhatra and Dhruva tribals traditionally offer iron horses, swings, trishuls (trident, the symbol of the Hindu god Shiva) to gods on fulfillment of their wishes. Exquisitely carved *diyas* are gifted to brides to take to their husband's home.

These artifacts, known locally as dhokra work, are predominantly hollow-cast and are produced by the lost-wax process, which has long been known to these pre-Aryan communities.

It is by the free and rapid way in which they construct a model, unlike the fastidious waxwork of their counterparts of the south, that the tribal metalworkers are able to achieve their exciting castings.

The blacksmiths from southern Madhya Pradesh forge and hammer iron into delightful range of oil lamps, tools and statues that depict animals, birds and men. Using only a few tools and a simple furnace of a handful of coals, the smiths twist and bend the hot iron into expressive shapes.

Such work now adorns many city homes and most foreigners love to carry a few pieces back to their country.

Emerging from the fogs of time, steadfast with centuries of changeless tradition, yet keeping tune with contemporary styles, the metal craft of Madhya Pradesh stands apart, in concept and workmanship alike.

Metal ornaments boxes of Bundelkhand, lamps of Sarguja, rice measure bowls, animal figurines of Raigarh, sculptures of Bastar are a few examples of the ingenuity of craftspersons of Madhya Pradesh. These metal images invested with peculiar indigenous socio-religous history are considered auspicious.

Ornaments & Jewellery

All forms of adornment are dear to the hearts of tribals. The adivasis of MP are no exception. The intricate and artistic twisting of thread was itself considered an embellishment to round or octahedronal metal beads used in tribal communities. They often weave cotton thread into a broad band as a textured or patterned base, then loop in buttons, beads or metallic droplets intermittently.

The people of this state also delight in silver ornaments. However, articles of particular value are only displayed on weddings and, to a lesser extent, when visiting fairs and festivals.

Ornaments made of beads, cowries and feathers are also part of tribal costumes. The major centres for folk ornaments are Tikamgarh, Jhabua and Sheopur-Kalan. The rural and tribal women folk of Malwa, Nimar and Bastar regions are exceptionally fond of ornaments, and both men and women wear them.

The folk jewellery of Madhya Pradesh is most distinctive, highly artistic, elaborate and varied. The various cultural regions have their own distinct styles. Jewellery from Chhattisgarh is available in a variety of gold, silver, bronze and mixed metals. Other major centres for folk ornaments are Tikamgarh, Jhabua and Sheopur-Kalan. Ornaments made of beads, cowries and feathers are part of tribal costumes.

Tribal metalsmiths often fashion ornaments by the age old process of cire perdue casting, or lost wax process. For each technique, there is a specialised craftsperson whose family has been practising this hereditary craft for over three to four generations.

The rural and tribal women folk of Malwa, Nimar and Bastar regions are exceptionally fond of ornaments, and both men and women wear ornaments.

Papier Mache

Papier Mache, a craft practiced since time immemorial, finds expression in varied forms. In Madhya Pradesh, the main centre for papier mache is Ujjain, but it is practised in Gwalior, Bhopal and Ratlam also.

The Nagvanshi community, which makes mud toys and dolls, is also engaged in making of papier mache articles. The traditional expression of this craft was creation of ornate articles like vases, figurines and icons.

Today, craftspersons in Bhopal and Gwalior make statues, birds, animals and decorative panels. In Ujjain, the craft of papier mache brings to life different kinds of splendidly crafted birds with the artisans using natural colours to create exact replicas of living birds.

Presently, the craftspersons are also experimenting with ways of creating decorative pottery and furniture in papier mache.

Stone Carving

India's stone carving tradition is perhaps one of the richest in the world. Guilds of masons and stone carvers have existed since the 7th century B.C. A system of apprenticeship was initially prevalent. Later, skills were handed down as family lore, from father to son.

The famous rock cut temples of Vidisha, the sculptured stone temples of Khajuraho, the monuments of Orchha and Gwalior, all stand testimony to the excellence and originality of the stone carvers of Madhya Pradesh.

Each region has a distinct style. Gwalior specializes in jali (lattice) work, Jabalpur and Tikamgarh in decorative items such as statues of animals and human figures and Bastar in icons of tribal gods and goddesses and memorial pillars.

Stuffed Leather Toys

With delightful looks in various forms, skillfully crafted and gaily painted, the stuffed leather toys of Madhya Pradesh are very attractive.

Leather work has been practised since a number of years in Madhya Pradesh. Craftspersons in Gwalior, Indore, Dewas and Bilaspur specialize in making leather shoes, jutties, leather bags, mushk, etc.

With passage of time, the craft has evolved and given rise to new products. Today, Indore and Dewas are making leather garments & Gwalior is making shoes on a big scale.

Pottery

Pottery has been called the lyric of handicrafts. It symbolises man's first attempt at craftmanship. The colours of terracotta articles and figures vary from pink, red, brown to light and dark grey. The terracotta products of each region in Madhya Pradesh have their own identity and distinctiveness.

The terracotta pottery of Madhya Pradesh is simply remarkable, especially that practised by the tribals of Bastar. Traditional statues of elephants, serpents, birds and horses from Bastar are incomparable in their simplicity and are offered to the local deity as an offering in lieu of sacrifice.

The art of moulding terracotta in Madhya Pradesh shows a mature ability, the pantheon being even more varied and localized. In the rural areas, it is common to see terracotta animal figures placed under trees and in shrines made by potters.

The famous traditional statues of elephants, serpents, birds and horses from Bastar are incomparable in simplicity. Similarly, the decorative roof tiles and rukha padki of Raigarh have no equal. The life-size images of human forms are among the finest examples of Bundelkhand terracotta.

The Bhils of Jhabua and adjacent Chhota Udaipur in Gujarat also trust in animal offerings made from clay. Their potters mould distinctive clay horses, camels, elephants, tigers and bullocks that are then offered to a village deity or to a revered animal itself such as the tiger.

Set down in the sacred grove that always lies in a secluded spot near the settlement, the terracotta animals are clustered together in a jumble of new and old, all eventually disintegrating and returning to the earth in their turn.

Sarguja, Raipur and Raigarh have a charming tradition of decorative roof top tiles, made partly by hand moulding and partly on the wheel. These tiles, shaped like half tubes, have perched on top of them figures of elephants, monkeys, bears, reptiles, gods and goddesses and are considered a status symbol among the rural people.

Woodcraft

The art of wood carving has flourished in many parts of Madhya Pradesh, and the beautifully embellished wooden ceilings, doors and lintels with finely carved designs are silent testimonials of its glory.

The wood carvers of Madhya Pradesh, with great sensitivity and skill transform different varieties of wood such as shish, teak, dhudi, sal and kikar into works of art. Besides the famous wooden memorials, the craftspersons of Bastar and Chattisgarh, Malwa, Nimar and Bundelkhand, Sheopur-Kalan, and Rewa also make pipes, masks, doors, window frames and sculptures.

Madhya Pradesh also offers a variety of painted and lacquered woodcraft items such as toys, boxes, bedposts, cradleposts and flower vases. The major centres of this art are Gwalior, Sheopur-Kalan (Morena), Rewa and Budhni (Raisen).

Textile Weaving

Ancient texts speak of Madhya Pradesh as a famous centre of weaving between 7th century and 2nd century BC. Among the finest textures of northern India are the Maheshwari and Chanderi saris.

Weavers settled in Maheshwar from Surat, Burhanpur and Banaras, at the insistence of Rani Ahilyabai Holkar of Indore, who supported the growth of handloom weaving, engaged in this activity. The Maheshwari sari is gossamer thin–a delicate blend of silk and cotton yarn–made in tiny checks or stripes with a coloured border. The Chanderi, widely woven in Guna, is also extremely fine but has a more intricately woven border (with motifs) than the Maheshwari.

The weavers in both Chanderi and Maheshwar are Muslims, while Hindus take on the trading. As with most handlooms and handicrafts of India, weaving these saris is mostly a family affair.

Tussar silk woven by the Devangan community of Madhya Pradesh is known by its Sanskrit name kosa. Raigarh and Champa are important centres for tussar silk saris and fabrics.

Textile Printing

Due to its strategic location as a central state that shares its border with many other states, Madhya Pradesh has absorbed influences from most of the textile traditions of India.

The tie-and-dye (bandhani) and block-printing traditions of Rajasthan and Gujarat are followed in Mandsaur, Indore and Ujjain. The Malwa and Nimar regions are renowned for their hand block-printed cotton while the textiles of Bagh, located in the Dhar district, are world-renowned.

Batik, a resist process in which the fabric is painted with molten wax and then dyed in cold dyes, is done on a large scale in Indore and Bherongarh. Multi-coloured batik saris, dupattas and bed sheets are popular for their contrasting colour schemes.

Zari Work

The craft of Zari work is concentrated in Bhopal, which is famous for its exquisite craftsmanship. Also practised in Gwalior and Indore, its origin can be traced back to 300 years.

Today, traditional articles have been replaced by modern purses, bags, tea cozies, and "jutties" or slippers.

PUNJAB HANDICRAFTS

Art is described as a creation or expression of something beautiful, especially in a visual form, and Arts and Crafts as a phrase means decorative designs and handicrafts.

In this field also, Punjab has the hoary and distinguished tradition which its people have maintained in spite of vicissitudes of time.

Take as simple a thing as mud for example. Plastering the walls with mud and drawing ferns, plants, several other fascinating motifs has been a way of life of the woman of Punjab.

They have also been making paper mache utensils for storing household necessities in colourful designs for a long time past, out of a paste made by mixing paper and various kinds of earth.

A few decades ago, *sarcanda*, a kind of tough, thick elastic grass used to grow in plenty at places which have now come under the plough. Out of this grass, roofs of all sizes (which provided air conditioning) were fashioned in circular shapes. After shaving, thin straws of this grass were woven into beautiful carpets and curtains. Another useful household contrivance called *chhaj* in Punjabi was manufactured out of sarcanda which is used for separating edible stuff from the grain.

Screens, used as a parting between wheat and hay, for instance, were also woven from this stuff. Baskets used for keeping haber dasbery (pins, cotton, buttons, needles, threads) in different shapes and colours and covers were contrived by young girls by using shaved sarcanda and coloured cotton thread which were taken by them as a part of dowry. In Punjabi, these are called *katnees*. One wedding song goes like this–*Tyari ho gayi patolaya teri katni nu phul lag gaye* which means arrangement for you have been made O beautiful one as katni has now blossomed forth'.

The state of Punjab has given some of the most attractive looking handicraft items to the world. It is sense of handicrafts being rooted deep into the soil of merry-making, hard work and creativity that makes the entire thing look so significant. Some of the artisans in Punjab also design handicrafts that reflect their joyous nature. Apart from this, it is the traditionality that forms the base of every craft work.

Punjab has traditionally rich collection of handicrafts to offer the world. While Phulkari is undoubtedly main attraction in the crafts of Punjab, there are several other beautiful, traditional crafts. Many of them amazing and highly specialized, are made all over the state.

Famous handicraft products like pidhis, jootis, durries and parandis are made all over Punjab. Used as household items or decoratives, these crafts reflect Punjab's colourful identity.

Girls are taught the art of weaving durries at a young age. The durries are woven in different sizes and patterns.

Skills of the craftsmen in Punjab continues to blossom and they produce a remarkable range of trays, mirror frames, dressing tables, easy chairs, sofa sets, handicrafted furniture dining tables, chairs and much more.

The dolls of Punjab, especially the Punjabi bride and bhangra dolls are colourful and beautifully crafted.

Different corners of Punjab are the traditional workshops where marvellous pieces of handicrafts are given life. Beside, phulkari, there are other captivating crafts which are groomed only in Punjab.

Pidhis and other Wood Works

The woodwork of Punjab has also been traditionally famous. Artistic beds are made with comfortable and skillful, backrests fitted with mirrors and carved colourful legs called pawas, and low seats called peeras. Peerian were made by carpenters in almost every village. Their skill has passed into folk songs–*raati rondi da bhij gaya Ial bhangoora* meaning "weeping last night my red swing became drenched".

At Kartarpur, Jalandhar and Hoshiarpur, craftsmen and women create pidhis (low, four-legged woven stools), which are both functional and artistic. In a marvelous display of skill, the pidhis are first carved out from wood, and then covered with lacquer and woven with threads of different colours.

Other lacquerware products of Punjab include table lamps, dolls, and attractive scratch work surahis. Wood workers at Hoshiarpur and Kartarpur specialize in making artistic furniture with intricate designs.

In those golden days, when artisans received royal patronage, the wood workers of Hoshiarpur, particularly, were specialists in inlaying ivory. With motifs and ornamentation drawn from life around them–patta (leaf), dodi (bud), jhari (bush), flowers and animals and birds–the wood workers created masterpieces that found their way to the homes of those who had an eye for skill and beauty.

Today, the march of time has taken its toll in terms of raw material–with ivory inlays being replaced by plastic. Yet, the skills of the craftsmen continue to blossom and they turn out a remarkable range of trays, mirror frames, dressing.

Furniture designed in Punjab, and boxes, toys and decorative pieces made out of wood, are exported. In giving lacquer finish to wood crafts, in adorning it with coloured mirror and in engraving wood, inlaying ivory (now white plastic only) the workmen of Punjab have been renowed.

The onslaught of modern technology is putting a premium on the arts and crafts in the present era and it will require special efforts to preserve them for posterity.

Punjabi Jootis

Colour, beauty and utility combine to form the central theme of the well-known leather jootis (shoes and slippers) of Punjab. Rich gold and multi-coloured threads are used to decorate and impart a royal touch to a variety of jootis crafted from leather of different shades. In many parts of Punjab, entire families continue to devote themselves to making jootis.

A good place to buy jootis is Patiala–once the proud capital of the Sikh Maharajas. One can find a stunning range of jootis embroidered with zari (gold thread), salma and tilla here.

Muktsar, near Faridkot, is also a good center for purchasing jootis. Known for the production of two varieties-khosa and kasuri, Muktsar is home to more than 50 families who specialize in making jootis.

Durries

Weaving of Durries (cotton bed or floor spreads) in myriad motifs and designs especially by young girls in the villages has been a long tradition in Punjab. These are also woven in stripes, cheek boards, and squares, motifs of birds, animals and even plants as a part of dowry.

In the villages, women weave durries (a pile less cotton spread, which can be used on a bed or on the floor). Girls are taught the art of weaving durries at a young age.

The durries are woven in different sizes, patterns like geometrical, animals, birds, leaves and flowers, and colours. Nikodar, Jalandhar, Hoshiarpur, Tarn Taran and Anandpur Sahib offer a vast variety of durries.

Carpet weaving is not as widespread as the weaving of durries, but the art of weaving carpets took root long ago in Punjab, with Amritsar being one of the oldest centers of carpet weaving in the country.

Parandis

Making *parandis* may not be as exotic as carpet weaving, but the parandi craftspeople have refined their art and now produce wonderfully attractive parandis in a number of colours and designs. Parandis can be purchased almost everywhere in Punjab, but Jalandhar, Amritsar, Nikodar, Hoshiarpur and Ludhiana are amongst the places where the greatest variety can be seen.

Dolls and Folk Toys Making

The earliest hand-made toys of Punjab can be traced back to the Indus Valley Civilization, dating from 2500 to 1700 B.C. These bear a remarkable resemblance to the traditional toys of a much later period which remained popular through the ages till recently when factory made toys found their way to the villages.

The traditional toys usually depict animals, equestrian figures and wheeled vehicles, all of which, though varying in quality and intended for different purposes. They can be used as playthings by the children and as decoration pieces by the adults.

Toys of cloth stuffed with cotton are still made by the women in the villages. Dolls, birds and animals are some of the common subjects. These are embellished with colourful additions of beads, buttons, feathers, tinsels and tassels and also with cowries. Sometimes, the body of the toy is appliqued.

The material used in this folk art reflects the dynamic spirit of improvisation. Besides their ornamental quality these toys have a sentimental value as well as emotional appeal.

The popularity of the clay toys is diminishing day-by-day but still there are to be seen sporadic instances of miniature dolls in clay, animals and kitchen utensils, roughly coloured with *kharia mitti* and decorated with motifs in bright colours.

Rivaling the parandis in popularity, are the dolls of Punjab, especially the Punjabi bride and the bhangra dolls. Colourful and beautifully crafted and dressed, dolls are made all over Punjab, but the most important center for doll making is Chandigarh.

Both collectively and individually, the crafts of Punjab symbolize many of the strengths of the state and the feel of the people of Punjab to come up with superb combinations of colour, beauty and utility bound together by the skill of the craftspeople. In the process, the buyer is served with a tasteful feast of crafts.

Other Folk Arts

Other noteworthy form of folk art in the Punjab, which originated in various rites and religious performances is drawing the image or some symbolic figure of a deity on the walls or the door of a house. Some people draw images of gods on their front door to protect themselves from the influence of evil spirits. Women are adept in making images of gods and goddesses of mud or dung when a special worship in connection with a fast or a festival takes place.

When the festival of Sanjhidevi is celebrated on the first Naurata, one of the walls of the house is smeared with dung and then the figure of Sanjhi Mai is drawn on it. She is adorned with ornaments. In the background one one side, the rising moon is shown and on the other the setting sun. Thereafter, she is worshipped for nine days.

Phulkari

The word phulkari (embroidered flowers) is normally used for all types of embroidery but the real phulkari work is not that in which the motifs are properly spread.

Needle work of Punjab is unique; it has beautiful names because of its associations with beautiful aspects of life and the beautiful designs which the dextrous fingers of Punjab's proverbially beautiful women create have such a wealth of forms and motifs that they defy enumeration.

Some of these are called baghs, literally a garden, Phulkaris, literally flower work, *rummals*, and scarfs. The patterns of needle work done on the bed spreads, *chunnis*, *dupattas* (these are head covers) and shirts and *salvars*, are still different.

Needle work on phulkaris is done on a deep coloured cotton cloth with striking silk threads. The threads are pierced upwards from underneath the cloth into free-hand motifs, while in the baghs and rummals, threads are worked on the top side only.

Phulkari work is one of the most fascinating expressions of the Punjabi folk art. Women have developed this art at the cost of some of their very precious moments of leisure. They have always been very fond of colour and have devoted a lot of their time to colourful embroidery and knitting.

It has also been customary for parents and relatives to give hand-embroidered clothes to girls in dowry. Punjabi women were known for embroidery with superb imagination.

Phulkari is something of which Punjab is justly proud and is also noted as the home of this embroidered and durable product. This is a kind of women's dress used as special cover to be worn over the shirt which women traditionally don.

It actually formed part of the brides trousseau and was associated with various ceremonies preliminary to the wedding during which it used to be embroidered. The cloth used for making this, is generally in red or maroon colour and the thread employed in the close embroidery is made of silk in gold, yellow, crimson red, blue and green colours.

In the phulkari work, the whole cloth is covered with closed embroidery and almost no space is left uncovered. The piece of cloth thus embroidered is called baag meaning a garden. If only the sides are covered it is called *chope.*

The background is generally maroon or scarlet and the silken thread used is mostly golden. Colour schemes show a rich sensitiveness. Some phulkaris are embroidered with various motifs of birds, animals, flowers and sometimes scenes of village life.

These were traditionally used for wear but now are exported as wall hangings and sewn as jackets, etc.

Mud Works

There is no limit to the creativity of Punjab's craftsmen. They have this panache for turning seemingly dull materials into masterpieces of art. For instance, a simple material like mud is used by craftsmen here to create fascinating motifs apart from plastering walls in lovely style.

Miscellaneous Crafts

These include making use of paper mache intensils for storing household necessities; use of *sarcanda*, a special type of grass to make roofs, carpets, curtains, *chhaj*, *katness* which are, infact, baskets used for keeping haber dasbery given as a part of dowry to girls and other household articles viz. *chiks*, *bohiey*, *pitarian*, *moorras* (a kind of chairs). However, these crafts are moving fast towards falling into wilderness.

HANDICRAFTS OF HARYANA

The name Haryana conjures up image of a green and fertile land; of tough and hard working people; of a vibrant and dynamic economy; of a society that respects tradition while at the same time looks with eagerness to the future and all that it may offer.

Haryana embodies the sole of the handicraft persons. Here, amidst the throb of modern machines, the ancient handicrafts are still alive.

Making handicrafts has never been the mainstream occupation of the people in Haryana. Most crafts have not evolved into art forms and have remained rooted to their original use and simplicity. Perhaps, people were always too involved in the hardships of agricultural life to spare time for crafts. Even when the Green Revolution made agriculture easier, people preferred to continue with agriculture, which was a familiar area, rather than venture into the unknown world of crafts.

Historically speaking, Haryana's craft traditions also never received any royal patronage, as did crafts in Rajasthan or Avadh.

Despite all these problems, Haryana has some interesting handicrafts on offer including pottery making, handloom, woven furniture, artistic pottery, and woodcarving.

Embroidery, Weaving and Handlooms

Haryana is quite famous for its woven work, be it shawls, durries, robes or lungis. The Haryana shawl is known as "phulkari". It is an offshoot of the shawl from Kashmir.

The Haryana shawl is a work of art in itself. Known as phulkari, it is a spectacular piece of clothing, full of magnificent colours and intricate embrodiery. Worn with a tight-fitting choli (blouse) and ghaghra (long skirt), it forms the basic winter wear for the women of Haryana.

A deviation from the phulakri is the bagh (garden). In this case, the entire cloth is covered with embrodiery inasmuch that the base cloth is hardly seen.

Traditionally, work on a phulkari commences from the time a daughter is born in the family and is given to her at her wedding.

Phulkari

Phulkari is made by female members of a house, and it takes a long time to make; sometimes even a few years.

Normally, only one woman works on the design so that the uniformity is maintained. However, it is no surprise that the other women also contribute in little ways to its creation.

Against a red background, motifs of birds, flowers and human figures are stitched into the cloth. The design is fed into the cloth from the reverse side using darning needles, one thread at a time, leaving a long stitch below to form the basic pattern.

The stitching is done in a vertical and horizontal pattern as well as variations from this standard format, so that when the phulkari is finally complete, the play of light on its shiny surface can do wonders. Satin and silk is also used frequently to enhance the effect.

Bagh

Bagh design almost always follows a geometric pattern, with green as the basic colour probably because mainly Muslims worked on them. Although lacking in technical finesse, it makes up for the loss by a colourful display of its design.

Everything goes into its design – elephants, houses, crops, the sun, the moon, kites, gardens, anything and everything.

The embrodiery is worked into *khaddar* (coarse cotton cloth) with silk thread. Khaddar is cheap and locally available everywhere in India, and in making a bagh, narrow pieces are used. Sometimes, two or three baghs will be stitched together to form a phulkari.

Chope

Another kind of shawl is the chope, a rather simple affair in comparison to the phulkari and bagh, and is presented to a new bride by her maternal grandmother. The darshan dwar shawl is gifted to a temple by a devotee whose wish has been fulfilled.

Durries Handicrafts

Haryana durries are rather coarse, although spectacular geometric designs adorn the entire rug. The Jats of Haryana are known to make durries with white triangles often set against a blue background. In Haryana, durrie making is concentrated in and around Panipat.

Karnal is a hot spot for bright robes and lungis (a skirt-like garment worn by men and originally invented by Gautam Buddha), a common garment worn by inhabitants of rural India.

Pottery

Pottery is essentially a village craft, and Haryana is essentially a village state. The potter's wheel, dating back to pre-Aryan times, is the most common feature of any village in India.

Although numerous kinds of wheels are used throughout India, in Haryana, the kick-operated type is common. With this contraption, you don't use your hands to turn the wheel as in normal cases; on the other hand, you use your foot. The actual wheel may be either of cement or stone.

The material for making earthen articles comes cheap, and from the earth itself. While the potter works on the wheel, he has a helper (usually his son or a relative) mixing clay, while a woman (his wife or a sister) makes intricate designs into the finished vessel or toy.

From utensils to toys to decorative pieces, clay forms the most essential ingredient on which the potter literally survives. Seasonal festivals call for the potter to get cracking – he has to make hundreds of toys like miniature cows, horses, people, houses and sepoys which are then sold in brightly decorated stalls along dusty lanes.

Brass & Metalware Handicrafts

Brass & Metalwares were probably the earliest non- ferrous metals, which man shaped into tools for lightness and resistance to corrosion.

The production process begins with melting old scrap or using sheer metal. Later, shaping is done while heating or pouring molten metal into a mould. The turning process on a lathe smoothens the article by scraping and brushing.

Attractive contrasts in colour and texture of metals are created through the techniques of inlay, overlay, applique and fusing of colours.

Punja Durrie/Block Printing Handicrafts

Cotton floor coverings or durries made in Haryana are by far the best on account of their rich hues and weaves in bewildering patterns.

The punja durries of Haryana are cool aesthetic and a hot selling item in the international market. The printing and painting of cotton cloth has won the hearts of millions in India and abroad.

Jute Handicrafts

Jute craft is new to Haryana and this craft is mainly practised in urban areas i.e. in Karnal district. Besides this, there are few handicraftsmen in Bhiwani, Hissar, Faridabad practing this craft.

The items mainly made with jute fibers are bags, curtains, jackets, mats, purses, floor covering, etc.

Sandal/Bone/Wood Carving Handicrafts

Early builders fashioned wood into different shapes such as birds, animals and the human figures. Later, these were carved on roots, pillars, pilasters, beams, brackets and corners. Sophisticated containers, chests, boxes, jewellery, trinkets, lamps, palanquins and images of gods, followed this.

The most commonly used wood in Haryana is rosewood, shesham and sandalwood. Articles made of bone include ornamental pins, bracelets, bangles, necklaces, perfume, jars and ear pins.

Jewellery Handicrafts

Haryana is famous for its jewellery, which is highly artistic and elaborate especially silver, bone and lac. It has the vigour and sturdiness in style associated with the children of the soil and the beauty of designs borrowed from simple motifs picked from the immediate environment.

The motifs have been developed into artistic, stylized patterns like the *mor-morni* pattern, which occurs repeatedly. It is amazing how many of the old designs have remained unaltered through the ages, particularly in folk jewellery.

For ornamentation repousse, chase, filigree and enamelling are and beads are blown into beautiful shapes and sizes.

Leather Craft (Tilla Juttis) Handicrafts

Tilla juttis of Haryana are sewn out of locally cured leather ornamented with silk, metal embroidery, or designs done in applique with thin leather pieces of different colours. The designs are extremely delicate and the colours bright.

An equally colourful item is the embroidered knucklepad.

Mudha/Basketry Handicrafts

Cane or rattan, as it is called, is a kind of climbing palm with many joined stems. The stems are dried after removing the green sheath. It is extraordinarily strong. Cane sticks twisted together are used as cables and cordage in country crafts.

Chairs called moorahs are made of bamboo and cane. They are a major export item and are made in many parts of Haryana.

Carpets Handicrafts

The great Mughal Emperor–Akbar, in the middle of 16th century, brought the art of carpet weaving into the Indian subcontinent. As one of the oldest and major industries, Indian carpets are known world over for their design, colour and craftsmanship.

Haryana has today emerged as a major carpet-producing centre, as a result of long years of research and practice.

Paintings

Haryana was always a rendezvous for various tribes, invaders, races, cultures and faiths, going right back to BC 2500, and it witnessed the merging of numerous styles of painting.

While references to paintings are to be found of the Aryan period, art actually flourished during the reign of the Guptas (5th century BC to 6th century AD). However, these are mostly concentrtated in Southern India, and nothing close to such magnificent art is to be found in Haryana.

Discoveries of earthenware and designs painted on them in black and white in Siswal district in Haryana are the first impressions of art in this state.

Mitathal and Banwali districts have also revealed that art did exist here, but definitely on a much smaller scale than that of the Deccan and Southern India. The drawings are mainly in horizontal and vertical lines, with a little more creativity allotted to floral art. During Harsha's reign, art and painting received special attention for some time as the king himself was a painter of sorts.

After Harsha's death, painting flourished for a while under the Rajputs, but the establishment of the Delhi Sultanate put an end to this.

The Sultans had no love for art – they were busy fighting wars and battles and never patronised painters. The Mughal empire was different and art reached its zenith during this time. Jahangir was a patron of art, and during his reign, the influence of the Persian painting style was happily married to the Indian style.

However, all that was happening in Delhi and Haryana was conveniently left out in the cold. There were rich jagirdars who liked paintings, and they engaged artisans and painters to do up their houses, celings, walls, and such other works.

Temples were another structure where the painter got to work, decorating everything within reach with landscapes, dances, hunting expeditions, wrestling bouts, birds, bees, and love scenes. Come the 18th century, and the Rewaris made sure that painters got enough work, albeit under Rajput style.

The god Krishna was a big hit in the villages – walls, doors, windows, and the like, all bore similarity with the Mughal and Kangra styles merging later with the Rajput style.

The walls of the palace of Maharaja Tej Singh in Mirpur in Gurgaon are adorned with paintings, following the Rajput pattern. The patterns on the walls express scenes from the Ramayana. The Matru Mad ki Piao in Gurgaon features mythological paintings, but these are slowly fading away.

The Asthal Bohar paintings are also in the Rajput style, and their influence can be seen even in the Shiva temples in Panchkula and Pinjore, Venumadhava temple in Kaul, the temples in Kaithal and Pabnama, the Kapil temple in Kilayat and the Sarsainth temple in Sirsa. The Rang Mahal in Pinjore is also decorated with wall paintings, an originality straight from the hands of Mughal painters.

The samadhas of Lala Balk Ram and Lala Jamuna Das in Jagadhari and Ambala are famous for their walls paintings from Hindu mythology. The entrances to both are flanked by heavily painted *dwarapalas*.

The Rajiwala temple near the samadhas also boasts of religious themes in its paintings. Its walls, cells and verandah have been subjected to the Jain style, while the Qila Mubarak, a two-storeyed Mughal structure is embellished with images of birds and flowers.

Kurukshetra's Bhadri Kali temple has religious themes and frescos running throughout its structure, with a broad frieze bordering the lower end. The second storey is covered with murals, as is the haveli (house) of Rani Chand Kaur in Pehowa, the temple of Shri Ram Radha in Pehowa and the temple of Baba Shrawan Nath. In fact, you'll find similar paintings in temples and holy Hindu places throughout Haryana.

The Persian style infused with script also gains prominence, especially with murals in which the Persian script is freely used. Elaborate detail forms the central theme within which verses from the Koran are written in various flowing styles, following the calligraphy method.

Mughal paintings also seeped into Hindu temples, especially in Kaithal, Kalayat and Rohtak. Here too, the subject matter is lifted right out of mythology and carry moral and spiritual messages.

In Rohtak, paintings have been found which are now in possession of the Manuscripts Department of Kurukshetra University. Liberal use of blue, pink, green, orange and red enhance the beauty of these paintings which are of the Lord Vishnu and his incarnations.

Sculpture

Rock and stone were the most common subjects for the development of art, right from the Maurya period to Harshavardhana to the Mughals and the British.

However, the Mughals put a stop to carving idols and images out of rock as this was against the very basis of Islam. They went a step further, destroying temples and any such figure which went against their beliefs.

Sculpture in Haryana was concentrated around central and northen parts and was basically religious in content. Lord Vishnu was the most important, and he and his incarnations were enough subjects for sculptors to practise their art. A figure of Vishnu found in Kurukshetra is a remarkable piece of art, showing the god with four arms gracefully reclining on the coils of Anantnag, the many-headed snake. This stone figure was probably made in the 10th century AD.

Gods formed the basis of sculpture in ancient Haryana, and likewise all over India. Sandstone was widely used, be it green, buff, grey or black. But, besides the images of Hindu gods and goddesses, Jain images from the Pratihara period (9th century) have also been found, all made of sandstone. The Buddha also surfaces once in a while, like in Rohtak where he was found seated cross-legged on a lotus pedestal made entirely of grey stone.

Himachal Pradesh Handicrafts

"Art strives to express; craft strives for excellence. Good art has good craft, good craft is artistic. Within every craft, there exists artists. Within every artist there is craft"–Ralph Reichenbach & Doug Madill.

Himachal has its own unique tradition of handicrafts. The range of crafts in Himachal is vast and shows many facets of artistic dexterity. The mind-boggling range includes fine woodwork, traditional leather embroidery, beautifully patterned carpets, traditional woolen shawls, textiles, wood carving, architecture and paintings.

The creative minds of the craftsmen of Himachal Pradesh have given birth to an astonishing range of handicrafts. Contributing a great deal to the glorious cultural heritage of Himachal Pradesh, the handicrafts have even earned international fame.

Celebrated in India and abroad for their fineness and beauty, the handicrafts of Himachal Pradesh fascinate many a tourist. From stone and metal statues to dolls, pottery, paintings, rugs, carpets, shawls and jewellery, Himachal Pradesh has a lot to offer.

It is amazing to see how these hilly people developed such great tradition of artistic excellence despite their tough life.

Tibetan craftsman often sell intricate and brightly coloured cloth paintings called Thangka Paintings. Usually depicting the Buddha and other deities in the wheel of life, Thangka reflects artistic dexterity and happens to be extremely popular with foreign tourists.

Extremely fine and valuable shawls are a specialty of Himachal. Its Kangra style of paintings and carpets are also famous. Himachalis simply love to dress up their garments, accessories, embroidery, woolen garments, shawls and leather craft is extremely valuable and popular.

The geographic isolation of Himachal has allowed its people to evolve their own unique tradition of handicrafts. The mind-boggling range includes fine woodwork, traditional leather embroidery, beautifully patterned carpets, traditional woollen shawls and lots of other things.

Wood Carving

Forests all over the state abound in pine and deodar, besides walnut, horse chestnut and wild black mulberry. Wood has been used to great effect in temples and lavishly built palaces. The steep-roofed pine temples of northern HP often bear relief figures carved on their outer walls.

Intricately carved seats, doors, windows and panels speak volumes of the craftspersons' skill. The Bhimakali temple of Sarahan is a perfect product of the kind.

Woodcarving is still a living tradition in HP. Pahari artisans use wood to make intricate jalis, trelliswork or perforated reliefs that filter light, transforming the interiors of a building with the play of light and shade and balancing mass with delicacy.

The carpenters of both villages and towns make beautiful objects of everyday use like vedis (low benches), bedlegs, cradles, bedsteads, low settees, boxes, ladles, churners, rolling pins, wooden utensils, charkhas (spinning wheels) and hukka nari (the pipe and body of the smoking pipe).

You might like to take back something from their range of fruit bowls, beermugs, wooden jewellery, decorative boxes and carved images. Bamboo and willow bark is also stripped and fashioned into sturdy trays and baskets.

Painting

To say that HP has a rich tradition of painting would be an understatement. While museums and art galleries preserve the famous miniature paintings of the region, traditional ritual paintings can be seen in most village houses, on the floors and walls.

Women draw magic diagrammatic designs called yantras on the thresholds on ceremonial occasions.

Floor paintings are white, done with rice paste, while wall paintings are colourful. The colours are from what the women use in their daily lives – red from kumkum (the liquid for bindi, the dot between the brows), yellow from turmeric powder, red ochre from golru (red clay), and so on.

In some places like Kangra, Mandi and Bilaspur, brilliant wall paintings are done in the torana griha (honeymoon room), where the newly married couple enjoy their first days of togetherness. This painting is known as kauhara or kamdeo. Temple walls, too, sometimes have bright motifs painted on them.

Various schools of miniature painting collectively called pahari, flourished between the 17th and 19th centuries in the sub-Himalayan states. The hilly region, then divided into 22 princely states, was ruled by Rajput kings or chieftains who were all great connoisseurs of art, with most of them maintaining ateliers.

The focal points of their lives were war, hunting, lineage, and the *zenana*. Also partial to love themes, especially the legends of Radha and Krishna, were liked by the Rajputs as depicted in their miniature paintings.

The early Pahari paintings of the mid-17th century were in the basholi style (dubbed so because of its association with the king of Basholi).

These are extraordinarily colourful and charged with vitality and emotion. Two persistent strains can be observed – a fondness for the portraits of the local rajas in plain white garments and for the gods of the Hindu pantheon.

The paintings bear resemblance to Rajasthani and Malwa paintings but this can be attributed to the fact that the kings of the princely states in Himachal were Rajputs.

Some of the telling characteristics are the use of extremely elegant two-dimensional architectural settings topped by domes or pavilions, bands of scrollwork pattern and the use of elaborately figured rugs.

There are many striking works in this genre as the basholi style, with its strong indigenous Indian element, is well suited to the portrayal of many-headed Shivas and many-armed Durgas (figures from the vast stockpile of Indian mythology).

The coming of painters from the Mughal court in the second quarter of the 18th century (due to the decline of the Mughal Empire) led to a complete transformation of the existing basholi style. There was a wholesale ferrying in of Mughal style and fashion, from dress to architecture to the arts. The resultant was the Guler-Kangra style.

The style owes a great deal to later Mughal painting, particularly in its receding planes, its fondness for quasi-realistic landscape and its frequent enlargement of the figures on the page.

This late Pahari style first appeared in Guler, and then in Kangra. Raja Goverdhan Singh (1744-1773) of Guler gave shelter to many artists.

Kangra School of Paintings

Under the ambitious Sansar Chand (1775-1823), the Kangra School flourished happily. It is said that Sansar's love for a gaddi (a tribe of Chamba-Kangra region) maiden drove him to commission the paintings.

Kangra Fort, where he held court for nearly 25 years, was once adorned with paintings and attracted art lovers from far and wide.

Later, he moved his capital to Nadaun and finally to Sujanpur Tira. The temples and palaces at each of these places were adorned with lovely miniatures. The 1905 earthquake damaged many of these buildings but you can still see some of the miniature wall paintings.

The Kangra style is by far the most poetic and lyrical of Indian styles, says art historian J. C. Harle.

His favourite subject here is 'the idealization of woman, in flowing sari, head half-covered with a shawl, demure but stately, passionate and shy'. The more complex many-figured compositions – usually larger and horizontal in format – tend to illustrate events from the Krishna legend – the cowherd god putting out a forest fire, subduing the serpent Kaliya, or stealing the clothes of gopis (milkmaids of Braj) while they were bathing in the river.

The ability to handle large groups of figures and landscapes with towns or clusters of houses in the distance is admirable. Apart from intricate brushwork, Kangra miniatures are characterized by the skillful use of brilliant mineral and vegetable extract colours that possess an enamel-like lustre. But the strangest thing about these hill paintings is that you'll never find snow-capped mountains in them!

Research shows that while the Kangra style became well-entrenched in the Hills, many offshoots emerged in regions like Kullu, Nurpur, Chamba and Mandi. The Bhuri Singh Museum in Chamba is best-known for its exquisite collection of Pahari miniatures.

Thangkas

Places with a Tibetan community often sell intricate and brightly coloured cloth paintings called thangkas.

These are actually ritual paintings displayed during certain Buddhist festivals, but they happen to be extremely popular with foreign tourists (and cost the earth too!).

Thangkas are scroll paintings on canvas, edged with a border of rich silk, usually depicting the Buddha and other deities and the wheel of life. The painting follows complex dicta like proportional grids for each diety and traditional vegetable or mineral colours are used.

The Norbulingka Institute at McLeodganj is the centre of learning this ancient art of Tibet.

Rugs & Carpets

Carpets and blankets are almost synonymous with Himachali furnishing. Their brilliant colours and traditional motifs can make you forget your Persian back home! You'll be spellbound by their appearance – Garudas (Vishnu's mount, the eagle) perched on flowering trees, dragons, swastikas (auspicious Hindu/Buddhist emblem), flutes (symbolizing happiness) and lotus blooms (signifying purity).

In the higher reaches of the state, hillfolk rear sheep and goats and weave the wool and hair into traditional blankets, rugs and namdas (heavy rugs). Namdas are made with beaten wool. In fact, men spinning wool by hand as they watch their flocks is a common sight in Himachal.

Fleecy soft blankets called gudmas are also very popular. They are made from the wool of the Giangi sheep. They come in natural wool colours and are finished with a red or black edging.

You'll have a lot of furnishings to choose from: thobis (floor coverings), karcha (mattresses), which are made from goat hair, pattoo cloth (like shawls), carpets and yarn made from soft wool.

Garments & Accessories

Himachalis simply love to dress up. Their everyday wear is so colourful that you'd think that they were dressed up for a festive occasion.

The Gujjars (a semi-nomadic tribe) wear kurtas (long shirts) which are delicately embroidered with circular and linear patterns.

The people of Chamba are majorly fond of all sorts of accessories, which include bright rumals (scarves) worn by the women, bangles and rings made of horsehair and brightly patterned grass shoes.

Traditional Footwear

Lahaul has its own traditional footwear. People wear the most interesting socks – we bet you've never seen anything like them before.

These handknit woollen socks are brilliantly patterned in bright and cheerful colours. Luckily for the rest of the world, they are sold in abundance in the bazaars of Himachal, along with gloves, mufflers and caps. The typical Kullu topi (cap), in shades of grey or brown and flat on the top, is rather striking too.

A band of colourful woven fabric brightens the front and the topi looks rather neat set at a rakish angle.

Embroidery

Embroidery seems to be the favourite pastime of pahari women, their nimble fingers busy with needle and thread on lazy afternoons. Houses in HP are replete with beautiful pieces like rumals (scarves), coverlets, handfans, caps, cholis (bodices), gaumukhi (prayer gloves) and such things.

The motifs are either from the traditional stock of miniature painting, the landscape or are innovations of the women themselves. This urge to create and live with beautiful pieces is very much a part of pahari culture.

The red and orange richly embroidered silk rumals (scarves) of Chamba are simply beautiful. The women of

Chamba have traditionally made them for a 1000 years now. These rumals are actually small shawls meant to be used as head coverings.

They often depict scenes from the Mahabharata, the Ramayana and the Raas-lila of Radha and Krishna. The embroidery is done in silk yarn on tussar cloth or fine cotton. The stitches are so fine that there is no evidence of knots or loose threads. As such, both sides of the rumal are alike.

The ground is usually white or cream, but the embroidery threads (usually red and orange) are in striking contrast. A finely embroidered rumal can take something like even a month to complete.

Woollen Garments

Wool is an auspicious thing in Himachal, and no ritual occasion goes without wearing woollen clothes. A quaint ritual during weddings, for instance, is to wrap the bride and groom in a woollen shawl to protect them from evil eyes.

Shawls

Extremely fine and valuable shawls are a speciality of Himachal and Kashmir. They are greatly sought after by tourists from all over the world.

In fact, shawl weaving is a major cottage industry in HP. These shawls, both plain and patterned, are made from the fine hair of pashmina goats. Pashm is the wool of a certain Asian species of mountain goat, Capra hircus.

The fine fleece used to make these shawls is that which grows beneath the rough outer hair. Did you know that the finest hair comes from the underbelly which is shed with the onset of summer?

The right mix of wool gives beautiful shades of grey, blue, mustard and black. Shawls in Kullu are often woven from the wool of angora rabbits. The borders of these plain-looking shawls are decorated with dazzling geometric designs. Shawls of Lahaul-Spiti, especially, are a riot of colours.

Leather craft

Traditional Chamba chappals (slippers), plain or embroidered, are exceptionally comfortable to wear.

They are embroidered with multicoloured threads – red, black, green, yellow and blue, and imitation zari (gold thread).

Tourists seem to love them and this inspires craftspersons to experiment with patterns and designs.

Apart from chappals, you can also pick from a range of shoes, sandals, socks and belts.

Jewellery

Chunky bead-and-metal jewellery of the hill people is usually in great demand. As with most tribal communities, the traditional attire includes ornaments for almost all parts of the body.

Markets abound with stalls selling amulets, pendants, necklaces, daggers and rings – you'll probably want to take everything home!

Fine jewellery is crafted out of silver and gold. The jewellers of the once–Rajput kingdoms of Kangra, Chamba, Mandi and Kullu–were famous for their enamelling skills.

They mainly worked with silver and were partial to deep blue and green enamelling. They created exquisite pieces like elliptical anklets, solid iron-headed bangles, hair ornaments, peepal leaf-shaped forehead ornaments, necklaces known as chandanhaars (a bunch of long silver chains linked by engraved or enamelled silver plaques) and pendants with motifs of the mother goddess.

An old Kangra pattern for silver anklets is a series of birds, archaic in design, connected by silver links. Unfortunately, most of this is old jewellery is no longer made. You could check it out in museums like the Kangra Art Museum in Dharamsala, the State Museum in Shimla and the Bhuri Singh Museum in Chamba.

Some of the jewellery that's made now and coin necklaces are extremely popular with pahari women. So much so that every pahari woman dreams of owning one.

Chokers called kach (made of silver beads and triangular plaques) and the collar-like *hansali* are also common. Heavy anklets, bangles and silver bracelets (kare) – solid or filled with shellac – with clasps in the shape of crocodile or lions heads are worn by all women.

In the Tibetan influenced Lahaul-Spiti, ornaments are studded with semi-precious stones like coral, turquoise, amber and mother-of-pearl.

Metalwork

In a land where religion rules daily life, worship is bound to be an elaborate process. Temples are replete with pretty objects needed for worship, all fine specimens of metalwork.

The metals used mainly are brass, copper, iron, tin and bell metal. Apart from the exquisite statuettes enshrined, there are several metal objects like bells with artistically designed handles, lamps, incense burners, low settees of silver or brass, vessels and ornate musical instruments in these temples.

In fact, the common lota (a small globular pot for storing water) itself is available in so many different forms all over the state that it's amazing. Similar things may be used as everyday items at home.

Some of the more affluent homes possess beautifully fashioned teapots, smoking pipes, carved panels, doorknobs and various other artifacts. Metal workers haven't lost their magic touch; this centuries old craft is still one of the most vital traditions of the state.

Another Metalcraft–Mohra

Another metalcraft unique to Himachal is the mohra. Mohras or metal plaques representing a deity are common in Kullu and Chamba.

Most of them represent Shiva, but masks of the mother goddess Devi and other deities are not uncommon. These plaques are usually made of bronze, brass or silver and consecrated by a pujari (priest) before being installed in a temple.

The head is sculpted in bold relief, while the neck and shoulders are more summarily treated.

Each village has its own mohra. Mohras have been made in Himachal for at least 1,400 years now. They are taken out of the temples on a palanquin in processions during religious festivals like the grand Kullu Dussehra.

Stonework

Thanks to the fair variety of stone found in this hilly region, stone carving has been explored to the fullest in Himachal. Numerous shikhara (spired) stone temples dot the landscape.

The Lakshminarayan temples of Chamba and the temples of Baijnath and Masrur in the Kangra Valley are some splendid specimens of the kind.

Beautifully carved memorial stone slabs called panihars are also found in several places, especially near temples and fountains.

Stone carvers in HP are hammering away at their blocks even today, producing several artifacts of domestic use widely available in the markets.

These include traditional stoves (angithi), circular pots for storing (kundi), pestle and mortar (dauri danda), mill stones (chakki) and other things. The centres of sculpting in Himachal are concentrated mainly in Mandi, Chamba, Kinnaur and the Shimla Hills.

Art and Handicrafts

Woollen Craft

Wool is considered sacred by Himachalis and wool weaving has been famous in Himachal Pradesh for ages. The state is known for its fine-quality shawls and caps. Pashmina is the most famous type of shawl, it is quite expensive as it is the finest quality of shawl available in India. The shawls with beautiful geometrical patterns and colours are popular with tourists. Carpets and blankets in several designs and colours are the other woollen crafts available in Himachal Pradesh.

Metal Craft

The best place to see the captivating metal art of Himachal Pradesh is its temples. The metal idols of the gods and goddesses in the temples are very beautiful. Metal is also used in an artistic way to make temple doors. Other metal wares available in the state are bells, incense burners, lamps, jars, flasks, tridents and canopies. Several household items made of metal are also available here. The towns of Bilaspur, Chamba, Kupa, Rekong Peo, Rohru, Sarahan and Jogindernagar are especially famous for their metal craft.

Stone Craft

Stone carving is an important tradition in Himachal Pradesh. The stone temples are the best examples of the art of stone craft. Exquisitely carved images inside the temples leave the onlookers awe-struck. Several household items such as traditional stove, circular pots, mill stones, etc. are also carved out of stone. Places such as Mandi, Chamba, Kinnaur and Shimla are known for stone craft.

Wood Craft

The craftsmen of Himachal Pradesh are expert in carving beautiful wooden objects such as doors, windows, panels, benches, beds, cradles, bedsteads, low settees, boxes, ladles, churners, utensils, jewellery, images, baskets, etc.

Paintings

Influenced by various themes like love, the legends of Krishna and Radha and hunting scenes, the paintings of Himachal Pradesh are an important part of its handicrafts.

Leather Crafts

The plain and embroidered footwear called Chamba chappals are famous in Himachal Pradesh. This colourful embroidered footwear looks very attractive. They are available in various designs and colours. Other leather crafts such as shoes and belts are also available in the state.

Jewellery

Beautiful silver and gold jewellery of Himachal Pradesh fascinate many a tourist. Coin necklaces are quite popular with tourists. But the jewellery famous during the times of Raja-Maharaja can only be seen in the museums of the state. The Kangra Art Museum in Dharamshala and the State Museum in Shimla are the best places to see the antique jewellery of Himachal Pradesh.

Handicrafts in Maharashtra

Maharashtra has a rich cultural heritage, which is an amalgamation of different cultures and traditions. The state exudes a vibrant spirit, which never dies. This spirit is visible in its traditional arts and crafts.

The cave paintings at Ajanta, Warli paintings and handicrafts of Maharashtra are clear evidences of the state's cultural legacy. These beyond comparison arts and crafts of Maharashtra are enticing and exotic.

The expertise of the artisans of Maharashtra can be seen in the fine art and craft finishes. The fine fabrics of mashru and himroo are clear examples of their highest level of weaving art. The fabrics which look like golden clothe are regarded to be one of the finest of their kind. The high level weaving know-how is also evident with the paithani and narayan peth sarees.

Bidriware is another well-appreciated craft of this state. It takes lots of skills and time in preparation.

The district of Kolhapur is famous for its jewellery and Kolhapuri chappals. Kolhapuri chappals are known for their quality, comfortability and low price.

Then come the paintings of warli tribes of Mumbai. It is even compared to the famous paintings of Madhubani, Bihar.

Maharashtra has a rich cultural heritage, which is an amalgamation of different cultures and traditions. The state exudes a vibrant spirit which never dies. This spirit is visible in its traditional arts and crafts.

Some of the well-known handicrafts of Maharashtra are:

Weaving

Maharashtra is also known for its strong textile history. There are different types of saris or materials available belonging to a particular area or region of the state, such as Kolhapur, Pune, and Aurangabad.

Mashru and Himru

Aurangabad is famous for Mashru and Himru fabrics. These two types of fabrics are made of cotton and silk having a shine like satin.

Himru shawls are less expensive and are made by using both silk and cotton threads. These threads help in producing beautiful multi-coloured designs on these shawls. The actual ornamental design is formed on the principle of extra weft figuring. The extra silk weft, left loose, makes the Himru shawl soft, which almost feels like silk.

Weavers were brought to Aurangabad from Banaras and Ahmedabad by Mohamed-bin-Tughlak and thus the Himru industry started.

Paithani Saris

The Paithani Saris are being woven from the past 2000 years. In the making of a Paithani sari, pure silk is used along with the zari or gold threads drawn from pure gold. It takes almost six months to one and a half years to weave an intricately brocaded Paithani sari.

Narayan Peth

The Narayan Peth sari is a traditional Maharashtrian sari, belonging to Sholapur. This is a beautifully woven sari in silk having contrast zari border, generally of 'rudraksha' motifs.

Kolhapuri Chappal - Leather Footwear

Kolhapuri chappal making is a major handicraft industry that employees over 20,000 craftspersons in the district. Kolhapuri chappals are flat, intricately patterned, handcrafted leather footwear traditionally made in Kolhapur by the community whose hereditary occupation is tanning and leather work.

Originally, the footwear was made for daily use by farmers and field workers but the simple ingenious design has reached out to a wider spectrum of people all over the world. The cords used to stitch the sandals are made of leather.

Surprisingly, no nails are used in their making. Made of buffalo hide, fine goat leather is used for the plaited strips that decorate their upper portion. Dyed in natural tan, deep maroon, mustard yellow and dark brown colours, they are decorated with leather braids and golden zari (tinsel) cords.

Though traditional designs have thong-like straps with a toe strap for further strength, the craftsmen now produce simple variants of these designs such as kachkadi, bakkalnali and pukari. Numerous designs, along with the introduction of new colours, have evolved over time to cater to contemporary demands.

Paintings

(i) Ajanta Paintings

The paintings in Ajanta Caves are outstandingly beautiful; they belong to the diffused art style of China & Japan. The Ajanta paintings were painted by the Buddhist monks who turned the stone walls into picture books of Buddha's life & teachings. These Buddhist artists have portrayed the costumes, ornaments & styles of the court life of their times.

(ii) Warli Paintings

Living in Thane district of Maharashtra, the Warli tribe is known for the sacred pictographs that they paint on the walls of their huts during wedding rituals.

As such, the Warlis style of paintings belong to the tribal people who live in the Thane district, situated in north of Mumbai.

Rice paste and straw was smeared on the walls as base and motifs inspired from their life, nature, epics, legends, local incidents and tales painted on it with a brush made of twigs.

These paintings are a part of their tradition and are painted by the womenfolk during wedding rituals, using rice paste and straw.

After the painting is complete, it is smeared on the walls of their huts. Now, these paintings are also done on paper and are available almost everywhere in India.

The Warli paintings are made on religious themes. They are painted in white on an austere brown surface decorated with occasional dots in red and yellow.

Men, animals and trees form a loose, rhythmic pattern across the entire sheet of a Warli painting.

Palaghata, the goddess of trees and plants symbolizing creative energy, is the central theme of these paintings. The visual energy of the Warli painting is attained through line drawings of multitudes of tiny human forms engaged in hunting, dancing or cultivating land with colour being not the main criteria.

In recent years, the medium of these painting has transferred to paper and cloth layered with cowdung paste which produces the characteristic natural and dull background with the motifs painted white.

Wooden Toys

Sawantwadi is popularly identified with wooden toys that are made from mango tree. Though the craft is traditionally done by the Chitari, other communities have also adopted this craft due to its commercial success.

The toys are made by several techniques: wood and lac turnery, by assembling flat shaped pieces and by sculpting solid wood.

Seasoned mango wood is turned into cylindrical shapes with chisels and, its surface finished. At least four to five toys are turned together on the lathe at a time. Before removing the turned items, lac mixed with colours is applied to the finished surface. These are separated and the base of each item is finished with a sander.

Toys are also made by cutting different profiles with the jigsaw, which are later assembled into a whole product. The cutout pieces are finished on a sander, smoothened with sandpaper, painted and assembled.

Ganjifa Cards

They are circular playing cards made from paper that is covered with a mixture of tamarind seed powder and oil, painted and coated with lac.

Darbari cards have decorative borders and Bazaar cards are without borders. It used to be a popular pastime at the Indian courts.

The classic Mughal ganjifa with its 96 cards and 8 suits penetrated into the social milieu of India and the Deccan that later, with its themes and characters from Hindu mythology, gained widespread acceptance.

The most popular was the Dashavatar depicting the ten incarnations of Vishnu.

Ganjifa cards were introduced in Sawantwadi. The Chitari community in Sawantwadi, known for their skill in lacware and wood craft, learnt to make these cards. Today, the cards are used as gift items and educational aids.

Silverware

Silver artifacts, an integral part of Maharashtrian religious ceremonies has now evolved into a flourishing trade. Untreated silver is first melted, allowed to take the desired shape and size in rectangular moulds, and intricate designs are created by using embossing tools.

Parts of the products are made separately and then soldered together. The final matt or gloss polishing is done with a brush using soapnut powder solution. Silver jewellery is an ancient craft of Hupri.

Silversmiths at Hupri specializing in making popular oxidized jewellery embellish it further with meenakari and patterns based on the delicate shape of the papal tree, the champak, babul and aonla flowers and the ambi (mango).

Bidriware

Bidriware is an ancient craft of Aurangabad, which uses zinc and copper as raw material. It also employs the intricate workmanship of pure silver, either brocaded, overlaid or inlaid on the metal surface. In the beginning, Bidriware items were used as *hookahs* or *paan daans*, but now they are more often sold as souvenirs.

Bidri is a specialized and refined technique using complicated sequences of inlay and enamelling found only in India that follows in essence the techniques of the Persian way of inlaying gold and silver on steel or copper.

It involves four distinct processes of casting, engraving, inlaying and finishing. The principle of sandcasting is integral to the manufacture of bidriware.

Once the object is made and smoothened with sandpaper and blackened, a *kalam* is used to chisel the required design, and then strands of silver wire are hammered into these grooves. If the design is chiseled into larger patterns, small pieces of silver and brass cut out from sheets are pressed in.

A black colour is given to the surface and rendered permanent by rubbing it with a mixture of earth and ammonium chloride after heating it slightly. When burnished with oil, the inlay is revealed.

Bidri uses a rust-proof and non-corrosive metal alloy which is believed to be an ingenious innovation introduced at Bidar.

This form of decoration is often worked on round containers such as bowls, as well as caskets, jewellery boxes and other small boxes and includes delightful combinations of fine lattice work interspersed with floral clusters, leaves and flowers.

There are two principle techniques - tarkashi (inlay of wire) and tehnishan (inlay of metal sheets).

Durrie Weaving

Satrangi, sataranji, striped flat weave durries are woven on frame looms in several districts of Maharashtra–which is one of the largest cotton-growing states of the country.

The weavers of the Maniyar community weave three types of durries–plain flat weave shataranji, jainamaaz, prayer mats, with single or multiple prayer niches, and chindi or rag durries.

They are woven in various sizes. Chindi durries are being woven by displaced mill workers from the Vidarbha region who have been assisted and trained by NGOs to produce these rugs. Cotton durries are used as floor spreads to sit or sleep on, and as prayer mat with the prayer niche placed in the direction of Mecca.

Banjara Embroidery

The nomadic banjara communities, who trace their origins in Rajasthan, create beautiful embellishments on cloth.

The Banjara women, locally referred to as Lamani, make symmetrical embroidery by lifting the wrap thread of the fabric with a fine needle and making triangles, diamonds and lozenges, parallel to the weft thread, giving the effect of an extra weft weave.

They specialize in making borders of long skirts that are part of their traditional costume. The base cloth is usually, handwoven madder (red-coloured cloth), over which embroidery is done in yellow, green, red, off-white and black.

Cowrie shells and tassels are also used with the embroidery. Since this embroidery is laborious and time-consuming, it is usually done when the women are free from their main occupation of harvesting sugarcane.

Bamboo Work

Bamboo workers of the Thakur community make baskets, fans, containers and ghoghada or rain shield that are treated to prevent attack from moths and to ensure durability making them popular with the locals.

The technique of basket weaving is similar to cloth weaving. A variety of techniques are used to make shapes.

Thakur, Mahadev Koli, Kokna and Warli are some of the tribal communities residing in Raigad and Thane districts that are engaged in bamboo work.

Brass Musical Instruments

Taal, Jhansh and Ghanta are metal instruments which accompany songs and rituals.

Taal and jhanjh are both circular paired brass percussion instruments played by striking the two heads together.

Taal is a small-sized instrument in which the pair is tied together with a string.

The jhanjh is like a cymbal and used during the community festivals and also during weddings.

They are now made by the sandcasting technique though until some years back they were made by beating the metal into the required shape.

Sawantwadi Crafts

Sawantwadi is famous for the craft of lacquerware, which was introduced here around the end of the 17th century. Various schools teaching this craft were started in Sawantwadi during the 18th and the 19th centuries.

Many of the artisans were moved from nearby Goa. The Sawantwadi lacquerware is now available in a wide range of products and concentrates on traditional hand painted and lacquered furniture and light fittings.

MSSIDC is the nodal agency for implementation of various schemes for development of handicrafts and to preserve the languishing arts of handicrafts in the State of Maharashtra. MSSIDC implements the schemes for development of handicrafts of the State Government as well as Government of India.

Handicraft artisans can register themselves with MSSIDC. MSSIDC also undertakes periodic surveys to register artisans. In addition to giving prime display space for selling at MSSIDC's Trimourti Emporia and annual exhibitions, MSSIDC provides training to next generation of younger artisans and supports artisans through assistance.

West Bengal Handicrafts

The immortal inheritance of Indian culture has moulded its artists of the people, joyful exciting, intricate in imagination, intuitively creating, but each with individuality of its own.

This is the expression that found birth in the traditional masters of arts and artifacts of West Bengal. Here, cheek by jowl are stacked the wonderful worlds of our weavers, potters, metal-wrights, shell-artists, carvers in wood, bone or stone.

West Bengal heritage of handicrafts is legendary. The exquisite texture of Baluchari sarees, silk and tasar textile from Murshidabad, Birbhum, Bankura, Hoogly and Nadia districts have become the choice of the century.

The fascinating handloom textiles of the same regions as mentioned above are now attracting world-wide attention. Besides the garment materials, jute products, wood and cane products, conch-shell products, brasswares and folk dolls and handicrafts belonging to different schools of art as Dokra art, etc. now embellish a large many drawing rooms.

And these amazing variety of creation, the aesthetic, varied, living pulsating life are expressed in vibrant collections of colour, hue, tone, shape and size.

Textile

Bengal Handlooms

For many centuries, Bengal has been the place where the best of handloom products have been made. It is famous worldwide for the fine fabrics like muslin, silk and cotton.

Different Varieties

There are at least six varieties of Bengal handlooms, each deriving its name from the village in which it originated, and each with its own distinctive style.

The undisputed queen of the range, however, is the fabled Jamdani, which in all its myriad local avtars continues to retain its original grandeur and sophistication.

The original version is referred to as Daccai Jamdani, although it is now produced in Navdeep and Dhattigram in West Bengal.

Daccai Jamdani

Daccai Jamdani is distinguished from its mutant cousins by its very fine texture resembling muslin and the elaborate and ornate workmanship.

In Bangladesh, weavers use fine Egyptian cotton, while the Indian weavers use only indigenous raw material. The single warp is usually ornamented with two extra weft followed by ground weft.

While the original Bangladeshi sari is almost invariably on a beige background, the Indian weavers are a little more adventurous in their choice of colour schemes.

The gossamer thin black Jamdani with its splash of multi-coloured linear or floral motifs sprinkled generously all over the body and border and crowned with an exquisitely designed elaborate pallu is a feast for the eyes.

The Daccai Jamdani is woven painstakingly by hand on the old-fashioned Jala loom, and many take even up to one year to weave a single sari. It feels supple to the touch and drapes gently to reveal the contours of the wearer.

Other Jamdanis

While the Daccai Jamdani is strictly a party affair, the other Jamdanis are much sought after by fashion-conscious working women for their elegance.

These are mostly Jamdani motifs on Tangail fabric and are generally known by the confusing nomenclature of

Tangail Jamdani. Although beige background is the most popular, these are available in a riot of colours, at affordable prices.

Tangail, Dhoneokali, Shantipuri and Begumpuri are other popular styles of Bengal handlooms in the lower price range. Of these, Tangail, which comes from Fulia, has a fine texture, with its 100s count fabric and highly stylized motifs, while Dhoneokali is known for its stripes and checks.

Artistic Leather Craft

A fine example of contemporary art and craft, the Bengal leather crafts owe their widespread popularity and development due to some innovative work done by gifted artists at Santiniketan.

Brass & Bell Metal

A many-splendoured craft of West Bengal was handed down to generations of metalworkers. From domestic utensils for everyday use to vessels for observance of rituals, the emphasis is always on strength of form.

Copper, one of the earliest known metals was transformed into alloys like bronze, brass and bell metal by Indian metallurgists of Harappan times.

Archaeological evidence indicates that Bengal's metallurgists too were practicing the art and science of metal workings as early as 2nd millennium B.C. Artisans of Bankura, Bishnupur, Ghatal and Chandanpur in Midnapore, have a superb lineage of shaped and engraved brass and bell metal work.

Cane & Bamboo

From the depths of time and the earliest chapters of civilization, comes a craft that endures. Bengal's very own tradition in creating everyday and fancy articles from bamboo and cane, is rich and varied. More than 35,000 artisans practise this craft in different districts of rural Bengal.

Wood Carvings

Wood is widely used for making toys and decorative panels. Kalighat dolls & Natungram wood carvings are worth mentioning. Image made in wood relate back to traditional icons & deities–some of them stylised to a modern look.

New materials and innovative techniques are being used by the artisans to produce useful and aesthetic products. Folk motifs and ingredients are being effectively used for a greater market.

Ceramic

This is a radition built up in contemporary times–several centuries of interaction with foreign craftsmen and a legacy left us by many years of British rule.

The craft, however, is today flourishing in and around Calcutta and in some places in Birbhum district.

New ceramic technologies have joined hands with a heritage of handicrafts to produce a range of fine, glazed ceramic products for decoration, dolly, toys, wall-hangings, household pottery and industrial applications.

Clay Dolls

Clay fantasies of real-life stylized, sometimes even graphic in their representations, mark traditional Indian clay dolls and toys. But the dolls and figurines of Krishnanagar in Bengal, are unique in their realism and the quality of their finish.

Patronized by Maharaja Krishnachandra himself in the late 18th century, they truly represent a breakaway from the traditional form.

Dokra

Nomadic tribes who roam the earth restlessly–what permanence do they leave us with, as a mark of their passage?

The Dokra or Dhokra group of tribal craftsmen who range through the landscapes of Bengal, Orissa, Madhya Pradesh and Andhra Pradesh – give us a timeless heritage of beautifully shaped and ornamented products of cast metals.

The Bikna group of Dokra artisans of Bankura and the Dariapur group of Burdwan were rehabilitated in the nineteen sixties. There are similar concentrations at Kharagpur in Midnapore and Malda.

Horn Work

The early pages of Indian civilization are full of descriptions of 'horn combs' which adorned the tresses of women in ancient times. In shining black and translucent shades of greys, Bengal horn work is still a fascinating craft.

Jute Products

Jute, the 'golden fibre' has traditionally been woven and knotted and braided by women of Bengal, often for domestic storage. Jute as a fabric was much popular in ancient times.

Today Bengal is not only a major producer of jute goods ranging from plush jute-blended carpets, to decorative tapestries, garden pot hangings, decorative handbags, bedspreads and more.

In 50 villages of the Kaliaganj area in West Dinajpur, the process of colouring, weaving of jute on single looms goes on, as the world outside turns once again to this wonderful natural fibre.

Masks & Puppets

Once upon a time, priests masqueraded as gods, demons or spirits. Sorcerers and wizards wove their spells. Today, they are more popular as items of interior decoration.

In Bengal, masks used by the Chhou dancers of Purulia and those who perform the Gambhira dances of Malda, actually represent the theatrical tradition. While the masks used in devil dances and other socio-religious festivals of Darjeeling and Tibet, are colourful relics of priesthood.

Papier Mache

Papier mache is not a craft traditional to this state. The Santiniketan School of artists did some pioneering work in introducing this craft in West Bengal.

Today quite a number of craftsmen in and around Calcutta have taken up the craft and their products mainly dolls and masks, have found a market for their beauty in designs and excellence in craftsmanship.

Sandalwood Carving

Once upon a time, elephant tusks were carved into great and tiny delicate pieces of art by master craftsmen of Khagra and Jiaganj in Murshidabad district.

But then, the elephant population stood threatened, ecological disaster became imminent and so a ban came upon ivory. That did not stop the wizardry of the craftsmen. Their deft fingers found the aromatic, oily sandalwood as an ideal substitute. And so, those legendary ivory creations grew in sandalwood.

International Textiles & Garment Fair is the first one-stop opportunity in India for textile professionals and exporters to discover what West Bengal has to offer. ITGF'99 is an unprecedented, high profile extravaganza, where hundreds of weavers and craftsmen come together to meet industry and trade participants and interact on the intricacies of production and concepts that can sell.

Arts and Crafts of Andhra Pradesh

Handicrafts have always been a remarkable feature of Indian art and crafts. Andhra Pradesh is yet another great site offering ample astounding handicrafts. The artisans still make these extraordinary handicrafts with dexterity.

Whether it is needle craft or bronze castings, metal craft or stone craft, Andhra Pradesh has a wide array of handicrafts that can become a part of your lifestyle.

The eminence of these handicrafts lies in their traditional method of creation. These handicrafts are loved and adored not only by Indians, but people from all parts of the world. Many inhabitants of the state still rely on the handicraft industry.

Andhra Pradesh is a land where handicraft lies in the heart and soul of people. From carvings to bronze castings, brassware, metal and stone work, Andhra people have created a special placc in the field of art.

The most famous thing here is the use of pearls in various designs of jewellery. And it is Hyderabad, which is well-known for this form of art.

Apart from this, Andhra Pradesh is full of various forms of crafts from nomadic and gypsies. One of them is Bidri craft, which is known to be the silver inlay on metal. There is also a use of vibrant colours in the handicrafts that goes with the lifestyle of people.

The crafts of Andhra Pradesh also have a place of artistic brassware, such as statues and carvings on brass and bronze.

Another art form to be checked out is Kondapalli toys. These toys are designed from softwood (Tella Poniki) with tamarind seed powder, sawdust and water colours. After the toys are carved on wood, the paste of tamarind, wood and sawdust is applied to gives various shapes.

Each and every handicraft form in Andhra Pradesh is well-known for its exclusive style. And this tends to bring close the customers and appreciators of all age groups.

The range of handicrafts is absolutely fantastic at Andhra Pradesh. They hold a special place in the culture and tradition of the state.

Handicrafts

Some of the most exquisite handicrafts are found in Andhra Pradesh. Many of them evolved from within the state whereas some were brought by the people coming to this magnificent state.

Banjara Needle Crafts (Embroidery)

The embroidery and mirror work, created by the 'banjaras' (Gypsies) on fabrics, have become a popular part of wardrobe in India. These people employ their dexterity in needle craft and create incredible designs on clothes.

The embroidery of this form is live and vibrant. Banjaras in Andhra Pradesh display their colourful lifestyle through their exuberant clothes. This work of art is known for its intricate and colourful designs.

Metal Works

There are different types of metal works practiced in Andhra Pradesh. Bronze works and brassware done in the state are famous all over the country.

Statues of gods and goddesses are made of bronze and for other metal crafts, brass is the main metal.

There is a form of metal work called Dokra which is prevalent in a small village called Adilabad. It is famous for the fact that no two items are similar and each has its own speciality.

Statues of tribal gods and figures of many animal are the main features of this art form. Another uniqueness of Dokra is that although it is primarily made of brass, it has a clay core inside the metal casting.

Pembarthi is another small village in Andhra Pradesh that is known throughout India for its exquisite brass handicrafts.

Bidri Craft

This craft belongs to the the city of Hyderabad in Andhra Pradesh. It basically involves silver inlay on metal, which is very exquisite. There are many legends related to its entry and exit into the country and then to Andhra Pradesh.

Bronze Castings

The famous bronze idols were based on the verses from the Shilpashastra. These verses were called dhyana. These verses instruct the craftsmen about the physical measurements, proportions, description of the deity, characteristics, symbolism and above all, aesthetics.

Budithi Brassware

The Budithi Brassware originated from a small village called Budithi in central Srikakulam, a district in Andhra Pradesh. This place is famous for creating beautiful shapes out of alloys. These shapes are also available in modern as well as antique style.

Pembarthi Metal Crafts

Pembarthi is a small village located in the state of Andhra Pradesh at about 100 kms from Hyderabad. The village is famed worldwide for its unmatched brassware tradition. This meticulous brass work art flourished during the reign of Kakatiyas empire.

Durgi Stone Craft

The famous Durgi stone craft originated in the Durgi. It is situated 10 kms from Macherla in Andhra Pradesh. There is a school of sculpture and stone carving located here, which imparts this ancient skill. Some of the masterpieces of Durgi stone craft is found at the Nagarjunakonda museum.

Kondapalli Toys

The famous Kondapalli toys are made of softwood, known as Tella Poniki. These toys are also made up of sawdust, tamarind seed powder, enamel gums and watercolours.

After the toy is carved on the wood, a paste made of tamarind, wood and sawdust is applied for giving further shapes and attaching limbs etc., to the toy. This art form belongs to the Kondapalli district of Andhra Pradesh.

Lacquer Ware

The lacquer craft is widely found in Etikoppaka in Andhra Pradesh. This place is one of the major centers of this craft.

The lacquer craft involves the application of lacquer on wood in pleasing shades to create a distinguishing appeal.

Folk Paintings

The start of painting in Andhra Pradesh has the most interesting legend behind it.

It is said that Lord Narayan was meditating when celestial dancing girls tried to disturb him with their beauty and grace. To teach them a lesson, Lord painted a portrait of a nymph. The portrait was so beautiful that no woman in heaven and earth could match the beauty of the lady in the painting. The celestial dancers were all put to shame when they saw the painting.

Lord Vishwakarma was then instructed on art so that he can impart the knowledge to people of earth.

The earliest paintings were all related to mythology and religion, which slowly started to change with time. Though tough to find nowadays, long painted scrolls are the most prized possessions of an art lover. You can find such scrolls in Cherial in Warangal District.

Nirmal Arts–Paintings & Toys

The Nirmal art is generally found in the Nirmal town, Adilabad district of Andhra Pradesh. Here, many craftsmen known as Nakash reside. They are involved in Niramal arts, in which scenes from the Hindu epics, Mahabharata and Ramayana are painted.

Veena Manufacturing

At Bobbili in Andhra Pradesh, the oldest musical instrument, Saraswati Veena is manufactured. This instrument is mentioned in almost all ancient texts. It is an integral part of Carnatic music, famous all over the world for its melody and harmony.

Handlooms

The handlooms of Andhra Pradesh are of excellent quality. It is also famous for its fine saris all over the world. Every region of the state has its own style and weave.

Chirala Textiles

The textiles of Chirala are quite famous. The Chirala textile is made by using a large quantity of oil, which is used in preparing yarn for weaving. After the fabric is ready, it is wrapped with wax & clay before being dyed in selected colours.

Dharmavaram Saris

The Dharmavaram in Andhra Pradesh is famous for silk saris all over the world. These saris are specially worn on functions. They have simple, plain borders without much contrast.

The borders of these saris are commonly broad having brocaded gold patterns. The borders also have butta and the pallus of the saris have exclusive designs.

Eluru Carpets

The Eluru in Andhra Pradesh is famous for its woolen pile carpet industry. This art from was brought to India by the Persians who migrated to Andhra Pradesh during the Muhammaddin regime. Later, they developed the carpet industry here.

Gadwal Saris

Gadwal located in Andhra Pradesh is famous all over the world for its beautiful saris. The body of the Sari is cotton whereas the border and pallu are in silk. The cotton and silk fabrics are woven separately and then attached together.

Ikat Weaving Handlooms

This is a skill that requires a lot of intricacy. It is a style of weaving, where the yarn is randomly dyed in natural zigzag or geometric patterns.

The Ikat weaving originated in Nalgonda district of Andhra Pradesh. This internationally acclaimed weaving form is now practiced mainly in Puttapaka, Pochampalli and Chautuppal villages of Andhra Pradesh.

Kalamkari and Block Printed Fabrics

Kalamkari is the art of painting on fabrics using a pen. The name kalamkari is derived from 'kalam' meaning pen and 'kari' means work.

Like all other art forms, this too started with designs of religious importance such as images of Gods and scenes from mythology.

The art also flourished under the temple guardianship where it was kept alive.

Earlier the colours for the designs were extracted plants like indigofera anil and rubia tinctorum, but now, artificially synthesized indigo and alizarine are used.

The main areas in Andhra Pradesh where Kalamkari is done are Machilipatnam and Srikalahasti.

The Kalamkari is a fabric famous all over the world for its beautiful vegetable colours used on the clothes. These fabrics include a range of special mythological designs for Hindus, prayer carpets for Mohammadans, tent lining cloth, chintz, table clothes and curtain clothes printed in attractive colours. This art form is found at Machilipatnam in Andhra Pradesh.

Mangalagiri Sarees

The Mangalagiri saris and dress materials are made from Mangalgiri cotton, which is quite popular here. Mangalagiri, located 12 kms from Vijayawada is also an important pilgrimage center in Andhra Pradesh.

Uppada Sarees Handlooms

The Uppada saris are produced in Uppada, a beach town located 20 kms from Kakinada. It is famous for attractively designed cotton saris. At Peddapuram, 20 kms from Kakinada one can buy delicately designed silk saris created by local artisans.

Budithi Brassware

In Srikakulam district, Budithi is a small village that is known for its astonishing brassware.

The items carved out of alloys range from traditional to modern ones. The exclusive art articulates in the form of traditional utensils and contemporary pots. Brass is commonly used to make the objects.

These objects are adorned with geometric patterns and floral designs.

Durgi Stone Craft

Durgi is a small town, located at a distance of 10 km from Macherla.

The traditional skill of making sculptures is still practiced and taught at the School of Sculpture and Stone Carving situated here. From generation to generation, these skills have been passed and the ancient methods are still observed to create the masterpieces of art.

Hyderabad Pearls

Hyderabad is one city that is extremely modern while still keeping its age old culture and traditions alive. Pearls in Hyderabad have been a part of Hyderabad since the time of Nizams. The rich Nizams got interested in Pearls and brought in the most expensive and exclusive pearls from all around the world.

Since then, Hyderabad is famously referred to as 'Pearl City of India'.

There are different types of pearls which are distinguished according to their shape and luster. The pearls are then used in various ornaments like bracelets, necklaces, earrings, rings, etc.

You can pick the best pearl-studded jewellery as a purchase from the many famous pearl shops in the Charminar shopping market which have been in operation since many years.

There are not many states in India that come close to giving the same kind of variety and same level of quality. The culturally rich past of Andhra Pradesh is still very evident in the arts and craft items, which gives a very exclusive feel to it. Tread through the traditional markets of Andhra Pradesh and gift yourself some exquisite memorabilia to take back home.

Goa Handicrafts

The handicrafts in Goa are of various types and are mostly made with the help of naturally available materials like clay, sea-shells, paper, bamboo and brass.

In fact, the handicraft division in Goa has attained extraordinary proportions mainly because of the workmanship, organization and skill of the craftsmen. The other reason for the flourishing of this division is because of the boom of tourism in Goa.

With the number of tourists multiplying in Goa, there has been increase in the rush to carry back traditional Goan souvenirs. The government too has taken steps to further the cause of crafts in Goa.

For this purpose, the Government of Goa has set up the Goa Handicrafts, Rural & Small Scale Industries Development Corporation Limited (GHRSSIDC). Now some 1,000 craftsmen are employed in about 500 units.

The uniqueness of Goan crafts lie in the background of Goa's chequered history.

The crafts of Goa mirror has influences of Hindu, Muslim and Christian origins. However, the crafts do not mirror the distinctive elements of the different cultures; rather, they present a unified artistic amalgam.

Apart from the materials mentioned above, wood, lacquer, jute, fabric, stone and coconut shells are also used to create some truly exquisite works of art.

Handicrafts of Goa are the most valuable assets of the beach state, which are not only ethnic, but their creative merit surpasses many costly trendy items of the present age. Goanese are very good at carving out showpieces out of natural stuff like coconut husk or palm leaves.

The items made by these craftsmen in Goa are made available at the Handicrafts Emporium in Panjim, tourist hotels, and other souvenir hubs.

Goa does not lag behind as far as local arts and crafts are concerned and with the superb craftsmanship of the local artisans, has managed to carve out a niche for itself in this highly competitive field.

Goa Hub presents a special feature on handicrafts of Goa, all for you. The local craftsmen in Goa, design articles from coconut husks, palm leaves, brass and wood, and colour them with vibrant coloured paints to make them eye-catchy.

These hand-made articles or handicrafts are amongst the prime attractions of Goa. These handicrafts not only contribute to the livelihood of the local people, but also play a vital role in Goa tourism.

Brass Work

While on a trip to Goa, you may see several artisans moulding brass into various designs and shapes. These items may include hanging oil lamps, statues, candle stands, ash-trays and the most famous handicraft of Goa, the lamp samai (a tree-like oil lamp with flower motifs). These artisans are considered geniuses at the art of moulding brass by hands, with such simplicity and tremendous beauty, which even modern techniques fail to achieve.

Goa's artisans mould brass into various designs and shapes. Some of them include a hanging oil lamp, statue, candle stands, ashtrays and the most famous handicraft of Goa, the lamp samai that is a tree-like oil lamp with flower motifs. The art of crafting brass metal still surprises modern techniques in simplicity and beauty even though it is generations old.

Wooden Lacquerware

In Goa, this art also known as 'wood turning', is a century old. Here, a variety of attractive toys and decorative-cum-utility items are created with great skill after special wood is manipulated. Some of the items created include corner stands, baby carts, cradles, etc.

Paper Machine

In this art, waste paper is put to good use and colourful items used in daily life are made such as jewellery boxes, wall hangings, pen stands and flower vases.

Terracotta Pottery

One of the arts that continues to lend character to Goan homes and in which each art piece is known for its artistic finish is terracotta pottery. It includes items such as pen holders, decorative flower pots, floral designs, ashtrays and figurines of saints and gods and it is also one of the earliest arts known to mankind.

Woodcarving

This intricate art that has adapted well to the changing times and is constantly evolving is one of the best examples of eastern and western influences on Goan culture. Items such as photo frames, idols, mirror frames, book shelves and boxes are carved by the Goan craftsmen today.

Seashell Craft

Beaches in Goa are a shell collector's delight and seashell craft has become a full-fledged art with recent design innovations. Some of the items produced are chandeliers, lampshades, curtains, coasters, mirror frames, ashtrays, etc.

Coir Products

Do not forget to buy the specially knotted mats, hand-made hats, masks and tough ropes made from cocnut husk. These coir products are considered one of the oldest handicrafts in Goa. The locals are expert in extracting husk from coconut shells. This natural substance is also used in making ashtrays, lamp shades, coasters, chandeliers, curtains, pot hangers, table mats, mirror frames, shopping bags, ladies purses and other traditional items.

Jute Macrame Craft

Jute, a cheap natural fibre composed of cellulose (plant fibre) and lignin (wood fibre), is often used by the craftsmen of Goa to design decorative bags, belts, wall hanging, lamp shades, flower pots, hangers, shopping bags, ladies purses, etc. Jute materials form the most unique crafts of India as jute is considered the best fibre in terms of strength.

Bamboo Craft

This art springs from the extreme rural areas of Goa by the Mahar community and is believed to be one of the oldest arts. Bamboo and cane crafts can be used as decorative items in houses. Earlier, this art was limited to bamboo carriers and baskets which were specially designed for the farmers and fishermen. These baskets were used to carry coconut, rice, paddy, fish, flowers, and the like.

As Goa turned into a major tourist hub, this art introduced several decorative items like flower pots, baskets, pen stands, lightweight furniture and letter holders.

Once you explore Goan beaches or the interiors, you find a majority of tribes indulging in the activity of making beautiful handicrafts. These crafts also include:

Crochet and Embroidery

Hand-made tablecloths, children and ladies garments, pillow and cushion covers, linen, curtains, etc. from thin cotton or silk threads form a part of this.

Other Crafts

Some of the other crafts in Goa include embroidery, crochet, jute macram–derived from an old lace form, fibre tone carving, batik prints, coconut carving that is a figure from a coconut shell, silver and imitation jewellery, fabric collage, cotton dolls and soft toys, metal embossing, wooden tapestry and artistic weaving.

Goa is well known on the world ornithology circuit as it has more than 400 bird species. Some of the commonly seen birds are cuckoos, pigeons, buzzards, eagles, ospreys, kites, doves, kestrels, kingfishers and woodpeckers. Most of the birding sites are near the Western Ghats forest, the paddy fields, river estuaries and beaches along the coastline. It has now become a very popular spot with professional bird-watchers from abroad, mainly UK, Scandinavia, and Denmark.

The attractiveness and stunning beauty of these hand-made items compel the visitors to buy them. All these items collectively contribute towards employment for the villagers and tribes of Goa.

The Goa Handicrafts, Rural & Small Scale Industries Development Corporation (GHRSSIDC), initiated in 1980, is the organisation that encourages and promotes the handicrafts of Goa and makes them available in various outlets.

Handicrafts of Karnataka

Karnataka, the state having rich cultural heritage, presents an enchanting range of objects of arts and crafts.

The craftsmen create masterpieces out of mere wood, metal, fabric or just good earth which capture hearts of millions. The patronage of the Maharajas for centuries, these traditional crafts are preserved, developed and promoted by the state.

Many great dynasties left their imprint upon the aesthetic development of Karnataka's art forms. The variety offered is really astonishing with presence of exquisite sandalwood carvings, intricate inlay work on rosewood, splendid bronzes, beautiful bidriware, colourful lacquerware toys, ethnic durries, batiks, stone-studded jewellery and incense sticks.

Arts and crafts of Karnataka always have been an inseparable part of people's life. Karnataka is among those states that still employ traditional methods for producing their arts and crafts.

In yesteryears as well, Karnataka has been the hallmark of excellence in craftsmanship. This is evident from the numerous temples that are present in Karnataka. They are living examples portraying the skills that the people of that era possessed.

The magic of hands has been passed down to the younger generation and that is visible in the paintings and other art works.

It is not one place that is excelling in this aspect, almost every part of Karnataka is famous for one thing or the other. like, Mysore is renowned for its paintings and silk apparels, Udupi is famous for its metal works. Many institutes have started in Karnataka where masters in different forms of arts and crafts impart their knowledge to upcoming artists.

Wood Works–The Craft of Wood Carving

Karnataka has come to occupy pride of place in the field of wood carving. Holding a vast densely populated forest reserves, the State provides enough raw material for its craftsmen who continue to employ age-old techniques for carving, inlay-work, coating, painting and lacquer articles in wood.

Ancient temple wood architecture is the foremost specimen of wood carving where wood has been used extensively and carved finely into delicate sculptures.

The ceilings and gateways of royal homes and the temples showcases hundreds of intricately carved images of gods and goddesses. Rosewood articles are a shopper's delight and tourists take home with them articles or sculptures carved out of rosewood; beautifully carved rosewood elephant being most famous of all.

Mysore craftsmen have acquired expertise in wood inlay-work making exquisite articles delineating picturesque beauty, tranquil scenes and lot more. The Maharaja's palace in Mysore and the mausoleum of Tipu Sultan in Srirangapattna are the foremost specimen of master craftsmanship where visitors get stunned by the startling delicacy in the work.

Woodwork in Karnataka has come of age in the last few decades. The most impressive work of wood can be seen in the numerous temples that adorn the face of Karnataka.

The intricate carvings done on the wooden ceilings and doors are simply remarkable. The craftsmen still use the traditional methods for carving and giving finishes to their works.

Idols of gods and goddesses are the most common works in wood that one can see in every household. Karnataka has a rich cover of forest which proves to be a good source for the raw material.

Rose wood articles are the most famous among tourists as well as people who can afford it. Don't forget to pick a well crafted rosewood image for yourself.

Ivory Carving

Ivory carving is another popular craft prevailing in the entire state. Articles carved delicately without excessively ornate image adjoining the figures, mostly showcase the figures of god and goddess. Some of Mysore's masterpieces in ivory are now preserved in the Heritage Museum in Russia and in the South Kensington Museum, London.

Stone Carvers

Shilpis, the stone carvers of Karnataka, are supreme of all, having won the master craftsman awards at the national level while others have been assigned to carve stone idols for Hindu temples abroad, especially in the USA.

Sandalwood Craft

Talking about sandalwood, Mysore charms the fragrance of this soft wood which is extensively used to produce beautiful art pieces. There are vast range of sandalwood product carved by highly skilled workers, the gudigar families of Shimoga, Uttara Kannada and Mysore districts specialize in this craft. Krishna images are very popular among the devout, besides articles like lamp shades, trays, jewel boxes, decorative articles, combs and even walking sticks with rosewood handles.

Mysore Silk

Mysore silk, with its unique sheen and regal look, amazing drape, pure yarn and zari, has held its own among all other silk fabrics from India and abroad. The contribution of Karnataka to India's silk industry is significant.

Karnataka's more than 200-year-old silk industry owes its origin to Tipu Sultan who ruled Mysore. He showed a very personal interest in sericulture and also established 21 centers in his dominion to rear the silk.

The very word silk has fascinated man for many centuries. It has become an inseparable part of the Kannada culture and tradition. No ritual is complete without the participants wearing silk in some form or another.

Today, Karnataka alone is contributing 75 per cent of mulberry silk to the nation's production. Presently, it is the Karnataka Silk Industries Corporation (KSIC) which holds aloft the State's supremacy in silk and silk products, from classy dress material, stoles, and furnishings to the most resplendent of saris. Silk is the main export material from Karnataka and Mysore is the main center for the production of mulberry silk in the state.

Mysore became the main center for silk as early as in the reign of Tipu Sultan. He was very much interested in the practice of sericulture and brought silkworms from Bengal. He set up more than 20 silkworm rearing center, giving Mysore a new industry.

And since then, it has only been on the rise. Like in other parts, Silk in Karnataka as well is used mainly for the production of silk saris. Although, shawls made of silk are also hugely popular in India.

Doll Making

Doll making is another craft famous in Karnataka evenly arranged on wooden platforms, decorated and displayed during the nine day Dusshera. Kinnal and Gokak in North Karnataka and Channapatna in the Bangalore/Mysore are famous for doll-making. The art of making puppet has galvanized many wood artisans and painters to produce a variety of puppets. Besides puppets made of wood, Karnataka also makes leather puppets which are more extensively used.

Metalware

Metal works in Karnataka is not confined to any particular area or city. While some regions are famous for bronze casting, others are known for bell metal works.

Bidar in Karnataka is a famous for bidriware–a craft done on a metal plate of zinc, copper, tin and lead. Bidri articles include ornamental jugs, bowls, plates pen holders, candle sticks and even paper knives. Nagamangala near Mysore is famous for its bronze items and Mangalore in the west coast boasts of domestic articles made of bell-metal.

Metalware in Karnataka has a rich and ancient tradition, Udupi–the temple town is famous for its small images and ritual objects, while Karkala–an ancient Jain center, is well-known for its Jain icons.

Metalwork industry is an important part of Karnataka people as numerous families are involved actively in it. Many articles for religious purposes are made of metal.

Karkala, famous for Jain statues and Udupi, are the major centers for such works. Mangalore is famous for the bell metal works and Nagamangala is famous for bronze casting. Most attractive pieces of bronze work are the human figures made out of it.

Mysore Paintings

Mysore Paintings are probably the oldest form of art works that have been carried onto the present era. Paintings in Mysore started way back in Ajanta period.

Rule of Vijayanagara dynasty was a major boost to and turned out to be a boon for this kind of painting. King

Mummadri Krishnaraja Wadiyar was the noted personality who worked towards the betterment of this art form.

The paintings are still made the way they were done in the earlier periods. Bright vegetable colours, lustrous gold leaves, and precise lines is what makes the Mysore paintings so unique and exquisite.

Fabulous Mysore paintings of Karnataka are another attractions that dates back to the carving of Ajanta caves. The soft lines, the smooth and elegant drawing of figures the sagacious use of bright vegetable colours and lustrous gold leaves, make the traditional paintings of Mysore very elegant and attractive and most demanding in international market. Chitrakala Parishat in Bangalore, showcasing masterpiece collection of old paintings, also runs a school teaching the art of traditional painting.

Recently, many institutes started by master painters, impart the knowledge and skills to the younger generation of artists so that they can increase the glory of Mysore paintings around the world.

The above description shows that, in Karnataka, the work of 'art' and 'craft' is evident in every sphere as even the objects of daily use, like the earthen pot, greatly portray the magnificent work of art.

The extensive magnitude of Karnataka's arts and crafts is easily to be seen in the palaces, royal homes and elite bungalows of the bygone era. It depicts the elegant delicacy and sense of supreme craftsmanship. Karnataka craft tradition has been followed through ages from father to son, which has encouraged and continuously helped to hamper a vast variety of handicrafts with their high degrees of perfection.

Government has set up many agencies and even design centers for encouraging handicraft designing that has ultimately resulted in upgrading of many craft traditions.

In the past, craftsmen of Karnataka have won many accolades from the kings and queens for their scintillating works. And today, their works are earning recognition around the world for the same magnificence. Just tread through the famous market streets to get the taste of this exquisiteness.

Assam Art & Craft

The richness of the art and handicrafts of Assam beautifully reflects the bountifulness of its culture. The craftsmen here have long perfected the art of creating wonderful objects from very ordinary products. The craftsmen make several handicrafts apart from the famous silk fabric and cane and bamboo products. Different regions of Assam are known for their different forms of art and handicrafts.

The people of Assam have traditionally been craftsmen from time immemorial. Though Assam is mostly known for its exquisite silks and the bamboo and cane products, several other crafts are also made here.

Cane and Bamboo

Practised since time immemorial, making products from cane and bamboo is a popular art form in Assam. Bamboo and Cane are grown in abundance here, and hence, most of the household articles in the homes of Assamese are made of cane and bamboo.

Even some of the houses are completely made from these natural products. Cane baskets, music instruments, jaapi (sunshade) and several other accessories are fashioned out of bamboo and cane.

Cane and bamboo have remained inseparable parts of life in Assam. They happen to be the two most commonly-used items in daily life, ranging from household implements to construction of dwelling houses to weaving accessories to musical instruments.

Handlooms

Silk fabric of Assam has earned immense recognition from all over the world. Several types of silk are available here but Muga silk occupies a prized place in the world of silk in Assam. It is produced in plenty here. Assam is home to the largest number of weavers in India. Beautiful and durable silk fabrics are available here.

Assam is the home of several types of silks, the most prominent and prestigious being muga, the golden silk exclusive only to this state. Muga apart, there is paat, as also eri, the latter being used in manufacture of warm clothes for winter. Of naturally rich golden colour, muga is the finest of India's wild silks. It is produced only in Assam.

Metal Crafts

In Assam, two types of metal crafts are available – bell metal and brass metal. They are not only used for making utensils and other household items but also for jewellery. Hajo and Sarthebari villages of Assam have established their names in the world of metal crafts.

Bell-metal and brass have been the most commonly used metals for the Assamese artisan. Traditional utensils and fancy articles designed by these artisans are found in every Assamese household. The xorai and bota have in use for centuries, to offer betelnut and *paan* while welcoming distinguished guests.

Woodcraft

Assam has always remained one of the most forest-covered states of the country, and the variety of wood and timber available here have formed a part of the people's culture and ecomony. An Assamese can identify the timber by touching it even in darkness, and can produce a series of items from it.

Masks

With tribal art and folk elements form the base of Assamese culture, masks have found an important place in the cultural activities of the people. Masks have been widely used in folk theatres and bhaonas with the materials ranging from terracotta to pith to metal, bamboo and wood.

Masks are an integral part of the art and culture of Assamese. Cultural activities like dance involves the use of masks. The masks are made of wood, terracotta or metal.

Toys

A wide variety of toys are made in Assam – clay toys, pith toys, wooden toys, bamboo toys, cloth toys and clay and mud toys. The most famous themes picked up for making toys are bride, groom and animals.

The toys of Assam have been broadly classified clay toys, pith, wooden and bamboo toys, and cloth and cloth-and-mud toys. While the human figure, especially dolls, brides and grooms, is the most common theme of all kinds of toys, a variety of animals forms have also dominated the clay-toys scene of Assam.

Pottery

Pottery is an amazing art form practised here from ages. The kumars and hiras are two traditional potter communities of Assam and while the kumars use the wheel to produce their pots, the hiras are probably the only potters in the world who do not use the wheel at all. They make incense holder, clay pots and several other decorative articles.

Pottery is probably as old as human civilisation itself. In Assam, pottery can be traced back to many centuries.

Jewellery

Assam is famous for its gold and silver jewellery. Other metals are also used for making jewellery.

Gold has always constituted the most-used metal for jewellery in Assam, while the use of silver and other metals too have been there for centuries. Gold was locally available, flowing down several Himalayan rivers, of which Subansiri is the most important.

The moment you step in Assam, you get to notice the different forms of arts and crafts that are prevalent in the state. Every single item that you see on the walls and windows of homes are a perfect example of the state's tradition in arts and crafts. You must have seen similar items produced in other parts of the world as well, but none are as original and creative as the articles you find in Assam.

Handicrafts of Kerala

Handicrafts of Kerala are either hereditary occupation or practised by amateurs who have great interest in art.

Kerala has the tradition of making beautiful handicrafts with ivory, bamboo, palm leaves, seashells, wood, coconut shells, clay, cloth, metals, stone etc.

Many old handicraft classics can be seen in palaces, old heritage homes, museums, etc. The artists are experts in making beautiful flower vases, ashtrays, ornamental plates, jewellery boxes, miniatùre boats, elephants, idols, kathakali masks, embroidery works, etc.

The ornaments, head gears and costumes for classical arts and ritual arts are entirely made by artists expertised in handicrafts.

They make all necessary materials for kathakali, theyyam, mudiyettu, koodiyattam, etc. They use the locally available turmeric, powdered rice, powdered leaves of acacia etc. for making excellent colours and combination of colours for painting faces of performers, which is a very good example of handicrafts of Kerala.

The handicrafts of Kerala are the flag bearers of their inimitable and glorious cultural heritage. It also reflects a society that is deeply religious. This is evident in the hundreds and thousands of Lord Krishna, Goddess Saraswati, Goddess Lakshmi, Lord Ganesh and the enigmatic Nataraj–in all his dancing frenzy–idols carved in rosewood and sandalwood. Kathakali, the colourful dance drama comprising histrionics, dancing, singing, dating back to the seventeenth century also finds representation in full-size moulds. The models of the famous snake-boat races of Kerala, steeped in mythological folklores, are also coveted souvenirs.

Brass and Bell metal Lamps

Kerala is famous for its metal art. In tandem with its cultural and religious roots, bell metal is used in casting several mythological events like the 'tandava dance' which is popularly known the 'gaja tandava' or 'gajasamhara' where Lord Shiva vanquishes a powerful demon.

Metal as a media of expression by the craftsman weather it is for creating objects to meet the religious commitments or for meeting the domestic necessities of common man, has the tradition going back to the second millennium B.C.

The studies also revealed that the metal alloys have been in use for workshop art in India from time immemorial, perhaps as old as lamps, bells and other temple requirements and utensils to meet the customary requirements of the public and are yet another form in which the metal craft is practised mainly in Kerala.

Angadipuram, Payannur and Trivandrum are the places to visit to acquire one of these Kerala trademarks.

Bell metal is an alloy of brass, tin and copper. Besides being used in churning out idols of deities, it is also used in fashioning out lamps in all sizes, household utensils like jugs, 'varpus', 'urli', that are an integral part of their tradition and binds their lives. Irinjalakuda and Trivandrumare are famous for their bell metal artisans.

Mirrors made out of polished metal are another marvel of craftsmanship and the place to check this out is a village called Aranmula near Chengannur.

Coconut Shell

Of all the materials used for carving, coconut shell is the hardest medium. Consequently, high degree of skill is required for carving coconut shell items.

The usual items of manufacture are cups, flower vases, snuff boxes, sugar basins, nut bowls, powder boxes and spoons. The brass broidered coconut shell articles which have come into existence is an admirable deviation from the usual coconut shell carving.

Ever since the Arabs took interest in the brass broidered coconut shell hookahs, the trade had maintained a certain continuity. The craft is mostly concentrated in Calicut district.

The shells are cut into proper sizes or shapes by using a handsaw. Specially made chisels are used for carving the shells.

Coir and Cane Products

Though Tripura is the most famous state for its bamboo products, Kerala churns out exquisite rattan and coir mattresses, painting adorned mats, floor furnishings and a host of other colourful and eco-friendly goodies. This should not come as a surprise as coir products form one of the most important cottage industries. Kollam and Calicut are renowned for coir products.

Rose Wood

The large number of temples scattered throughout and the doors, windows and ceilings of most of the ancient houses are testimonials of high level of craftsmanship and tradition of rosewood carving. Statuettes and relief work were of a high order of perfection in wood craft.

The main theme of carving in those days was drawn out of mythology. With the cessation of the temple building activities in the state by 18th century and urged by the necessities of the modern society, the ancient wood craft of Kerala took a surprisingly new form to carve items like elephant, tiger, deer, etc. in different poses to suit as paper weight, book ends, lamp stands, etc.

Decorative furniture was produced in large quantities besides the individual ones to suit to figures with realistic appeal of different tastes.

Ivory Work

The carving of the ivory is another example of the traditional art of Kerala. Besides the predominant mythological characters that forms fodder for the artisans, a wide variety of ivory carved showpieces are also cherished as mementoes.

The craftsmen often use buffalo horns for their art. Working wonders with the wood comes naturally to a group of highly talented artists who borrow generously from their music and dance tradition. It may, however, not elicit a favorable response from the PETA folks.

Lacquerware

Metal and woodcraft join hands to churn out exquisite decorative lacquerware. Rosewood and sandalwood are carved out in different shapes and sizes and given a lacquer finish and the final showpiece is adorned with precious metals. This art thrives in the Ernakulam district.

Sandalwood Carving

The fragrant sandalwood is carved into a host of products, including ashtrays, decorated boxes, candle stands, and figures of elephants, rhinoceros and Kathakali dance postures, and so on.

Alike the rosewood carving industry, this industry is also primarily concentrated in Trivandrum, Trichur, Ernakulam and Cochin.

Textiles

The land of Kathakali and coconuts has earned a place for itself on the world map for the exquisite collection of textiles. The flowing silks, kancheepurams and such other items are among the must buys.

Wooden toys

Besides chiseling wood for carving out mythological characters, wooden toys are also among the sought after souvenirs.

Nettor Box

These boxes are traditionally used for preserving the kathakali costumes. These are normally being painted for artistic appeal. Brass cut out design and hinges fitted for these boxes to use them are used for keeping valuables known as 'abharana petti'. Mainly, rosewood is used for manufacture.

Screw Pine

Screw pine mat weaving is one of the major cottage industries in Kerala. Three types of mats are woven with screw pine leaves.

As regards the history of this craft, it can be said that screw pine mat weaving has existed for more than 800 years.

Embroidery on screw pine mats is a commendable deviation from the ordinary cloth embroidery.

These craft concentration areas are Karunagapalli taluk of Kollam district; Mavelikkara & Karthikapalli taluks of Alappuzha district; Thazava, Vachrai and Vallikunnam panchayaths and some villages in Thiruvananthapuram & Kottayam Districts.

Horn Carving

Horn carving in Kerala has been in existence from time immemorial. The craft is mainly concentrated in Thiruvananthapuram. Artisans belonging to viswakarma community are mainly practicing this craft.

A wide range of utility and decorative items like flower set, birds, animals, combs & cigarette cases, etc. are made out of horn.

Bamboo Reed Paintings; Bamboo Mat Paintings

Bamboo mat painting is one of the major craft which requires more concentration and devotion as well as an artistic mind with the craft person.

Most of the paintings are gods, goddess, animals, birds, scenery, etc. in different sizes and in attractive colours.

The craftpersons initially make mat of required size as canvas for drawing the sketch according to the required painting, finishing with bamboo reed frames at bottom and top with a tag for handing to complete the painting.

Lace and Embrodiery

Essentially, an alien craft, this industry was introduced sometime early in the Christian era by a colony of Syrians who settled in Kerala.

The present form of embroidery is of a recent origin and it is believed that the London Mission Society gave a start to it during first quarter of the 19th century.

The main concentration for embroidery and lace work are Eravipuram, Changanassery, Kottayam, Pala, Parrasala, Trissur and Cannoor.

In the matter of pillow lace, the entire lace work is done by passing fine thread attached to wooden pages around pins fixed on a cardboard, while in embroidery work, the designs are first drawn on the cloth by hand or copied through a stencil.

The embroidery work is done only after selecting the different colours to form an attractive pattern.

Laminated Wood Craft

The laminated woodcraft originated in and around Ernakulam district in Kerala around 1975. Rosewood, plywood, whitewood and brass metal pieces are the main raw materials used in the craft.

The rosewood and whitewood are cut into required sizes and pasted on the plywood pieces according to the various designs by using araldite as adhesive. After drying, the entire piece is fixed into the lathe machine for turning.

Generally, sheenlac is used for final polishing. The brass metal pieces are fixed in different designs to make the final product ready. The product rarely includes anjali face, dancing lady, peacock, candle stand, star wheel, kathakali heads, wheel of furniture, key stand, and butterfly, etc.

Joint Wood Articles

Having recent origin, this craft is only concentrated in and around Quilandi of Calicut District.

Rosewood, coconut stem and soft wood (karimuruku) are the three varieties of wood used as raw material for making the laminated joint wood table mats.

The wood is sliced into small sizes of diamond shape by using table saw machine, holes are made crosswise, jointed together by using nylon thread to form the mats of different shapes and sizes.

The mats are given a coating of mansion polish by using cotton cloth and after sometime rubber to get fine finishing. Star mat, flower mat, oblong mat, stripped mat are the most popular designs.

The laminated joint wood table mats are used as table mats as well as wall decorates.

Rather than an art, the handicrafts have evolved into a small scale industry in Kerala. The making, domestic selling and exporting are increasing and now there are many institutes giving training in handicrafts.

Tamil Nadu Handicrafts

Tamilnadu has a rich history of culture and tradition that has evolved over centuries. Perhaps, the most profused flowering of the Tamil culture is in the handicrafts of Tamilnadu.

The famous arts and crafts of Tamil Nadu, in its earlier stages were highly influenced by the temple economy that prevailed for a long time in this part of the country. These rich temples of the region were like budding ground for the craftsmen who used get constant construction work in these temples and helping them to regularly upgrade their knowledge and experience.

Flights of fancy are tempered by tradition. Imagination and creativity find expression in the skill of loving, caring, disciplined hands. The crafts of Tamilnadu speak with subtle beauty. They add grace and beauty to lifestyles the world over.

By ceaselessly promoting the various ethnic art forms, simultaneously preserving antique artifacts from Chola and Pandya dynasties by reproducing their replicas, Tamilnadu has become a world-known destination for pilgrims of art in search of fine handiworks of India, such as life-like stone sculptures, celestial figures in bronze, brass lamps, rosewood carvings, sandalwood carvings, countrywood carvings, Tanjore art plates, Tanjore picture paintings, and much more. Herein, we have collected brief descriptions of major handicraft specialities of Tamil Nadu.

Many items typically found in Hindu temples such as wooden, silver and golden chariots, wooden ornamental doors, kavachams, vahanams, bells, idols, dwajasthambams, silver sheeting work, gold cladding work on copper sheeting work, gold/silver kavasams for deities are sold in various handicraft centers of the state and central government.

Pattamadai mats

These beautiful reed mats crafted out of korai grass with cotton or silk in the weft are made in Pattamadai village in Tirunelveli district of Tamilnadu.

The traditional colours used are red, green and black and the weaves range from medium colour to 140 counts in the silk or pattu mat. The old pattern consisted mainly of stripes at the two ends or streaks through the body.

Design inputs by modern designers has led to the making of contemporary mats which are greatly in demand both in the international and national markets.

Today, apart from the sophisticated pattamdai pai, Pattamadai weavers also craft korai grass shopping bags, place mats, runners, office folders, etc.

Kanchipuram Saris

The gorgeous and very popular Kanchipuram silk saris which weavers claim descent from sage Markanda have distinctive designs such as sun, moon, swans, peacocks, etc., woven into the body in gold thread and characteristic contrast borders.

The very distinctive pallav has a different wrap and is often woven separately and joined to the body.

The best of kanchipuram saris have a rich repertoire of delicately wrought designs, a thick sensuous feel and outstanding woven borders in gold or intricate threadwork.

A contemporary look is achieved with less density of motifs or introduction of a new colour pallete.

Jewellery

Just like other parts of the country, Tamil nadu has its own traditional jewellery–especially, the stone-encrusted jewellery, which reached its peak here.

The ornaments, which are popular here are the oddiyaanam (gold waist belt), vanki (armlet) and jimiki (eardrop), which are traditionally crafted and finished with great dexterity.

The jimiki is a bell-shaped ear jewel set in coloured stones with pearls hanging at the lower end, and hangs from the lotus shaped kammal of diamonds or rubies worn on the lower lobe of the ear.

Other beautiful jewel that Tamil women wear are maattal, adigai, maangaamaalai, thaali or mangalasuthra, kaasumaalai, puduchcheri golusu, and gajja golusu.

Chola Bronzes

The ancient craft of bronze or "panchaloha" casting of icons which reached its apogee of excellence under the Cholas is done by the cire per due or lost wax method.

The icon is first made in wax and three layers of clay applied on the wax model which is then allowed to dry. When perfectly dry, the clay-coated mould is heated over an open ground oven and the molten wax forced out through appropriate holes in the icons.

When the mould is completely drained of wax, molten metal is poured into the mould and allowed to set. The mould is broken after a few days and the bronze icon emerges.

Chiselling, detailing and polishing follow. The icon is then complete, the only one of its kind in creation.

The best bronze icons are still made in the old Chola centres of Swamimalai, Madurai and Tiruchirapalli strictly according to shilpa shastra rules.

Tanjore Gold Leaf Painting

Featuring the pantheon of Hindu gods and goddesses and stories from Ramayana and Krishna leela themes, the classic Tanjore paintings present perfect harmony and rhythm in composition and blending of colours.

The speciality of Tanjore paintings, which originated in the courts of the Marhatta rulers of Thanjavur, lies in their ornamentation.

Gold leaf, gilted metal pieces and semi-precious stones decorate and embellish the figures on the paintings.

The best of Tanjore gold leaf paintings are available in Chennai where traditional artists with an eye to authenticity and detailing reproduce superior Tanjores using the original vegetable pigments.

Famous Paintings of Tanjore

The well-known Tanjore paintings are the most important handicrafts of Tamil Nadu. These paintings painted on wood, glass, mica, ivory and on walls, are defined by the use of thin sheet of gold along with primary colours, stylized modeling effects by shading the inside of the contours. Jewels, drapery and architectural elements like finely executed pillars, rich canopies, garlands of ropes and chandeliers are slightly raised by the use of special plaster covered with pure gold leaf and embedded with semi-precious stone of different colours.

Painting on ivory, mica, and the more difficult genre of glass paintings, were all introduced in the 18th century. Whereas the religious paintings are highly decorative and flat, the paintings of the women are highly conventionalized with an element of reality infused in the portraits.

Pottery

The famous art of pottery has been practiced here from ancient times, which is expressed in the manufacture of the famous Ayyannar horses.

The horses are said to protect each village from evil. The large terracotta horses are made in Salem and Pudukottai.

The horses were originally made and fired individually. But with increasing popularity of terracotta art items, the moulds began to be put into use.

Papier Mache

In Tamil Nadu, waste paper pulp is hand beaten into a soft substance mixed with local clay to be rolled out into thin malleable sheets.

Life sized dolls, scenes from the epics, icons of gods and goddesses, masks and animal forms are among the many colourful papier mache toys handcrafted in Tamil Nadu.

After fashioning the form of the article out of papier mache pulp, the articles are dipped into a thin solution of paper pulp and white clay and then painted in oil or water colour.

Stonecraft

Through the ages, the best talent in stone craftsmenship went into stone carving of images and structures made for the temples by hereditary sthapatis belonging to the vishwakarma community.

The stone icons are carved by the sthapatis according to the precise measurements, proportions and rules of shilpasastras.

One can see the best of Tamil Nadu's stonecraft skills at Mahabalipuram, the superb chiselling, detailing and even humour in Arjuna's penance with Arjuna standing in the traditional penance pose on one leg, arms upraised surrounded by a cat standing in the same pose as Arjuna; by a stag scratching its nose, etc! The traditional icon making of Tamil nadu has been given a new lease of life at the Mahabalipuram School of Traditional Architecture.

Today, Mahabalipuram is full of units creating granite and soapstone sculptures both religious and secular, garden lights, nameplates, etc.

Pottery

Vellore in North Arcot district is famous for black and red earthenwares. Usilampatti in Madurai district has black pottery painted over with a special yellow substance which has an old tradition.

Panruti in South Arcot is famous for a large variety of claywork that include small and large figures of deities, toys, etc.

Karigiri in South Arcot is most famous for its unique style of pottery. The base of this pottery is made with a local semi-vitreous white low fusing china clay with high plasticity known as namakatte — as it has been used for nama — cast mark.

The distinctiveness of this type of pottery lies in its highly artistic shapes, original colours in glazes and excellent ornamentation.

Every article of this type of earthenware is distinctive. Even the very common clay pipe chillum is made into a noteworthy item both through its elegant shape and its deep blue or green glaze.

Other noteworthy items are water jugs, tableware items including tea and dinner sets, ashtrays, beautifully decorated flower vases and decorative animal figures made as paperweights.

Pottery from Karukurichi in Tirunelveli district is popular for its technical superiority and novel and attractive shapes.

Red, black and grey clay are used for the base. This clay body looks brighter after a coating of red ochre. This is done for all common items of use.

Woodcraft

In Tamil Nadu there are a number of places noted for wood craft. Virudunagar is famous for the traditional style. It has now started making articles for household use.

Devakottai and Karaikkudi make traditional panels in different sizes. Small shrines finely carved with wood known as kavadi have exquisite designs and serve as votive offerings to the deity that devotees carry on their heads as they go singing or chanting.

Panels from some of these old kavadis are detached and are now used as wall decorations. Nagercoil and Suchindram have traditional carvers who also make figures.

Madurai is famous for its rosewood carvings. The style is marked by its bold forms, the details being minutely and painstakingly worked out.

Tables with the top covered with floral motifs or lovely parrots or panels with epic scenes are most outstanding examples of this type of craft.

Embroidery

The Toda women of the Nilgiri region have evolved a very rich distinctive style of embroidery called pugar which means flower.

Geometrical patterns are stitched on long shawls called poothkuli that are worn in Roman style by the menfolk. The designs are mostly symbolic ranging from floral motifs to animal and human figures.

There is a unique style of applique work done in Tanjore for decoration on temple hangings, especially those adorning the carved chariots used in processions.

They are tubular in form as they hang down the side of the charriot. The designs are appliqued with several traditional signs and motifs including images of gods and goddesses.

Durries

The Bhawani durries of Coimbatore district date back to a couple of centuries. They are woven in cotton and silk.

On a cotton base, cotton stripes or traditional designs are woven and on silk base, the designs are woven in silk.

This place was initially famous for silk durries but now staple has taken its place for economic reasons.

Metalware

Nachiarcoil in Thanjavur district is famous for a light brown sand called vandal on the banks of the river Cauvery that is ideally suited for making moulds.

Owing to the growing scarcity of copper, the bell-metal workers of the state have now switched to brassware.

Some of the articles cast are vases in different shapes, tumblers, water containers, ornamented spitoons, food cases, bells, candlestands, kerosene lamps, picnic carriers, and a large variety of lamps.

Of these, a few items like tumblers, food cases and milk containers are in bell-metal and the rest are in brass. A special jar with a cashewnut design and named after it has become a kind of hallmark of Nachiarcoil.

Musical Instruments

Music and dance played an important role in the life of Tamil Nadu. Thus, the making of musical instruments became a major craft, here.

Most of the centers for this craft are situated around Thanjavur, which is also the hometown of many famous musicians of the country.

According to the Tamil classic, the Silappadikaaram, there's an ancient Tamil instrument, the wooden Yaazh in the shape of boats, fishes, and crocodiles, which is similar to the harp or lute.

This instrument has been replaced by the more versatile Veena, made of jackwood. The various parts of this instrument are, the kudam (pot), top plank, neck and yaali.

These are first assembled and a mixture of honey wax and black powder is applied to the top plank. Then it is further processed for completion. In Thanjavur, there are families that are into the trade of manufacturing veenas for generations.

Other musical instruments are the Thamburas with their wooden bases, the flute or kuzhal–a wind instrument associated with Lord Krishna. It is popularly known as Vangiyam, made of bamboo, sandalwood, bronze, sengaali and karungaali woods.

The famous arts and crafts of Tamil Nadu, in its earlier stages was highly influenced by the temple economy that prevailed for a long time in this part of the country. These rich temples of the region were like budding ground for the craftsmen who used to get constant construction work in these temples and helping them to regularly upgrade their knowledge and experience.

North-eastern States

North-East India is the abode of a large number of tribes and sub-tribes. They possess a vigorous craft tradition and every tribe excels in craftsmanship. The superiority manifests itself in the various craft items which stand the evidence of their dexterity.

The crafts of North-East India viz. Arunachal Pradesh, Assam, Manipur, Meghalaya, Mizoram, Nagaland, Tripura have a rich craft tradition that speculates on their creations. Each state presents their speciality in craftsmanship. Arunachal Pradesh presents an ambit of crafts including carpet-making, masks, painted wood vessels, bamboo and cane crafts, weaving, woodcarvings, jewellery. Other miscellaneous crafts like handmade pottery, brass cutting, silver works, etc. are also being presented by the artisans of Arunachal Pradesh. They also make numerous articles with goat hair, ivory, boar's tusks, beads of agate, and other stones as well as of brass and glass.

The crafts of North-East India have a rich variety with the people of Assam having excelled in them. The cyclorama of crafts encompass handloom weaving, cane and bamboo works, sholapith, brass and bell metal works, ivory, wood-work, sholapith, pottery and fiber craft. Handloom weaving comprises the culture of endi, muga and mulberry silk.

The crafts of North-East India have a spectacular range of variety. The artisans of Manipur have contributed to the richness and variety of Indian culture with its peculiar blend of tribal traditions and vaishnavism. Of the numerous colourful crafts of Manipur, their textiles, strong bell metal bowls, cane and bamboo and mats made of spongy reeds can be traced as having rich artistry. One of the states of North-East India, Manipur is also well-known for its gold and gold plated jewellery–earrings, necklace, armlets and bracelets.

Beautiful dolls and toys of straw and clay are also remarkable craftsmanship of Manipur.

The North-East Indian crafts are made wealthier by decent crafts of the Nagaland that incorporate weaving, basketry, woodwork and jewellery making, pot making, products made out of shell and beads, birds' wings and flowers, woodcarvings generally associated with the religious beliefs and practices, apart from preparing objects for daily use, like utensils, etc.

The North-East Indian crafts have been enriched by the distinct craftsmanship of Meghalaya which is known for various art and crafts and is culturally very rich in the area of dance and music as well. Cane and bamboo hold a prime place.

Artistic textile weaving and woodcarving is practiced in Garo hills. Silk weaving of Endi silk is very famous. Carpet weaving, ornaments, musical instruments are other specialities. But the unique craft of this state is Pineapple fiber articles in which fiber from its leaves is utilized for making various types of nets, bags and purses. Being the domicile of a plenty of skilled artisans, Mizoram showcases decent variations in crafts like weaving, bamboo and cane craft, pipes, jewellery and musical instruments, bamboo and cane work.

With a huge number of tribes as its residents, Tripura keeps the tradition of a large array of crafts that adds to the glory of the North-East Indian crafts. Handloom is the most important craft of the state. The foremost feature of Tripura handloom is vertical and horizontal stripes with scattered embroidery in different colours. It is followed by cane and bamboo craft. The well admired handicraft items are bamboo screens, lamp stands, tablemats, sholapith, woodcarving, silver ornaments and other crafts that are practiced. The people of this state follow simplicity as the hallmark as evident from brass and bell-metal articles of Tripura.

The crafts of North-East India has a vast variety as artistry differs from one state to another and each carries a distinct style that stands alone in the Indian market. The culture and the dexterity of the people add variety to the rich tradition of crafts of North-East India and broadly of India.

Handicrafts of Delhi

Delhi is a city full of skilled artisans, who are proficient in handicrafts of the city. Shahjanabad, which we today know as Old Delhi, possesses a rich heritage of handicrafts. This is so because the Mughals were great patrons of works of arts and crafts. You can visit the Matia Mahal's Pahadi Bhojla to see numerous jewelers' shop. These shops are full of exclusively made necklaces and bangles that are carved out of the bones of buffaloes and camels. This is indeed an exotic art form.

Quality has always been the prime concern at Delhi handicrafts. There are quality checks at every step of production. The dedicated team of craftsmen understand the latest trends and makes the jewelery accordingly thus making them all the more demanding in the market. Each of the products is developed under the strict supervision of our quality control personnels. The craftsmen are determined to give good quality products at most competitive prices, thus, enabling them to create a niche for themselves in the market. They are a team of extremely talented craftsmen and designers who work in close coordination, thus delivering the best results in terms of productivity and quality.

Delhi handicrafts has a long and important history and it ideally reflects the culture of India. Different forms of Delhi handicrafts, which have evolved through ages, enjoy great popularity even today.

Decorative lacquerwork on bangles is a very ancient form of art, yet it is still thriving in the city of Shahjanabad. The handicrafts of Delhi also include embroidering on the saris or dresses. Embroidering with golden threads is known as zardozi. The craftsmen of Delhi create exclusive designs on velvet, silk, tissue materials, etc.

The silver paper which we use to cover and protect our food is prepared in Old Delhi. You can visit the Matia Mahal in Delhi where you will find many craftsmen, busy in beating silver in thin sheets by hand. A little searching through the alleys can lead you to those small workshops of great craftsmanship.

The very popular meenakari work is also found in Delhi. It is a work in which the paint is embossed on silver or gold, which makes it appear like a precious stone. The other handicrafts of Delhi include beautiful and attractive pottery. The potters in Delhi fashion wonderful pots to quench your thirst, especially in the hot summers, and also fulfil your aesthetic sense. They also create exquisite clay and paper-mache dolls. These dolls made of clay can be used as decorations, as a toy or even clay idols, at the time of different festivals. The places in Delhi where you can get these indigenous materials are Hauz Khas, Chandni Chowk, Ajmeri Gate, Paharganj and Ramakrishna Puram. You will also find a rich collection of good quality belts in Delhi. They are created in an exclusive style to suit the needs of the young generation.

They are made out of wooden beads and some other materials like stones, etc., and are available to you in different styles, designs, size and in a fashionable outlook. The handicrafts of Delhi do not stop here only. Delhi is a city rich in handmade articles. You will also find perfumes (attars), incense sticks, brass molding, earthenware figures, and many more articles here, which will exude the aroma of a Delhi gone long by.

Delhi handicrafts stand as brilliant specimen of Indian handicrafts as a whole.

Handicrafts Shopping in Delhi

It is important for the tourists to know about best places in Delhi to shop for handicraft goods. Although, these products can be found in almost all parts of the city, there are certain shops that are worth visiting. Some of the most popular handicraft shops of Delhi are Ambapali Bihar Emporium, Bharati Delhi Emporium, Central Cottage Industries Emporium, Indian Handicrafts Emporium, Handloom House, Khadi Gramodyog Bhavan, Amrita Carpets and Crafts, AAR Exports, Concept Handicrafts, Lepakshi Andhra Pradesh Emporium and Asian Handicrafts, to name a few.

Popular as paradise for shopaholics, Delhi is the ultimate destination for handicraft lovers. Since Delhi is home to some of the finest handicraft bazaars, markets, showrooms and government emporiums, you can get the most exquisite and authentic range of Indian crafts. Due to its proximity to Rajasthan, Delhi could be referred to as the next handicrafts hub in India. The Delhi handicrafts and handlooms include exclusive textiles, artifacts, and antique jewellery. Most of the handicraft showrooms in Delhi are stacked with the widest range of khadi fabrics, chikankari work sarees, handmade jewellery with precious and semi-precious stones, stone carvings and hand-knotted carpets.

Delhi Haat, Sri Aurobindo Marg, Opposite INA Market: Located in South Delhi, it is an ideal place to spend some time while admiring the great array of handicrafts, jewellery, garments and artifacts representing the workmanship of almost all parts of the country.

Delhi Haat is one of the best places in Delhi to shop for amazing handicraft products. Coming to this market, the tourists can actually grasp true essence and rich heritage of Delhi handicrafts. The visitors are simply fascinated with the wide variety of artistically crafted products that is sold in this market. Delhi Haat acts as a platform in between the craftsman and the buyers. Different types of handicrafts products are sold in this market such as nicely decorated camel hide footwear, sandalwood and rosewood carvings, draperies, zardozi and embroidery work, gems metal craft, brassware, potteries and many more.

Ambapali Bihar Emporium, Baba Kharak Singh Marg: Located in Central Delhi, it is a house of handicrafts & handlooms of Bihar. Madhubani, a popular art form of Bihar, can be sourced from here.

Delhi Emporium, Baba Kharak Singh Marg: One of the prestigious emporium, it has a mix of handicrafts, sleek wooden-carved furniture, leather handbags and apparels, alongwith a modest range of delicate jewellery, precious and semi-precious stones.

Central Cottage Industries Emporium, Janpath: Popularly known as Cottage Emporium, this is the largest store of exotic and authentic Indian crafts. The Indian handicrafts and handlooms include exclusive textiles and articles sourced from artisans and sold at fixed price.

Handloom House, Connaught Place: An undertaking of the Government of India, the shop's speciality is handlooms. Here, you can choose lovely chikankari work sarees and suit fabrics, handloom shirts and stylish silk scarves for men. A large variety in ikat prints are also available.

Indian Handicrafts Emporium (Near Qutub Minar): An award winning emporium, it is a treasure house of Indian culture, art and crafts articles. It is also one of the largest expository on Indian handcrafted art objects and handmade jewellery with precious and semi-precious stones.

Khadi Gramodyog Bhavan, Connaught Place: A newly constructed multi-level swanky showroom in Central Delhi, Khadi was Mahatma Gandhi's favourite fabric. Here, you can find everything related to khadi textile. 10% discount is available for the 90 day period starting with Gandhi's birthday on October 2nd.

Lepakshi Andhra Pradesh Emporium, Baba Kharak Singh Marg: A complete house of handicrafts and handlooms from Andhra Pradesh, here you can get a change to pick from an exclusive range of Dharmavaram, Pochampaili, Narayanpet, Magalgiri, Venkatgiri silks and cotton sarees.

Amrita Carpets and Crafts, http://www.indiamart.com/amrita: It is a professionally managed organization in South Delhi. They are manufacturer and exporter of pure silk carpets, hand-knotted carpets, woolen carpets, durries, furniture/exclusive stone carving & traditional handicrafts, precious and semi-precious jewellery and much more.

Indian Tribal Craft

Indian tribal craft is an astounding section in modern Indian times, which slowly has taken a cosmopolitan appearance. The final get-up that such tribal crafts receive to adorn and deck sophisticated Indian city homes, can perhaps only be described after a thorough admiration. Indian tribal crafts are available in every area of decoration and embellishment, with numerous irresistible choices, heightening ones urge to buy tribal goods.

Crafted to perfection, such tribals crafts leave one spoilt for choice. The amount of pressure and physical exertion that goes to make an item look dazzling, is manifest through the daily lives of tribal aborigines.

Some of the numerous tribal crafts manufactured in India include: antiques, art, baskets, papier mache, ceramics, clock making, embroidery, block printing, decorative painting, glass work, fabric, furniture, gifts, home decor, jewellery, leather crafts, metal crafts, paper crafts, pottery, puppets, stone, and wood works.

Indian tribal crafts verily mirror the lives of their users, their food and its source, their observances to pacify indefinite forces which incorporate their arts and crafts, music and dance. Majority of Indian tribals inhabited in far-off forests and had kept distance from the nearby agricultural villages. The confrontations and combats that ensued in the following years, made the tribals recede to other hinterlands and resort to other professions, like fishing, hunting and cattle-grazing.

Religion plays a dominant role in tribal day-to-day life. It is wholly expressed through art and reflects its use in their crafts. Indian tribal craft is generally ritualistic, rubbing off a distinct line between the artist and the art lover. It is encased within the consciousness of the tribe and transforms according to developments in the tribe.

Tribal crafts are dependent on the local plant ecosystem. For instance, the use of bamboo for making bows, arrows, vessels and habitations doubtlessly lent to the conservation of bamboo grass. Implements, like the digging stick and bow and arrow, canoes and boats, dwelling houses, each an essential craft item, were dependent on plants and trees.

The other popular raw material used by Indian tribals in their craft-making is mud. Mud is in fact utilised in umpteen artifacts, like, pottery, storage jars, figures of deities, votive offerings, decorations and burial urns and other objects.

One of the bare essentials, tribal habitations are constructed of mud. Fascinatingly, clay images are moulded not of the deity but as offerings to the deity. Terracotta is yet another material that can be seen in regular usage in tribal crafts in India. The figures are a central part of a total ritualistic portrayal of the rites of passage.

What tells apart Indian tribal craft is the quality of usefulness which is integral to its creation. Whether it is a pot to carry water, a storage jar, a bow and arrow, a basket to carry goods or a votive offering, the object always has a role to play, a purpose intrinsic to its creation and existence.

The shapes and forms of tribal crafts are, fascinatingly, deduced from basketry, as are the ornamentations on pottery. Basketry is the most popular and available of tribal crafts, being highly diverse, with its origins impossible to outline.

Indian tribes have rich craft traditions which are as diversified as the basketry of Arunachal Pradesh, metal casting of Madhya Pradesh, terracotta votive offerings and decorations of Gujarat. In this regard, the tribes of the Nilgiri Hills deserve a special mention with their astonishing and crafty works in Indian tribal craftwork.

Although each tribe of the Nilgiris is fully integrated, there is a distinct delineation in their craft production, making them essentially dependent on each-other.

The Todas are the most enthralling and captivating tribe of the Nilgiris. The Toda women are expert in coiffing an intricate embroidery on the surface of plain cotton material. Their embroidery consists of geometrical designs such as zigzag bands, triangles, squares and dots. The embroidered cloth is utilised as a shawl and is named as a putkuli.

Todas also wear intricately patterned silver jewellery. The Todas serve as the leading band in Indian tribal crafts, with expertise in cane crafting. The most noteworthy is the multi-forked churning stick used in their dairy-based traditions. One end of a long cane is split into multiple forks and covered with a bud-like structure. Used in their funeral rites, they mould a cane twig into an non-figurative buffalo head as a substitute for buffalo sacrifice.

Indian tribal crafts rests heavily on the Kotas, legendary as musicians and serving as essential manufacturers of musical equipment like hard drum, tambourine and brass cymbals resembling oboes. This particular instrument is beaten with a suck and pipes. Kotas are expert musicians and the only artisans in the Nilgiris. They are professional blacksmiths who make iron implements both for household as well as agricultural usage.

The Kotas also manufacture iron knives and bill hooks. They manufacture ropes and umbrellas from buffalo hide, jewellery like anklets, rings and necklaces out of brass and necklaces from glass beads and cowry shells. Kotas are also expert potters who use the wheel to develop clay vessels out of the locally offered black clay. To this, they add white clay in equal proportions to create masterpiece.

Sometimes they glaze the end product to develop glazed pottery. In comparison to the Kotas who are the most crafty people amongst all the Nilgiris tribes and receive payment in kind, the others sink into irrelevance.

The Irulas, yet another tribe creating history in Indian tribal crafts, make and use the conch, drum, dwarf pipe (kwale), long flute (buhin) and nagasore in their dances for rain and fine harvest. While they manufacture glass bead necklaces and brass earrings and anklets, their striking craft is the plaited palm leaf straw ornaments, used as necklaces and anklets.

The Panlya tribe possess very few crafts, music or dance. They use the drum (thudi) and musical horn (cheemam) for ritualistic ceremonies. They are the labour caste among the Nilgiri tribals. The Kurumbas and Mulla Kurumbas are hunter-gatherers, also noted for their basketry. The Kattunayakan, another hunting tribe, are collectors of wild honey and wax.

With the exception of the Todas who are lacto-vegetarians, all the others are devoted hunters. The common weapon is the bow, manufactured from bent bamboo and rope and arrow. Other implements encompass wooden ground-digging sticks and plain tools. The basketry items include woven triangular head cover (as a defend from rains), carry-baskets with handles for gathering minor forest productions and bulky baskets for storage.

The natural environment of the Nilgiris, has undoubtedly impressed upon material culture in Indian tribal crafts profoundly. The hilly terrain, intense rains, cold winters and constant fear of elephants have kept their crafts simple, light and ordinary. Bamboo is the most important material, followed by clay, wood, palm leaf and metal. The last although is rare, owing to the non-availability of raw material.

Unlike tribals in other parts of India like the north-east, internecine wars are rare and even unheard of. Each tribe has a function to perform: the Todas are buffalo herders and supplier of dairy products, the Kotas are artisans and craftsmen, the Irulas serve as hunters, with Paniyas living as labourers and so on.

CHAPTER-7

HANDICRAFTS AND TOURISM

What is the relationship between tourism and the development of handicrafts? One can find intricate, yet positive relationship, between tourism and handicrafts. This is elucidated by means of two case studies–one from the South-Western region of the United States of America and the other one from Thailand.

As far as USA is concerned the studies done by Lewis I. Deitch show – The South-Western part of the USA is inhabited mostly by the original inhabitants of the region– the American Indians. They passed through various phases in their long history. Their multi ethnic stock consisted of the Pueblos, the Apaches, the Navajos, etc. The Pueblos were more advanced and by the early 1600 AD, when they came into contact with the Spaniards, they already knew the arts of pottery, baskets, cotton cloths, jewellery, etc.

The Navajo Indians were less artistically developed but were quick to learn both from the Pueblos and the Spanish. The Spanish introduced sheep in this area and the Navajos took to the domestication of sheep at a large scale. The wool weaving developed as a consequence and by the mid-19th century, their weaving skills reached a high level of excellence.

Apart from the jewellery made from silver, those made of turquoitlse, coral and shell were also developed among the Navajos and Puebles. But the more traditional crafts like pottery-making and basketry faced extinction when the metal pots were introduced by the white people.

The development of tourism in this region heralded a new era in many ways for the inhabitants of this region. It had a great effect on their crafts tradition as well. The sale of the existing handicrafts increased and it encouraged them to go for further refinement to establish their products. We shall discuss now some of their handicrafts and the changes brought in by the growing contacts with the tourists.

a) Navajo Rugs

These rugs were woven by the Navajo Indians, particularly their women folk, from the sheep and goat wool. Initially, with the increasing tourist traffic, the demand for them increased phenomenally leading to the increased volume of production. This led to a decline in the quality of craftsmanship and production of inferior rugs. Due to this, their popularity began to decline and the genuine buyers started to lose interest. This brought the realization among the craftsmen and the merchants that this over-production of substandard goods was doing more harm than good to their trade. Innovations in designs, use of quality raw materials and introduction of new colour patterns infused this traditional handicraft with new vigour and vitality. The prices increased but so did the buyers willing to purchase it at a higher price.

b) Jewellery

As happened with the rugs, the increased demand for various items of jewellery due to tourism caused a deterioration in their quality. At the same time, however, it also promoted distinctive regional styles which led to their nation-wide recognition: The problem of quality was also overcome later on after the stabilization of the market.

c) Pottery and Basketry

These dying crafts of the American Indians were revived under the impact of tourism. Although, they never became as famous as their rugs or jewellery, their demands increased and small pottery pieces became tourist items.

The impact of tourism on the arts and crafts of the American Indians has been quite positive. It has not only increased their earnings but also has led to artistic refinement. The quality of today's products is much higher than those in the 19th century. This impetus has been provided by the growing tourist market. It is true that in some cases, it has also given boost to imitation products which are sometimes sold as genuine items. But, the overall impact of tourism on the local handicrafts production has been positive.

As far as Thailand is concerned, the studies done by Eric Cohen show – In Thailand tourism has developed rapidly. Between 1960 and 1990, the number of tourists coming to Thailand increased more than sixty times. While in 1960 only 80,000 foreign tourists came to that country, in 1973, there were one million tourists and by 1990, the number reached 5.3 millions. This phenomenal growth in international tourism was accompanied by equally significant development, of domestic tourism. The improvement in road system prompted the tourists to move around in cars to various tourist resorts. This increasing touristic activities in various areas induced the Thai Government to promote Thai arts and crafts.

The main traditional craft producing areas in Thailand are located away from the tourist centres and the craftsmen, therefore, were forced to deal with the intermediaries in order to reach the tourist markets. The development of road network, increase in tourist traffic, growing motorization and the helping hand of the government led to the emergence of touristic craft ribbons. These ribbons consist of shops along the roads selling mostly tourist crafts. Although specialization has not developed to that extent as to exclude the non-tourists, the crafts pieces sold from these shops on the ribbon are mostly oriented towards the tourists.

Two types of ribbon development has taken place in Thailand. One is the localized ribbon which develop simply and on a single road. It is, initially, quite short and offers one type of products. This type of ribbon normally links a village to a small town on the main road. The shops along such ribbon are mostly locally-owned. With further development, some heterogeneity is introduced–in the variety of products offered. The shops also show some kind of heterogeneous composition with the outsiders setting up some establishments which are larger in size.

Another type of ribbon is the ramified ribbon. It is longer stretching and more complex consisting of several roads linking many craft-producing villages to the major artery road leading into an urban centre. Such craft ribbons contain variety of shops having heterogeneous products. The shops near the villages are mostly owned by the locals while those on the highway are owned by outsiders.

The growth of these crafts has given tremendous fillip to the production of crafts in Thailand. The volume of production and sale has increased tremendously. Moreover, the craftsmen have benefited from direct interaction with the tourists. The role of the intermediaries has been reduced to some extent.

The tourists have also derived benefits from such interaction. They can now observe the process of craft production first hand and this has made these ribbons as centres of tourist attraction. The arts and crafts of Thailand have gained international reputation and many declining traditional crafts have revived due to the availability of both national and international markets.

It is true that the, role of the middlemen is still important and a large part of the benefit accruing from the increased production and sale of the crafts has gone to them. Nevertheless, the craftsmen and their crafts have also greatly benefited from these developments.

The Indian Story

Bounded by the majestic Himalayan ranges in the north and edged by an endless stretch of golden beaches, India is a vivid kaleidoscope of landscapes, magnificent historical sites and royal cities, misty mountain retreats, colourful people, rich cultures and festivities. Modern India is home alike to the tribal with his anachronistic lifestyle and to the sophisticated urban jet-setter. It is a land where temple elephants exist amicably with the microchip. Its ancient monuments are the backdrop for the world's largest democracy.

Handicraft and tourism sectors are correlated. Handicraft market is a favoured shopping haunt for locals and tourists alike. Souvenirs galore await you and rest assured there is something for everyone.

Start with the cheap trinkets, which make excellent gifts for friends and family. These include keychains, beaded bracelets and necklaces and bookmarks. You will be spoilt for choice with miles and miles of beautiful gorgeous pearl jewellery and handicrafts. You can purchase loose pearls or stunning brooches, necklaces and earrings, available at almost every stall you visit in the vast market of handicraft in whole of India.

For those with an eye for ornate wooden carvings, you have come to the right place. The market has an endless variety of carved crafts, including exotic wooden masks, picture frames and even stunning wall panels. The best thing about the handicraft market in India is that you never know what piece of treasure you might unravel during your visit. The most important tip when visiting the market is to bargain, bargain, bargain! Pick up some local lingo to improve your bargaining skills and you might even walk away a steal.

The Government of India is taking several steps to manufacture and popularise Indian handicrafts. The latest one is the introduction of 'Ladli'–a vocational training program for abused, orphaned and destitute children. For most of these children, the alternative to Ladli is begging, child labour or prostitution. At Ladli, they learn jewellery-making and skills such as tailoring and stitch-work. They also study other subjects, including English, Drawing and Dance. The benefit to the children is far greater than education and employability; they also gain confidence, social skills and self-esteem. Ladli is a place where emotional damage and stresses of extreme poverty can in some way be healed.

The first centre was established for girls in August 2005; a centre for boys was opened in February, 2006 and eventually a centre opened in the heart of city (Hathroi) in August, 2007. These centres are located in Jaipur and are projects of I-India – a local, non-profit, non-governmental organisation whose donors include UNICEF, Finland and the Government of India. Ladli is currently attended by about seventy five girls and fifty boys. The Organisation is expanding every day with its intention to help more and more such people.

The interrelationship between handicraft and tourism industries have great impact on the economy. The handicraft sector contributes nearly six percent to the GDP.

Today, tourism, textiles and costumes are closely linked. One can not separate cultural tourism and textiles. Special visits of tourists are arranged to famous textile centres to give them first hand knowledge about the traditional methods of weaving and printing in India.

Besides, special interest tour/packages are also organised to traditional weaving centres. Specific crafts museums are established where the artifacts are displayed. The famous Calico museum of Ahmedabad, where rare art pieces relating to costumes, textiles, and textile technology, artisans' tools, etc. are preserved, is an important place of tourist attraction.

Handloom is the present day craze. In each tourism promotional brochure, textiles of the particular region forms the foremost place. Even the foreign tourist who come to visit India love to buy Indian handwoven textiles. Increasing demand of Indian handwoven textiles in the world market is an ample proof of the interest taken by foreign tourists in Indian textiles.

When a tourist visits a place, the first thing he/she would like to do is to roam in the market and enjoy watching local costumes and textiles. The increase in the textile demand during the tourist season is clear indicator that tourist is attracted towards the local costumes and textiles. Tourists love to take textiles pieces/garments, etc. as a souvenir for their friends and relatives.

The tourism industry is occupied with roles like that of a leading employment generator, a foreign currency earner and that of handicraft industry's promoter. It is opined that the tourism and handicraft sectors are apparently linked and added that handicrafts greatly attract tourists who look upon them and purchase them as travel gifts or souvenirs.

In India, in the last fifty years, the handicrafts are basically produced for the export market. The domestic market is very small. Nine broad categories of articles have dominated the exports: hand printed textiles, art metalware, woodware, hand-knotted carpets, imitation jewellery, shawls, zari, embroidered goods and miscellaneous handicrafts. Out of these, the share of hand-printed—textiles, woolen carpets, art metalware and woodware are the largest. Their proportion has been the same throughout this period.

Tourism has also helped in the promotion of traditional crafts in India. In Kashmir, which till recently, has been attracting a large number of both the domestic and foreign tourists, the value of handicraft production has gone up.

Similar growth has been witnessed in many areas of Rajasthan, Kerala and the states where growth in tourist traffic has been substantial. Traditional handicraft items from Orissa, North-East region, Gujarat, Maharashtra, etc. have been popularized among both the domestic and foreign tourists.

Despite this potential, we find that India's actual share in world's handicrafts exports has not been upto the mark. It is largely due to:

a) **Lack of proper infrastructure**: The handicrafts production in India is mostly in unorganized sector. Lack of transport and other communication network leads to information gap. So, whenever there is an increase in demand, large quantities of goods are produced without any regard to quality. This lowers the value of the product in the market ultimately damaging the craft.

   At another level, infrastructural problems include problems in procurement of proper raw materials, lack of publicity and lack of literacy and skill in marketing.

b) **Use of outdated tools**: Indian handicrafts are still produced by using centuries-old tools and techniques. For example, Indian potters still use the hand-driven wheel for making potteries whereas the use of mechanised wheel can increase production manifold.

Similarly, the use of mechanised jenny can increase the production of yarn tremendously.

c) **Lack of market research**: Market research is generally undeveloped in the area of Indian handicrafts. The artisans simply go on producing their specialized goods on the demands of the merchants who then decide where to sell these products. Lack of marketing strategy may lead to dumping of goods in one area while they are unavailable in another. This ultimately leads to drop in production and losses to both the merchants and craftsmen.

d) **Middlemen**: A very large number of middlemen are thriving at the.expense of both the consumers and the artisans. They not only artificially hike the prices but also sell fake products in the name of the originals. The artisans normally lack avenues to directly approach the customers. If the facilities are created whereby the producers can have direct access to the market, this will not only benefit the artisans but will make available the genuine and cheaper products to the customers.

Artisanal productions in India have had a very long history stretching back to the Harappan Civilization. It continued to prosper and grow during the ancient and medieval periods reaching great heights under the Mughal rule. It branched out into new areas and developed new specializations.

In the post-independence India, the importance of handicrafts has been well recognized by the government which has made many efforts to promote it. There are, however, many factors such as lack of transport facilities, capital, literacy, market research, new designs, etc. which are inhibiting its fast growth. It is in these areas that the support from the government and non-governmental organisations has become necessary. Moreover, the development of tourism is playing an improtant role in this regard.

Thus, India's domestic handicraft market is lead by sales to tourists. It is believed that the volume of handicraft sales in domestic markets is double than that of exports. Also, the tourists back home tacitly promote handicrafts of the countries they visit.

If you're planning a holiday to India, looking for hotels and accommodation and events information, or simply interested in India as a country, you are sure to find many insights on the multifaceted travel options to India here.The timeless mystery and beauty of India can be experienced only by visiting this ancient Land. There's just one thing you'll need to travel through 5000 years of culture and tradition– a comfortable pair of shoes.

Today, handloom industry is the largest sector. It accounts for nearly 30 per cent of the total textile production in the country. There are about 3.8 million handlooms and about 10 million people depend on them. Thus, with such vast stakes involved, naturally, this sector has to attract the prime attention of the Government of India. Today, handloom sector is an important component of the policy of 'self sufficiency.'

Successive Five Year Plans provided support to the handloom sector.

The Parliament has passed the handlooms Act in 1985. It resulted in the establisluncnt of three regional enforcement offices at Delhi, Pune, and Coimbatore. It also launched an intensive programme for publicity and promotion. For the promotion and development of silk industry, separate Central Silk Board (CSB) was constituted in 1949. Uptil now, CSB has established two research institutes for mulberry in Mysore and Berhampur and one for tasar at Ranchi.

But still, lot more is to be done to protect and develop this sector. Sericulturists face more problems in marketing their cocoons for they are forced to sell the cocoons at the prevailing prices, as the moth emerges piercing out of the cocoon on the ninth or tenth day of the cocoon formation thus rendering the cocoon useless. Still more is to be done to ensure that the real profit reaches the weavers. Weavers also face credit problems. They need to get, both, short-term and long-term loan on easy terms.

Interesting Places to Buy Handicrafts in India

There's something undoubtedly magical about Indian handicrafts. Unique, intricate, eye-catching and expressive, each item has a story behind it. It's impossible to come to India and return home empty-handed. Forget the ubiquitous handicraft emporiums and check out these five interesting places to buy handicrafts in India.

1. Dili Haat, Delhi

When it comes to shopping for handicrafts in India, you can't beat Dili Haat. A joint initiative of the New Delhi Municipal Corporation and the Delhi Tourism and Transportation Department, it's one of the best markets in Delhi. Deliberately made to feel like a traditional weekly village market, Dili Haat offers an exciting blend of inexpensive handicrafts from all over India, food, and cultural and music performances.

2. Kala Madhyam, Bangalore

Kala Madhyam: Kala Madhyam supports traditional (folk and tribal) Indian artists and artisans. From the rugged beauty of Kutch to the ethereal hill country of Arunachal Pradesh, the wide variety of handicrafts at Kala Madhyam come from every corner of India. They include Bastar metal art figures, Manipur black pottery, ceramic and marble sculptures, paintings, jewellery, wall hangings, and clothing. However, the specialty at Kala Madhyam is wall murals.

They are simply magnificent. Don't miss the annual Arts Mela held towards the end of the year.

3. Anokhi, Jaipur

Anokhi: Anokhi was founded in 1970 and is renowned for its high quality, block-printed textiles. In fact, the store is so popular that it has outlets in major cities across India. What makes visiting Anokhi so interesting is the Anokhi Museum, located near Amber Fort in Jaipur. It's at the museum that you'll really get to appreciate the art of block printing. The Anokhi Museum has daily block carving and printing demonstrations, as well as slide shows and short film documentaries on printing and dyeing. One and two day workshops are also on offer for those who want to learn the art. These workshops cater to all skill levels, and you'll get hands-on experience working alongside craftsmen. See the Anokhi Museum website for more information.

4. MESH, Delhi and Hyderabad

MESH: MESH works with groups of disabled artisans, and they produce beautiful handicrafts. Very attractive and well-made items include bags, bed covers, cushion covers, hair accessories, home decor, toys, and cards. MESH has its own Design Studio, where items are developed. Find out more about the handcrafting process in the MESH Design Studio blog.

5. Khazana, Taj Hotels

Sharell Cook: If you're looking for distinctive handicrafts with a touch of luxury, you'll find them in the Taj hotel group's Khazana boutiques. Located at key Taj hotels in major cities across India, Khazana showcases premium handicrafts from leading and emerging Indian artisans. These include finely woven silks and saris, stone studded jewellery, evening bags, paintings, and home furnishings. In Mumbai, the signature store is located at the Taj Lands End in Bandra. There are also Khazana boutiques in Delhi, Goa, Chennai, Bangalore, and Hyderabad. A total of 14 stores are expected to be open by 2011. The first palace store, in the new Taj Falaknuma Palace Hyderabad, promises to be something special.

CHAPTER-8

Epilogue

In India, for instance, the handicraft industry contributes $5.6 billion to the national economy and employs close to 20 million individuals on a full-time basis. Moreover, increasing globalization and the expansion of free trade means that the impact of tourism for poverty alleviation will become even more significant among developing countries.

Tourists travel to learn – to experience personally – with their hands and eyes. The fundamental connection between handicrafts and tourism resonate particularly well in India, with ancient human settlement and abundantly rich culture. Handicrafts instil a sense of hand-made and the unique richness of artisan craftsmanship.

Tourists purchase handcrafted souvenirs to represent their memories of connecting with and participating in other cultures. Through the purchase of locally made items, tourists create craft economy, upon which artisans often depend for their livehoods, encourage the production of natural products and bind communities together. At the very least, every traveller makes the purchase of a souvenir to share what they have learned with friends and family.

The travel industry has also recognized the importance of linking craft with tourism by investing in handicrafts for room furnishings and for lobby, lounge, and spa and restaurant decor. That is why handicraft activities can increase the average length of stay by adding a day or more to a travel itinerary.

Learning and participating have become a paramount element of travel, as proven by the success of study and culture tours and special interest tours with crafts as a central focus. Shopping is no longer simply a form of entertainment, but a link to a foreign culture that greatly enriches the travel experience.

The Pushkar Fair in Rajasthan, Suraj Kund Craft Mela and others like these in India, have become a delightful carnival of culture and crafts, complementing traditional markets. Craftsmen perform skilled and essential repairs, and in a natural way, preserve tradition and culture by making them familiar and popular.

The patronage of tourists helps such techniques survive through sales. Without a market, many traditional skills could eventually fade due to lack of demand. Tourism provides an opportunity to preserve the traditions that comprise the fabric of cultural heritage.

Tourists want to enjoy the shopping experience. They expect to buy a product that relates to their visit, perhaps to a specific site, or that embodies some aspect of the culture they have seen and experienced.

Tourists seek information – guide books with sections on local shopping, maps, trend magazines, and informative, easily downloadable websites. Flight magazines can educate arriving tourists and direct them to featured locations.

A look at the figures on foreign and domestic visitors to handicraft production centres in countries such as India as well as their sales figures indicate that handicrafts are considered as art and cultural symbols of these countries. They can be important factors in attracting tourists, because every piece of handicraft demonstrates the historic, social, and cultural features of a country, region, or location in which it was produced and can play a significant role in introducing original, native art.

There are many reasons to encourage a link between tourism and handicraft production. Benefits can be categorized into three broad groups:

- Economic
- Social
- Sustainability

Handicrafts have much appeal as an economic stimulator with low barriers to entry that enable people to enter this sector with minimal capital and debt load. Government programs to provide seeding loans, training programs and assistance with the legal requirements to establish enterprises often yield positive results.

Crafts enable members of agricultural communities to supplement their income with off-season employment. Importantly, they provide much needed employment and income opportunities for people traditionally excluded from local economies, including women, members of ethnic minorities, young people, unskilled workers, people with disabilities and the elderly.

Crafts may also provide important income streams for museums and historic sites. Handicraft tourism can help diversify local economies, especially in rural areas of the less developed world.

Handicraft production is a socially responsible, sustainable activity that can eliminate much of the exploitation of unskilled workers found in so many parts of the world. As people directly involved in the production and distribution of the handicrafts, workers also have a direct say in how they are treated.

The production of handicrafts allows a number of individuals to benefit from tourism without necessarily having direct involvement in the industry, enabling many people to achieve a balance between home duties and income generation.

Tourism may also provide an alternative market for goods traditionally produced within the community that are now in decline, providing a means of retaining employment.

Further, tourist interest in some handicrafts may foster renewed interest from the local market, leading to a revitalization of some businesses.

Crafts also provide an opportunity for communities to reconnect to their cultural heritage, disappearing traditions, activities and cultural practices.

Creating a positive link between the tourism sector and local communities is a further benefit of handicraft tourism. The industry is increasingly developing a social ethic with many operators in rural communities realizing that they must contribute something back to the community.

The contribution to the sustainable use of heritage assets is one benefit that is often overlooked.

Souveniring of artifacts and the illicit trade in antiquities continue to pose a threat to our collective tangible cultural heritage.

Fostering a craft industry to produce copy relics for sale to tourists enables them to acquire an authentic souvenir, generate income for local communities and conserve cultural heritage in situ, a triple benefit.

While handicrafts and tourism obviously create a variety of synergies that can benefit the resident, the community and the tourist, this practice is not without its risks. Successful and truly sustainable handicraft tourism involves being aware of these risks and developing program to mitigate them.

An over-riding question is who really benefits from handicraft tourism? In some cases, an unequal relationship exists, whereby the consumer and end retailer seem to gain a disproportionate benefit, while the artisan him or herself gains little. The more are the steps in the distribution process, the higher is the end price. But, the artisan may see little of this price. The establishment of co-operatives is one solution that has worked for many aboriginal communities in many parts of India. The co-operatives assume responsibility for all or part of the distribution, and thus, its members retain more benefits directly. But, personal observation suggests that many of them are poorly run and not as profitable as they could be.

Pricing strategies emerge as a second issue. Often, local artisans are unaware of the true value that the consumer places on the handicraft, the retail price charged overseas, base prices of local economic conditions in the tourists' home community apart from having little knowledge of the various approaches to pricing. As a result, they charge a cost-plus price rather than a price that reflects the true craftsmanship and scarcity value of the item. Many handicrafts purchased at source are grossly under-priced. This problem is not unique to handicrafts, but it is common along all micro businesses in the tourism and hospitality industry.

The popularity handicrafts amongst tourists may be a double-edged sword that can lead to increased income, but may also result in the exploitation of the producers. How does the individual artisan cope with high demand for popular items, especially if cooperatives or wholesalers have accepted orders for these items?

Few have the ability to industrialize their production process and so most end up simply working more hours.

Demand pressures may convert an enjoyable part-time activity into a laborious full-time job where the returns do not match the effort.

The generic tourism literature also suggests that craft production can result in the commoditization of culture for tourist use, the trivialization of local culture, the transformation of skilled craftsman into trinket makers and, ultimately to the creation or fostering of ethnic and/or gender stereotypes. Others may suggest that rather than fostering a re-birth of traditional culture, it may lead to the suppression of diversity and to the loss of traditional skills as craftsman and women have to shift their emphasis to the production of the most popular tourist goods.

The theft of cultural identity and traditions poses an even greater threat. Artists with no connection to a community may copy a style of painting or other artwork and may produce 'authentic' goods for the tourist market. Tourists may think they are buying authentic goods from traditional craftsmen when, in fact, they are purchasing copies of art work from people that have no cultural connection to the works being produced. This issue has arisen repeatedly with the production and sale of aboriginal art works of India.

Finally, government also needs to examine its motivations for encouraging communities to become involved in community tourism. Tourism is often identified as an economic opportunity for rural communities not because there is any real tourism potential but because there is little potential for any other activity. Fostering community tourism represents a feel-good, low investment option whereby central governments can be seen to be doing something, and yet in reality are doing little.

Crafts and tourism can form a beneficial partnership that enhances the tourism experience and benefits of local communities. But, such a partnership also creates the potential for the loss of control by the craft workers themselves over the intellectual property rights, production and distribution process.

Successful and sustainable craft tourism must seek to balance the benefits and minimize the risks. Government agencies can play an important role in fostering a sustainable tourism craft sector. In this regard, the need of the time is:

- Encouraging socially responsible tourism as a respect for culture
- Actively working to stop the trade in antiquities by promoting the production of authentic copy artifacts
- Insisting on fair dealing between tourists and locals especially in relation to price
- Assisting producers to copyright and protect designs, or styles of production
- Licensing authentic producers/artisans
- Educating and training artisans in sales and marketing
- Providing a marketing platform
- Selling goods through official outlets in government owned museums, etc
- Stopping the trade of fake goods produced by individuals with no legitimate connection to the heritage being sold
- Increasing consultation with local communities to determine if and how craft tourism can be developed
- Respecting the rights and traditions of minority groups.

Bibliography

Agrawala, V.S., *The Heritage of Indian Art*, New Delhi: Ministry of Information and Broadcasting 1964

Aashi, Manohar, *Tribal arts and crafts of Madhya Pradesh*,1996

Abbasi, Shams, Mrs., *Popular types of Sindhi embroidery*. Hyderabad: Mehran Arts Council, 1966

Abdul Ali, Abul Faiz Muhammad, *The silk industry in Bengal in the days of John Company*. Poona: Indian Historical Records Commission , Vol. 7, 1925

Abidi, Nigar Fatima Home-base production: a case of women weavers in a village of eastern Uttar Pradesh, India. IN Gupta, Amit Kumar editor. *Women and societthe developmental perspective*. New Delhi: Criterion Publications, 1986

Academy of Fine Arts, Calcutta, All India Association of Fine Art Bombay. Exhibition of Contemporary Indian Art & Crafts in the United States of America, Calcutta: International Press 1954

Academy of Fine Arts, Calcutta, *Old Textiles of India,* Calcutta: Academy of Fine Arts, Calcutta 1963

Acharya, G V Acharya, G V, *Catalogue of the Coine in the Prince of Wales Museum of Western India*, Bombay: 1935

Acharya, R. M. and C. L. Arora, *Evolving fine wool braids in IndiaWool and woolen of India*, vol. 9, July, 1972

Ackermann, Phyllis, *Indian Embroidery*, London: Embroidery, Vol. 3, No. 1 1934

Aga Oglu, M., *A fragment of a rare Indian carpet*, Bulletin of the Detroit Institute of Arts, vol.XIII, no.1.October 1931.

Agarwal, S. U. ,*Textiles, Craft horizons*, vol. 19, July, 1959

Agarwala, Virendra, Textiles, ours are the world's best, *Illustarted weekly of India*, vol. 93,1972

Agrawal, Banu, Metalware of Mughal period, *Salar Jung Museum Research Journal*, 21-22, 1987

Agrawal, D. P. , The Copper Bronze Age in India, New Delhi: Munshiram Manoharlal 1971

Agrawal, Yashodhara, *Silk Brocades*, New Delhi: 2003

Agrawal, Yashodhra, The Ganga-Jamuni metalware of Banares, *Salar Jung Museum Research Journal* - 21-22, 1987

Aashi, Manohar , *Tribal arts and crafts of Madhya Pradesh*, 1996

Abayasekara, Anne. ,Curio notes, The batik printing arts of Ceylon." *Arts of Asia*, vol. 3, no. 1 pp. 70-72. 1973

Abbasi , Shams, Mrs. ,Popular types of Sindhi embroidery. *Hyderabad: Mehran Arts Council,* pp. 37-39. 1966

Abdul Ali, Abul Faiz Muhammad ,The silk industry in Bengal in the days of John Company. *Poona: Indian Historical Records Commission* , Vol. 7, 1925

Abedin, Zainul , Amader Shilpakala (Our Arts and Crafts) , Mashik Mohammadi, *Ashar* 1958

Abidi, Nigar Fatima, Home-base production: a case of women weavers in a village of eastern Uttar Pradesh, India. IN Gupta, Amit Kumar editor. *Women and society: the developmental perspective.* New Delhi: Criterion Publications, pp 324-355 1986

Academy of Fine Arts, Calcutta , All India Association of Fine Art Bombay. Exhibition of Contemporary Indian, Art & Crafts in the United States of America,Calcutta: International Press 1954

Academy of Fine Arts, Calcutta, Old Textiles of India, Calcutta: Academy of Fine Arts, Calcutta 1963

Acharekar, M R, *Rupadiarshini : The Indian Approch to Human forms*, Bombay: Rekha Publication. 2nd ed. . . 1958

Acharya, G V Acharya, G V, *Catalogue of the Coine in the Prince of Wales Museum of Western India*,Bombay: 1935

Acharya, Prasanna Kumar, *MANASARA SERIES* VOL. I TO VII.

Acharya, R. M. and C. L. Arora *Evolving fine wool braids in India, Wool and woolen of India*, vol. 9, July, pp 15-21 1972

Ackermann, Phyllis Indian Embroidery, *London: Embroidery,* Vol. 3, No. 1 1934

Adam, Leonhard *Primitive Art*, London: Cassell 1963

Adams, Barbara S *Traditional Bhutanese Textiles* Bangkok: White Orchid Press 1984

Adams, Monni Dress and Design in Highland Southeast Asia: the Hmong (Miao) and the Yao. Washington, D.C.: *Textile Museum Journal*, Vol. 4, no. 1 1946

Adhikary, Swapan Das A bibliographical note on the pat painting of Bengal, Calcutta: Folklore, 1973

Adkinson, Robert *Sacred Symbols: Peoples, Religions, Mysteries.* United Kingdom: 2009

Aga Oglu, M. A fragment of a rare Indian carpet, *Bulletin of the Detroit Institute of Arts*, vol.XIII, no.1.October 1931 1931

Agarwal, S. U. *Textiles Craft horizons*, vol. 19, July pp 20-23 1959

Agarwala, Virendra Textiles, ours are the world's best, *Illustarted weekly of India*, vol. 93.1972

Agrawal, Banu Metalware of Mughal period, *Salar Jung Museum Research Journal*, 1987

Agrawal, D. P. *The Copper Bronze Age in India*, New Delhi: Munshiram Manoharlal 1971

Agrawal, S N & Kar, D P *Saura Paintings of Orissa*. 2004

Agrawal, V.S. *Indian Miniatures : An Album*. Calcutta: Govt. of India 1961

Agrawal, Yashodhara *Silk Brocades*. New Delhi: 2003

Agrawal, Yashodhara. "Benares brocades: varying themes." IN Dhamija, Jasleen, editor. *The woven silks of India*. Bombay: Marg,

Agrawal, Yashodhra The Ganga-Jamuni metalware of Banares, *Salar Jung Museum Research Journal*,1987

Agrawala, R. C. *Glimpses of evidence of ancient handicrafts of Rajasthan based on excavations*, Marg Publcations, Mumbai: Marg, 1964-65, XVIII(1)

Agrawala, R. C. Unpublished sculptures and terracottas in the National, Museum, New Delhi and some allied problems, *East and West*, XVII(3–4), 1967

Agrawala, V. S. References to textiles in Bana's Harshacharita, *Journal of Indian Textile History* - IV: 65-68 1959

Agrawala, V.S. *The Heritage of Indian Art*, New Delhi: Ministry of Information and Broadcasting 1964

Agrawala, Vasudeva S. *A note on the Stavaraka cloth Ancient India*, vol. 4, pp 178-179

Barnard, Nicholas: *Arts and Crafts of India,* 1993, Conran Octopu Limited, London.

Basu, Indrani (7/11/2010). "Crafts village waits for Michelle". *The Times of India*.

Bhandari, Dhingra, Dr. Vandana, Sudha (1998). *Textiles and Crafts of India*. New Delhi: Prakash Book Depot.

Balraj & George Michell, *Human and Divine 2000 years of Indian Sculpture*, 2000

Barber, E. J. W. (1991). *Prehistoric Textiles*. Princeton University Press.

Burnham, Dorothy K. (1980). *Warp and Weft: A Textile Terminology.* Royal Ontario Museam.

B Binyon, Helen (1966). *Puppetry Today*. London: Studio Vista Limited.

Beaton, Mabel; Les Beaton (1948). *Marionettes: A Hobby for Everyone*. New York.

Bhattacharya, Manoshi. 2008. *The Royal Rajputs: Strange Tales and Stranger Truths*. Rupa & Co, New Delhi.

Barnard I Nicholas, *Arts and Crafts of India*,1993, Conran Octopus Limited, London.

Balinese Textiles; Brigitta Hauser-Schaublin, Marie-Louise Nabhollz-kartaschoff, Urs Ramseyer. British Museum Press. ISBN 0-7141-2505-9

Balakrishnan,Usha R. *JEWELS OF THE NIZAMS*. Photographs by Bharath Ramamrurtham.,New Delhi:

Balaram, Padmini Tolat, Anagami Nagas: the brave and the beautifu,l *India Magazine*, 1991-92, 12(11)

Balaram, Padmini Tolat, Textiles that speak.*India Magazine,* 1993-94, 14(2)

Baldizzone, G. & Tziana, *Tribes of India*. Preface by Dominique Lapierre,Text by Pecian Quigley and Vinay Srivastav, 2000

Balfour, Edward G., *The Cyclopaedia of India, and of Eastern and Southern Asia*: Commercial, Industrial, and Scientific. 3 Vols., London,: Bernard Quaritch 1885

Balfour-Paul, Jenny, I*ndigo*.London: British Museum Press (1998)

Baloch, N. A., ed., The Traditional Arts and Crafts of Hyderabad Region:Being the *Proceedings of the Seminar Held under the Auspices of the Mehran Arts Council, Hyderabad*, on May 22, 1966. Hyderabad, Pakistan: Mehran Arts Council 1966

Balraj Khanna & Aziz Kurtha, *Art of Modern India*

Bandopadhyay, Biswanath, *Hira potters of Assam. Man in India*, 1961, XLI(1):

Banerjee, Mukulika & Deniel Miller, *The Sari*. New York: Oxford 2003

Banerjee, N. N, Dyes and Dyeing in Bengal, *Journal of Indian Art and Industry*

Banerjee, Utpal K, *Indian Puppets,* New Delhi: 2006

Banerjei, N. N., Dyes and dyeing in Bengal, New Delhi: *Journal of Indian Art and Industry,* 1897, VII(59): 11-20 (Reprinted in *Art in Industry through the Ages: Monograph Series on Bengal*, Navrang, 1976

Banerjei, N. N., *Monograph on the woollen fabrics of Bengal, Art in Industry through the Ages*: Monograph, New Delhi: Navrang 1976

Banerjei, N. N., The cotton fabrics of Bengal, *Journal of Indian Art and Industry*, 1900, VIII(68)

Banerji, Adris, Phulkari, a folk art of the Panjab, *Marg*, 1954-55, VIII(3)

Banerji, Amiya, *The lacquer craft of Ilambazar, Art in Industry*, 1965, VIII(1)

Banerji, Arundhati, *Terracotta art expression in Indian sub-continent*, Roopa-Lekha, 1984, LVI.

Banerji, R D, Eastern Indian School of Mediaval Sculpture : *Archaeological Survey of India*,.1933

Bansal, Asha, and Sunanda. M. Phadke, *Profile of the traditional handloom shawl weaving industry in Himachal Pradesh*, India, Ars textrina, vol. 301998

Bapu, S., Kolam, the art of housewives, *Asia Magazine,* May, 1962, 27

Barbhaiya, Bihari, *Batik*. Baroda: 1968

Barbier, Jean-Paul, *Art of Nagaland,* Los Angeles: Los Angeles County Museum of Art 14

Barker, Alfred F., *A report on the cottage textile industries of Kashmir and their prospective development.*, Leeds: University of Leeds, 1933

Barker, Alfred F., The textile industries of Kashmir, *Journal of the Royal Society of Arts,* 1932, LXXX(4134)

Barnard, Nicholas, *Arts and Crafts of India*, London: Conran Octopus 1993

Barnard, Nicholas and Gladstone Soloman W E, *Masterpieces of Mogul Art: Essays on Miniature Painting and Architecture under the Moguls*, Mumbai: 1932

Barnard, Nick, *Indian Jewellery,* The V & A Collection. Photo By Ian Thomas, Hangkong: 2008

Barnes, Ruth *Fragments of splendour: Indian resist-dyed textiles* from the P. E. berrCollection in the Ashmolean Museum, The Ash molean, 1992, 22(Spring-Summer).

Barnes, Ruth, *Indian Block-Printed Cotton* Fragments in the Kelsey Museum, the University of Michigan, Kelsey Museum

Studies, Volume 8, Ann Arbor, MI: The University of Michigan Press 1993

Barnes, Ruth, *Indian block-printed textiles in Egypt*: the Newberry Collection in the Ashmolean Museum,Oxford New York: Clarendon Press 1997

Barrett, Douglas, *A group of medieval Indian ivories,Oriental Art*, 1955, N. S. I(2).

Barrow, Amanda, *tapestry of memoirs. Shuttle, spindle & dyepot*, vol. 26, Winter, 1994/95

Barua, Nilima, Textile and design,*Art in industry*, vol. 4, no. 4, 1954

Basham, A. L., *The Wonder That Was India*, New York: Taplinger Publishing Co., 3rd rev. ed. 1968

Collier, Ann M (1970). *A Handbook of Textiles.* Pergamon Press.

Crowfoot, Grace (1936/1937). *"Of the Warp-Weighted Loom"*. The Annual of the British School at Athens 37.

Currell, David (1992). *An Introduction to Puppets and Puppetmaking.* London: New Burlington Books, Quintet Publishing Limited.

Condra, Jill (2008). *The Greenwood Encyclopedia of Clothing Through World History*. Westport, CT, USA: Greenwood Press.

Collier, Billie J. (2009). *Understanding Textiles.* Upper Saddle River, N.J.: Pearson Prentice Hall.

Cable, Vincent, Ann Weston and L. C. Jain, *The Commerce of Culture: Experience of Indian Handicrafts,* New Delhi: Lancer International 1986

Caldwell, Dorothy, *Stitching Women's Lives: Sujuni and Khatwa from Bihar.*, Peterborough: Canad Museum of Textiles 2000

Calico Museum, *Block Prints: Calico Museum, India, Ahmedabad*: Calico Museum 1951

Calico Museum of Textiles, *A Select Bibliography of Indian Textiles*, John Irwin, ed. Ahmedabad: Calico Museum of Textiles 1975

Calico Museum, Ahmedabad, *Treasures of Indian Textiles, Atlantic Highlands*, NJ: Humanities Press 1982

Campbell, J.M.. ed., Muslim and Parsi *Castes and Tribes of Gujarat*, Gurgaon: Vintage Books. (1990) [1899]

Caplan, A. *An important carved emerald from the Mogul period of India*, Lapidary Journal 24869

Carmen, Kagal, Shilpkar. The craftsman,1998

Carmichaal, David Freemantle; Dist, Gazetteer A.P Ed., *A manual of the Dist. Vizagapatnam in the Presidency of Madras,* 1994

Census of India, Assam. Vol. 3. Pt. 10d. Endi *silk industry of Assam.* 172p, 1961

Census of India, *Bandhani or Tie and Dye Sari of Jamnagar*, V, VII-A, 21, Census of India, 1901.

Census of India, 1951, *West Bengal: The Artisan Castes of West Bengal and Their Craft*, Sudhansu Kumar Ray, Calcutta, 1953.

Census of India, 1961, *Bibliography of Indian Arts and Crafts*, I, Part XI(ii) Delhi: Manager of Publications 1968

Census of India, 1961, *Bibliography of Small Scale and Cottage Industries and Handicrafts,* I, Part IX, No. 1. Delhi: Manager of Publications 1969

Census of India, 1961, *Embroidered Vestments*, VII, Part VII-A., New Delhi: 1961

Census of India, 1961, *Ivory Works in India through the Ages up to the End of the 19th Century*, I, Monograph Series, Part VII-A, No 5, New Delhi: Gov't of India 1967

Census of India, 1961, *The Laws Governing Craftsmen and Their Crafts from Ancient Days til Today in India,* I, Monograph Series, Part VII-A, No. 2., Delhi: Manager of Publications 1966.

Census of India, 1961 (Andhra Pradesh) *Selected Crafts of Andhra Pradesh: Bidriware, Wooden Toys, Himroo Fabrics of Hyderabad City*, II,Part VII-A, No. 3, Delhi: Manager of Publications 1967

Census of India, 1961 (Andhra Pradesh), *Selected Crafts of Andhra Pradesh: Crochet Lace Industry, Studded Brass Bangles of Hyderabad City, Brass and Bronze Industry*, II, Part VII-A, No. 2 Delhi: Manager of Publications 1965

Census of India, 1961 (Andhra Pradesh). *Selected Crafts of Andhra Pradesh: Filagaree Industry,* Leather Puppet Dolls, Kalamkari Temple Cloth Paintings of Kalahasti, Kalamkari Cloth Paintings of *Masulipatnam, Woollen Pile Carpet Industry,* II, Part VII-A, No. 1, Delhi: Manager of Publications,1964

Census of India, 1961 (Assam), *Selected Handicrafts of Assam,* III, Part VI, Delhi: Manager of Publications 1966

Census of India, 1961 (Bihar), *Selected Crafts of Bihar: Stoneware Craft of Patharkatti Village,* IV, Part VII-A, No. 1. Patna, 1969.

Census of India, 1961 (Delhi), *Selected Crafts of Delhi: Village Pottery,* XIX, Part VII-A, No. 2.Delhi: Manager of Publications 1967

Census of India, 1961 (Gujarat), *Selected Crafts of Gujarat: Agate Industry of Cambay*, V, Part VII-A, No. 1.Delhi: Manager of Publications 1964

Census of India, 1961 (Gujarat), *Selected Crafts of Gujarat: Bandhani or Tie and Dye Sari of Jamnagar*, V, Part VII-A, No. 21, Delhi: Manager of Publications 1969

Chaudhary, S.N., *Employment of women: with special reference to embroidery work*, New Delhi: Deep & Deep Publications, 1994

Chaudhuri, K.N., *The structure of the Indian textile industry in the seventeenth and eighteenth centuries.* IN Roy, Tirthankar, editor. Cloth and Commerce: textiles in colonial India New Delhi: SagePublications 1996

Chaudhuri, S., *An Exhibition of Folk and Tribal Images of India,* New Delhi: Lalit Kala Akademi 1970

Chetty, G. K. Ramanathan, *Gems and Jewellery*, Madras: Kalakshetra Publications Press 1980

Chhiber, Neelam, Stone Craft of India, 2 volumes. Chennai: Crafts Council of India. 2004

Chishti, Iftikhar Mulk, *From architeture to textiles: Jali*, India Magazine, vol. 9, no. 2, 1989

Chishti, Rta Kapur, Saris of India - Vol: II Bihar and West Bengal, 1995

Chishti, Rta Kapur and Amba Sanyal, *Saris of India*: Madhya Pradesh, Delhi: Wiley Eastern Ltd. and Amr Vastra Kosh 1989

Chitra, V. R. and Viswanathan, Takumalla, *Cottage industries of India, guidebook and symposium*. Madras: Shilpi Publications, 1948

Chondhury, R.C.R., *The principles and practice of dyeing,* Daca: 1923

Choondal, Chummar, *Kerala's rich heritage of folk art,* Indian Express, March 2, Delhi Edition, 1969

Choondal, Chummar, *Some folk arts of Kerala: paavakoothu, chavittunatakam, kummatti, Malayalam Literary Survey,* 1981, 5.

Chopra, P.N., *Dress, toilets, and ornaments during Mughal period* IN Proceedings of Indian History

Congress. Fifteenth session, Gwalior. 1952

Choudhury, Anil Roy, *Bidri Ware*, Hyderabad: Salar Jung Museum 1961

Choudhury, R. D., *Decorative elements in the art of Assam—a survey, Decorative Arts of India,* M. L. Nigam, ed., Hyderabad: Salar Jung Museum 1987.

Churchill, D. C., *The hand-loom in Ahmednagar. IN Industrial conference*, 3rd, 1907, Surat. The industrial conference held at Surat, December 1907. Full text of papers read at it and submitted to it. Madras: G. A. Natesan, 1907

Clarke, C. Purdon, *The Process Employed in Casting Brass Chains in Rajputana*, Journal of the Iron and Steel Institute 11 1886

Dhamija, Jasleen. *"From then till Now"*. India Together. Civil Society Information Exchange Pvt. Ltd.

Dahiya, Neelima, *Arts and Crafts in Northern India: From Earliest Times to c. 200 B.C.* Delhi: B. R. Publishing Corporation 1986

Dallapiccola, A .L., *Indian Art in detail*, Ahmedabad: 2007

Dalmia, Yashodhara, *Art and religion amongst the Warlis, Art and Life in India*: The Last Four Decades, Josef James, ed., Delhi: B. R. Publishing Corp.

Dalmia, Yashodhara ed., *Contemporary Indian Art*. Other Realities, 2002

Dar, S. N., *Costumes of India and Pakistan*, Bombay: D. B. Taraporevala Sons & Co. Ltd 1969

Dar, S.R., *History of Wood-work in Punjab*, Lahore: Manson, C.F. 1976

Darrah, Henry Zouch, *The eri silk of Assam.*, Assam Secretariat Press, 1890

Das Gupta, Kalyan Kumar, *Wood carvings of Arunachal Pradesh and Nagaland*, Indological Studies: Essays in Memory of Shri S. P. Singhal, Devendra Handa, ed., Delhi: Caxton Publications 1987.

Das Gupta, Kalyan Kumar, *Wood carvings of Bihar, Studies in Art and Archaeology of Bihar*-Bengal: Nalinikanta Satavarsiki, Debala Mitra and Gouriswar Bhattacharya, eds., Delhi: Sri Satguru Publications, 1989.

Das Gupta, Kalyan Kumar, *Wood Carvings of Eastern India,* Calcutta: Firma KLM Private Ltd. 1990

Das Gupta, Priya, *Forgotten arts of India, Decorations: fibre, thread, metal, beads, mirrors and colours in the hands of the folk make fairy tales,* Marg, 1968-69, XXII(4)

Das, A. K., *Baskets: a utilitarian craft*, India Magazine, 1991-92, 12(12)

Das, A. K., *Tribal Art and Craft, Delhi:* Agam Kala Prakashan 1979

Das, Bhuban Mohan, *A note on the Hira potters of Assam*, Man in India, 1956, XXXVI(3)

Das, Chobe Raghunath, *Tie and dye work manufactured at Baran, in the Kotah State*, Journal of Indian Art and Industry, 1888, II(23)

Dongerkery, K., *The Place of Embroidery in Indian Crafts*, Mumbai: Marg Publications, Vol. XVII, No. 22, March 1964

Dongerkery, Kamala S., *Place of embroidery in Indian crafts*, Marg, 1963-64, XVII(2)

Dongerkery, Kamala S., *The Indian Sari*, New Delhi: All India Handicrafts Board, Ministry of Commerce and Industry, Gov't of India

Doshi, Saryu, ed., *Heritage of Karnataka*, Mumbai: Marg Publications 1988

Dow, George Francis, *The Paisley shawl with some account of the shawl made in Kashmir*. Old-time New England, vol. 11 1921

Dubois, J. A. (Abbé), *Hindu Manners, Customs and Ceremonies,* Oxford: Clarendon Press 1897; 3rd ed., 1928

Elliott, Inger McCabe. (1984) *Batik : fabled cloth of Java photographs, Brian Brake ; contributions, Paramita Abdurachman, Susan Blum, Iwan Tirta ; design, Kiyoshi Kanai*. New York : Clarkson N. Potter.

Eileen Rose Busby, *Royal Winton Porcelain: Ceramics Fit for a King*, Antique Publishers, 1998.

Edwards, Eiluned, *Textiles and Dress of Gujarat*, 2011, Mapin Publishing Pvt. Ltd, Ahmedabad.

Fraser-Lu, Sylvia.(1986) *Indonesian batik : processes, patterns, and places Singapore* : Oxford University Press. ISB

G. K. Ghosh, Shukla Ghosh, 2000. *Ikat textiles of India*. 2000

Gahlot, Sukhvirsingh. 1992. *RAJASTHAN: Historical & Cultural.* J. S. Gahlot Research Institute, Jodhpur.

Guy, John. *Indian Textiles in the East.* London, Thames & Hudson, 2009, p. 10..

G.Cook, *Handbook of Textile Fibres:I. Natural Fibres,* 5th edition, Merrow Publishing Co., Durham, England, 1984.

Guy, John. *Woven Cargoes: Indian Textiles in the East.* New York: Thames & Hudson, 1998.

Gillow, Barnard, John, Nicholas (1991). *Indian Textiles.* London: Thames & Hudson Ltd.

Gandhi, M. P. ,*A Monograph on Handloom Weaving Industry in India*, Bombay: Gandhi & Co. 1948

Gandhi, Manmohan Purushottam. *The handloom industry in India.* Sect. III. IN Cottage industries of India, guidebook and symposium. Calcutta: G. N Mitra, 1931

Gangoli, O.C., *Indian Terra-cotta Art*, Calcutta, Allahabad and Bombay: Rupa & Co 1959

Gangoly, O. C., *A collection of Indian brasses and bronzes*, Rupam, 1927.

Gangoly, O. C., *Indian Terracotta Art*, New York: G. Wittenborn 1959

Gangoly, O. C., *South Indian lamps*, Journal of Indian Art and Industry, 1916, XVII(136).

Gangoly, O. C., *The story of a cotton printed fabric from Orissa,* Journal of the Bihar and Orissa Research Society, 1919, V(Part III)

Ganguli, Kalyan Kumar, *Chamba rumal*, Journal of the Indian Society of Oriental Art, 1943, XI.

Ganguli, Kalyan Kumar, *Clay ornaments from Sisupalgarh*, Proceedings of Indian Historical Congress, 1947- 48, 10:208

Ganguli, Kalyan Kumar, *Folk art of Bengal,* All Indian Folklore Conference Souvenir, Calcutta, 1964.

Ganguly, Kalyan Kumar, *The Artisan Castes of West Bengal and their Crafts*, Tribes and Castes of West Bengal, Census - 1951

Ganju, M., *Textile Industry of Kashmir*, Srinagar: 1945

Gans-Ruedin, E., *Indian Carpets*, New York: Rizzoli International Publications, Inc. 1984

Gavin, Traude and Barnes, Ruth, *Textiles and the trade in Indian cloth: inspiration and perception.*, Textile history , vol. 30 (1999)

General Editor : Martand Singh. Compiled and edited by Rta Kapur Chishti, *Saris of India,* Vol. 2: Bihar and West Bengal, New Delhi: 1996

Gupta, Charu Smita Gupta , *Zardozi - Glittering gold embroidery*, 1996

Gupta, K. C., *Progress and Prospects of Pottery Industry in India,* Delhi: Mittal Publications 1988

Gupta, Samarendranath, "*Phulkari work in the Punjab*."Modern review, vol. 11 (1912).

Gupte, B. A., *Embroidery*, Journal of Indian Art and Industry, 1888, II(18)

Guy, John and Deborah Swallow, *Arts of India: 1550-1900.* Exhibition Catalogue, London: Victoria and Albert Museum 1990

Handloom construction: *Practical guide to constructing viable handlooms*, Joan Koster,1978

Hobsbawm, Eric, "*The Age of Revolution*", (London 1962; repr. 2008), p.45.

Handlooms: Practical guide to constructing viable handlooms, Joan Koster,1978

Habib, Irfan, *Notes on the Indian textile industry in the seventeenth century.* IN Essays in honour of Prof. S.C. Sarkar. New delhi: People's Publishing House 1976

Harris, Kathleen, "*Indian embroidery, chikan or white work.*"Embroideress, no. 50.

Harris, Peter, *The Kashmir shawl: lessons in history and studies in technology.*Ars texts-ina, vol, 16 (1991)

lumenthal, Eileen, *Puppetry and Puppets*, Thames & Hudson, 2005.

Jo Anne P. Welsh, *Chintz Ceramics*, 3rd ed., Schiffer Publishing, 2000.

Kumar, Ritu. *Costumes and Textiles of Royal India.* London: Christie's Books, 1999.

Kelly L. Moran, *Shelley Chintz: Unlocking the Secrets of the Pattern Books*, Thaxted Cottage, 1999.

Latshaw, George (2000). *The Complete Book of Puppetry.* London: Dover Publications.

Lynton, Linda, Madhubani painting, *Arts of Asia,* 1995, 25(2).

Lynton, Linda, *The assimilation of European designs into twentieth century Indian saris* - Contact, Crossover, Continuity: Proceedings of the Fourth Biennial Symposium of the Textile Society of America, 1994, Los Angeles: Textile Society of America 1994, 207-16

Lynton, Linda, *The Sari: Styles, Patterns, History, Techniques*, New York: Harry N. Abrams, Inc. 1995

Lynton, Linda, "*Victorian and Edwardian designs in East Indian handwoven saris*, "Surface design, vol. 18, no. 1, (1993)

Lyons, Tryna, *The Artists of Nathadwara. The Practice of Painting in Rajasthan*, 2004

Lynton, Linda, Madhubani painting, Arts of Asia, 1995, 25(2):112-121

Lynton, Linda, *Shisha embroidery: the mirrorwork of Gujarat, Piecework*, 1994, II(6)

Lynton, Linda, *The assimilation of European designs into twentieth century Indian saris* - Contact, Crossover, Continuity: Proceedings of the Fourth Biennial Symposium of the Textile Society of America, 1994, Los Angeles: Textile Society of America 1994.

Lynton, Linda, The Sari - Style Patterns - History - Techniques

Lynton, Linda, *The Sari: Styles, Patterns, History, Techniques*, New York: Harry N. Abrams, Inc. 1995

Lynton, Linda, "*The origins and significance of the Assamese sun tree. Motif,*" Ars textrina, vol. 2 (1993)

Lynton, Linda, "*Victorian and Edwardian designs in East Indian handwoven saris,* "Surface design, vol. 18, no. 1. (1993)

Lynton, Linda, *The wild silk saris of eastern India.Arts of Asia*, vol. 22, no. 5, 1992.

Lyons, Tryna, *The Artists of Nathadwara. The Practice of Painting in Rajasthan*, 2004

Lynton, Linda, Madhubani painting, *Arts of Asia,* 1995, 25(2):112-121

Lynton, Linda, *Shisha embroidery: the mirrorwork of Gujarat,* Piecework, 1994, II(6)

Lynton, Linda, *The assimilation of European designs into twentieth century Indian saris* - Contact, Crossover, Continuity: Proceedings of the Fourth Biennial Symposium of the Textile Society of America, 1994, Los Angeles: Textile Society of America 1994.

Lynton, Linda, *The Sari: Styles, Patterns, History, Techniques*, New York: Harry N. Abrams, Inc. 1995

Lynton, Linda, "*The origins and significance of the Assamese sun tree. Motif,*" Ars textrina, vol. 20 (1993).

Lynton, Linda, "*Victorian and Edwardian designs in East Indian handwoven saris,* "Surface design, vol. 18, no. 1 pp. 18- 21. 95. (1993)

Lynton, Linda, *The wild silk saris of eastern India.* Arts of Asia, vol. 22, no. 5. 1992.

Lyons, Tryna, *The Artists of Nathadwara. The Practice of Painting in Rajasthan*, 2004

Marsden, Richard (1895). *Cotton Weaving: Its Development, Principles, and Practice.* George Bell & Sons. . Retrieved Feb 2009.

Mass, William (1990). "*The Decline of a Technology Leader:Capabilty, strategy and shuttleless Weaving*". Business and Economic History.

Masters, Robert E.L. and Houston, Jean *Psychedelic Art* New York:1968 A Balance House book—printed by Grove Press, Inc.

McDowell, Colin (1984). *McDowell's Directory of Twentieth Century Fashion.* Frederick Muller.

Mathur, P.C., 1995. *Social and Economic Dynamics of Rajasthan Politics* (Jaipur, Aaalekh)

Mattiebelle Gittinger and H. Leedom Lefforts,*Textiles and the Thai Experience in South-East Asia,* Washington, DC 1992.

Maclagan, E. D. , *Monograph on the Gold and Silver Works of the Punjab* 1888-89 Lahore: Civil and Military Gazette Press 1890

Maffey, J. L. , *A Monograph on Wood Carving in the United Provinces of Agra and Oudh*, Allahabad: Gov't. Press 1903

Mago, Pran Nath, *Design in rural life*, Design, New Delhi, 1967.

Mago, Pran Nath, *Murals and mosaics from villages around Delhi* Design, New Delhi, 1967, 11(8)

Mago, Pran Nath, *Pottery in 'Homage to Himachal Pradesh'* Marg, 1969-70, XXIII(2)

Mahapatra, P. K., *The Folk Cults of Bengal*, Calcutta: Indian Publications 1972

Mahapatra, Sitakant K., *Orissa in 'Tribal Arts of Eastern India*, Marg, 1991-92, XLIII(4)

Maheshwari, J. K. and R. M. Painuli, *Plants used in tribal craft* by Sahariyas of Madhya Pradesh, Folklore, 1990, 31(12):239-43

Mailey, Jean E., *Indian textiles in the Museum's collection,* Chronicle of the Museum for the Arts of Decoration, 1953, 2(5)

Maira, Varun, *Dholavira : A Harappan Metropolis*, 2009

Maity, P. K., *Folk-Rituals of Eastern India*, New Delhi: Abhinav Publications 1988

Maity, S K, *Masterpieces of Hoysala Art*: Haledid, Belur , Somnathpur,1978

Majmudar, M. R., *Cultural History of Gujarat*, Bombay: Popular Prakashan 1965

Malathi, K. N., *Rangoli: computerising an ancient art*, India Magazine, 1990-91, 11(10)

Malkin, Michael R., *Traditional and Folk Puppets of the World,* South Brunswick: A. S. Barnes & Co., 1977

Mallinson, Jane; Nancy Donnelly & Ly Hang, H'Mong *Batik: A Textile Techniqe from Laos,* Chiang Mai 1996

Manchandra, B., *Designs of Manipur handlooms,* Imphal: Manipur Government Emporium, 15p. 1960.

Marg, *American collections of asian art*. Marg 1986.

Marg, *Changing Vision-Lasting Image*. Calcutta through 500 years, Marg 1990

Marg, *Design in traditional jewellery*: Central India, Rajasthan, Marg, 1952-53, VI(3)

Marg, *Embroideries of India*, Marg, 1963-64, XVII(2)

Marg, *Handlooms*, Marg, 1961-62, XV(4)

Marg, *Himachal heritage*, Marg, 1969-70, XXIII(2)

Marg, *Homage to kalamkari*, Marg, 1977-78, XXXI(4)

Marg, *Lac*,Marg, 1965-66, XIX(3)

Marg, *Pottery* (Sardar Gurcharan Singh), Marg, 1956-57, X(2):72

Maclagan, E. D. , *Monograph on the Gold and Silver Works of the Punjab 1888-89* Lahore: Civil and Military Gazette Press 1890

Maconochie, E. ,*Monograph on the pottery and glass industries in the Bombay Presidency* - Art in Industry through the Ages: Monograph Series on Bombay Presidency, New Delhi: Navrang 1976,

Maduro, Renaldo, *The Brahmin painters of Nathdwara, Rajasthan – Ethnic and Tourist Arts*: Cultural Expressions from the Fourth World, Nelson H. H. Graburn, ed., Los Angeles: University of California Press, 1976

Maffey, J. L. , *A Monograph on Wood Carving in the United Provinces of Agra and Oudh*, Allahabad: Gov't. Press 1903

Mago, Pran Nath, *Design in rural life*, Design, New Delhi, 1967.

Mago, Pran Nath, *Jewellery of Rajasthan*, Marg, 1964-65, XVIII(1)

Mago, Pran Nath, *Murals and mosaics from villages around Delhi* Design, New Delhi, 1967, 11(8):22

Mago, Pran Nath, *Pottery in 'Homage to Himachal Pradesh'* Marg, 1969-70, XXIII(2)

Mago, Pran Nath, *The mural art of the Meos* Design, New Delhi, 1971, 15(2)

Mahapatra, P. K., *The Folk Cults of Bengal*, Calcutta: Indian Publications 1972

Mahapatra, Sitakant, *Art and ritual: a study of Saora pictograms – Dimensions of Indian* Art: Pupul Jayakar Seventy, Lokesh Chandra and Jyotindra Jain, eds. Delhi: Agam Kala Prakashan, 1986.

Mahapatra, Sitakant K., *Orissa in 'Tribal Arts of Eastern India*, Marg, 1991-92, XLIII(4)

Maharaj, Sarat, *Arachne's genre: towards inter-cultural studies in textiles*.Journal of design History , vol. 4, no. 2 (1991).

Maheshwari, J. K. and R. M. Painuli, *Plants used in tribal craft* by Sahariyas of Madhya Pradesh, Folklore, 1990, 31(12)

Maheswari, C.S. Uma, *Dress and Jewellery of Women : Satavahana to Kakatiya*, 1995

Mailey, Jean E., *Indian textiles in the Museum's collection,* Chronicle of the Museum for the Arts of Decoration, 1953, 2(5)

Maira, Varun, *Dholavira : A Harappan Metropolis*, 2009

Maity, P. K., *Folk-Rituals of Eastern India*, New Delhi: Abhinav Publications 1988

Maity, S K, *Masterpieces of Hoysala Art: Haledid, Belur* , Somnathpur 1978

Majid, A., *Monograph on Wood Carving in Assam*, 1903

Majithia, Joan, *Creations in clay: the terracottas of Gorakhpur*, India Magazine, 1982-83, 3(4)

Majmudar, M. R., *Cultural History of Gujarat*, Bombay: Popular Prakashan 1965

Majmudar, M. R., *Gujarat, its Art-Heritage*, Bombay: University of Bombay 1968

Malathi, K. N., *Rangoli: computerising an ancient art*, India Magazine, 1990-91, 11(10)

Malkin, Michael R., *Traditional and Folk Puppets of the World*, South Brunswick: A. S. Barnes & Co., 1977

Mallinson, Jane; Nancy Donnelly & Ly Hang, H'Mong *Batik: A TextileTechniqe from Laos*, Chiang Mai 1996

Manchanda, Jaishree, *Traditional Fabrics of India*, New Delhi: Samkaleen Prakashan

Manchandra, B., *Designs of Manipur handlooms*, Imphal: Manipur Government Emporium, 1960.

Manohar, Aashi, ed., *Tribal Arts and Crafts of Madhya Pradesh*, Ahmedabad: Mapin Publishing Pvt. Ltd., with Vanya Prakashan 1996

Manson, C.F., *Note on the Lac Industry in the Santal Parganas.* The IndianForester 7 (1883)

March, Kathryn *Weaving, writing, and gender*. Paper presented at WennerGren Symposium, Cloth and the organization of human Experience,1993

Marg, *American collections of asian art*. Marg 1986.

Marg, *Bihar handicrafts*, Marg, 1966-67, XX(1)

Marg, *Carpets of India*, Marg, 1964-65, XVIII(4)

Marg, *Changing Vision-Lasting Image. Calcutta through 500 years*, Marg 1990

Marg, *Design in traditional jewellery: Central India, Rajasthan*, Marg, 1952-53, VI(3)

Marg, *Design in traditional jewellery: the Punjab,* Marg, 1952-53, VI(1)

Marg, *Embroideries of India*, Marg, 1963-64, XVII(2)

Marg, *Goa-Cultural patterns*. Marg 1983

Marg, *Handlooms*, Marg, 1961-62, XV(4)

Marg, *Haryana crafts*, Marg, 1975-76, XXIX(1)

Marg, *Himachal heritage*, Marg, 1969-70, XXIII(2)

Marg, *Homage to kalamkar*i, Marg, 1977-78, XXXI(4)

Marg, *Lac*,Marg, 1965-66, XIX(3)

Marg, *Pottery* (Sardar Gurcharan Singh), Marg, 1956-57, X(2):72

Maclagan, E. D. , *Monograph on the Gold and Silver Works of the Punjab 1888-89 Lahore*: Civil and Military Gazette Press 1890

Maconochie, E. ,*Monograph on the pottery and glass industries in the Bombay Presidency - Art in Industry through the Ages*: Monograph Series on Bombay Presidency, New Delhi: Navrang 1976,

Maduro, Renaldo, *The Brahmin painters of Nathdwara, Rajasthan – Ethnic and Tourist Arts*: Cultural Expressions from the Fourth World,

Mago, Pran Nath, *Design in rural life*, Design, New Delhi, 1967.

Mago, Pran Nath, *Murals and mosaics from villages around Delh*i Design, New Delhi, 1967, 11(8):22-25

Mago, Pran Nath, *Pottery in 'Homage to Himachal Pradesh'* Marg, 1969-70, XXIII(2)

Mahapatra, P. K., *The Folk Cults of Bengal*, Calcutta: Indian Publications 1972

Mahapatra, Sitakant, *Art and ritual: a study of Saora pictograms – Dimensions of Indian Art*: Pupul Jayakar Seventy, Lokesh Chandra and Jyotindra Jain, eds. Delhi: Agam Kala Prakashan, 1986,

Maharaj, Sarat, *Arachne's genre: towards inter-cultural studies in textiles.*Journal of design History , vol. 4, no. 2 (1991)

Maheshwari, J. K. and R. M. Painuli, *Plants used in tribal craft by Sahariyas of Madhya Pradesh,* Folklore, 1990, 31(12)

Maheswari, C.S. Uma, *Dress and Jewellery of Women* : Satavahana to Kakatiya,1995

Mailey, Jean E., *Indian textiles in the Museum's collection*Chronicle of the Museum for the Arts of Decoration, 1953, 2(5)

Naidu, M. Reddappa and Krishna, Nanditha, *Textiles, IN Arts and crafts of Tamil Nadu*, Ahmedabad: Mapin Publishing 1992

Naik, Shailaja D., *Traditional Embroideries of India*,1996

Nambiar, Balan and Eberhard Fischer, *Patola / virali pattu—from Gujarat to Kerala: new information on double ikat textiles in South India*, Asiatische Studien/Etudes asiatiques, 1987, XLI(2)

Nanavati, J. M., M. P. Vora and M. A. Dhaky, *The Embroidery and Bead Work of Kutch and Saurashtra,* Baroda: Department of Archaeology, Gujarat State 1966

Nandagopal, Choodamani, *The traditional jewellery of Karnataka – Decorative Arts of India*, M. L. Nigam, ed. Hyderabad: Salar Jung Museum 1987.

Nandagopal, Choodamani; Edited by M.L. Nigam, *The Traditional Jewellery of Karnataka. In Decorative Arts of India* Hyderabad: Salar Jung Museum 1987

Naik, Shailaja D., *Folk Embroidery and Traditional Handloom Weaving*, 1997

Naik, Shailaja D., *Traditional Embroideries of India*, 1996

Nandagopal, Choodamani, *The traditional jewellery of Karnataka – Decorative Arts of India*, M. L. Nigam, ed. Hyderabad: Salar Jung Museum 1987

Nandagopal, Choodamani; Edited by M.L. Nigam,*The raditional Jewellery of Karnataka. In Decorative Arts of India* Hyderabad: Salar Jung Museum 1987

Nandi, S. ,*The art of ivory in Murshidabad*, Indian Museum Bulletin, 1969, IV(1):93-99

Nandi, Santibhusan and D. S. Tyagi , *Forms of villages - Peasant Life in India: A Study in Indian Unity and Diversity*, Nirmal Kumar Bose, ed. Calcutta: Anthropological Survey of India 1967, 1–5

Nandini, Rajesh, *Phulkari*, Illustrated Weekly of India, 1974, XCV(41):49-51

Nanekar, K. R , *Handloom industry in Madhya Pradesh*, Nagpur: Magpur University, 186p 1968

Naqvi, Hameeda Khatoon, *Dyeing of cotton goods in the Mughal Hindustan* (1556-1803),Journal of Indian Textile History, 1967, VII:45-56

Naqvi, Hameeda Khatoon, *Mughal Hindustan: Cities and Industries 1556-1803*.Karachi: National Book Foundation, 2nd ed. 1974

Narain, Jai, *A note on the associated antiquities of ochre-coloured pottery*, Journal of the Oriental Institute, Baroda, 1979, XXIX(1–2)

Narasimhiah, B.,*The russet-coated painted ware: a reassessment abou its origin and pattern of distribution*, Journal of Indian History, 1975, LIII(Part III):

Narayan Rao, M . V. ,*"Indian printed textiles"*, Roopa-lekha, vol. 44

Narayan, Gitam, *Crafts India,Madras*: Crafts Council of India 1986

Narayana Rao, M. V. , *Handicrafts of Karnataka,* Journal of Industry and Trade, 1975, XXV(10

Narayanan, Gita , *Crafts India '86,Madras*: Crafts Council of India 1986

Narula, Vibha, *Cotton sarees of Bijapur and Dharwad.*, Ahmedabad: National Institute of Design, 1992

Nath, Aman, *Blue ceramicsIndia* Magazine, 1986-87, 7(1)

Nath, Aman & Francis Waiziarg, *Arts and Crafts of Rajasthan*, 1994

Nath, Aman and Francis Wacziarg, eds., *Arts and Crafts of Rajasthan*, Ahmedabad, New York: Mapin Publishing Pvt. Ltd. 1987

Nath, Bihrendra , *A critical study of terracottas from Bihar - History and Culture:* B. P. Sinha Felicitation Volume, Bhagwant Sahai, ed., Delhi: Ramanand Vidya Bhawan 1987.

Nath, G. Nanja, *Toys from Lucknow and Kondapalli*, Art in Industry, 1963, VII(3)

Nath, T.K., *Bamboo Cane and Assam*, Assam: Sponsors: Industrial

National Council for Applied Economic Research, *Census of Handicraft Artisans 1995-96*, New Delhi: National Council for Applied Economic Research 1998

National Council for Applied Economic Research, *Economic Status of Handicraft Artisans*, New Delhi: National Council for Applied Economic Research 1991the story of Kamalekamini in the Indian Museum, Indian Museum Bulletin, 1970, V(2)

Nandi, S. ,*The art of ivory in Murshidabad*, Indian Museum Bulletin, 1969, IV(1)

Nandini, Rajesh, *Phulkari*, Illustrated Weekly of India, 1974, XCV(41)

Nanekar, K. R ,*Handloom industry in Madhya Pradesh*, Nagpur: Magpur University, 1968

Narain, Jai *A note on the associated antiquities of ochre-coloured pottery*, Journal of the Oriental Institute, Baroda, 1979, XXIX(1–2)

People of India Rajasthan, Volume XXXVIII Part Two edited by B.K Lavania, D. K Samanta, S K Mandal & N.N Vyas, Popular Prakashan

People of India Gujarat, Volume XXI Part Three edited by R.B Lal, P.B.S.V Padmanabham, G Krishnan & M Azeez Mohideen

Pellew, Charles E. (1909). *"Tied and Dyed Work: An Oriental Process with American Variations"*. Craftsman 16

QuaChee & eM.K. (2005) *Batik Inspirations*: Featuring Top Batik Designers.

Riazuddin, Akhtar, *History of Handicrafts: Pakistan-India*, Islamabad: National Hijra Council 1988

Richards, F. J., *Suggestions for the classification of Indian pottery* (abstract), Man in India, 1924, IV(1–2)

Richter, Anne, *Jewelery of Southeast Asia*, 2000

Ridley, Michael, *Oriental Art: India, Nepal and Tibet for Pleasure and Investment*, New York: Arco 1970

Rivers, Victoria Z., "*Culture cut apart? Rural Indian embroideries and commodization.* " Marg, vol. 49, no. 3, (1998)

Rivett-Carnac, J. H., *On some specimens of Indian metal work*, Journal of Indian Art and Industry, 1902, IX.

Rao, K . S, *Handmade art textiles*, Patna : Government Press, 1931

Robinson, Stuart; Patricia Robertson (1967). *Exploring Puppetry*. London: Mills & Boon Limited.

R.K. Gupta; S.R. Bakshi (1 January 2008). *Studies In Indian History: Rajasthan Through The Ages The Heritage Of Rajputs* (Set Of 5 Vols.). Sarup & Sons.

Raghavendra Rathore's collection, Rathore, Jodhpur"*Rajasthan is now on the world ramp*", 25 October 2011 I The Times of India and Jun 19, 2008, *Fabric dyeing belongs to the Chippa caste of Rajasthan*.

Rao, K . S, *Handmade art textiles*. Patna : Government Press, 12p . 1931

"*Rajasthan is now on the world ramp*". The Times of India. Jun 19, 2012.

Singh, Kavita, *New Insight into Sikh art*, Marg 2003

Sinclair, Anita (1995). *The Puppetry Handbook*. Richmond, Victoria, Australia: Richard Lee Publishing.

Somani, Ram Vallabh. 1993. *History of Rajasthan*. Jain Pustak Mandir, Jaipur.

Sardar, Marika. "*Indian Textiles: Trade and Production*". In Heilbrunn Timeline of Art History. New York: The Metropolitan Museum of Art, 2000.

Susan Scott, *The Charlton Standard Catalogue of Chintz*, 3rd ed. Charlton Press, 1999.

Sainsbury, W.N., *The Fine Arts in India in the Reign of James I* – vol. II, January-May 1864. The Fine Arts Quarterly Review

Sakhai, Essie, Persian rugs and carpets. *The fabric of life*. Edited by Ian Bennett, 2008

Sakhai, Essie, *The Story of Carpets*. London: Studio Editions, an imprint of Random House, UK ltd. 2000.

Saksena, Jogendra, Mandana, *A Folk Art of Rajasthan*. New Delhi: Crafts Museum 1985

Sahay, Sachidanand, *Indian Costume, Coiffure and Ornament*, New Delhi: Munshiram Manoharlal Publishers 1975

Singh, Kavita, *New Insight into Sikh art*, Marg 2003

Sahay, Sachidanand, *Technique of terracotta art* - Dr. Satkari Mookerji Felicitation Volume, B. P. Sinha, et al., eds.,Varanasi: Chowkhamba Sanskrit Series 1969.

Sahoo, Basudeb, ed., *Arts and Artisans of Orissa*, Bhubaneswar: Satenetra Publications 1981

Sakhai, Essie, *Persian rugs and carpets*. The fabric of life. Edited by Ian Bennett, 2008

Sakhai, Essie, *The Story of Carpets*. London: Studio Editions, an imprint of Random House, UK ltd. 2000.

Sandberg, Gosta, *Indigo textiles: technique and history*, London: A&C Black, 1989

Sandhya Raman, Gupta, Aarti and Varkey, Mini, *Traditional Garments of Udaipur, Banswara and Dungarpur* ,1992

Sangar, S. P., "*Cloth fabrics of the Coromandel coast in the seventh century*." Panjab University research bulletin (arts), vol. 5, no. 1 (1974)

Sangar, S. P., " *Broach Textiles in the seventeenth century*", Journal of Oriental Institute (Baroda), vol 19, no. 1-2, 1979

Sangar, S.P., "*Bengal Textiles in the seventeenth century*", Punjab University Research Bulletin: arts, vol. 12, no. 1-2, 1981

Sangar, S. P., "*Cloth fabrics of the Coromandel coast in the seventh century.*" Panjab University research bulletin (arts), vol. 5, no. 1 (1974)

Sangar, S. P., "*Broach Textiles in the seventeenth century*", Journal of Oriental Institute (Baroda), vol 19, no. 1-2, 1979

Sanyal, Hitesranjan, *The nature of peasant culture in India: a study of the pat painting and clay sculpture of Bengal, Folk,* Copenhagen, 1984.

Sarabhai, Mrinalini, *Patolas and Resist-Dyed Fabrics of India,* Ahmedabad: Mapin Publishing Pvt. Ltd. 1988

Sanghvi, Lily, *Toda Embroidery*, Inside Outside, Oct 1955

Tod, James & Crooke, William. 1829. *Annals and Antiquities of Rajast'han or the Central and Western Rajpoot States of India,.* Numerous reprints, including 3 Vols. Reprint: Low Price Publications, Delhi. 1990. (set of 3 vols.)

Tortora, Phyllis G. (2009). *Survey of Historic Costume.* New York: Fairchild Books.

Traditional Ornaments of Kerala, Kerala: The Kera Tewari, Laxmi G., *A Splendor of Worship: Women's Fasts, Rituals, Stories and Art*, New Delhi: Manohar 1991

Thakur, Jai Narain, *Silk industry in Bihar*. Journal of the Bihar Research Society, vol. 58, 1972

Thakurta, Srimati Guha, ed., Mahamaya: *Crafts and Craftsmen of Eastern India*. Calcutta: Crafts Council of West Bengal; Philadelphia: Port of History Museum 1986la State Handicrafts Apex Cooperative Society, *Treasures of Indian Textiles: Calico Museum,* Ahmedabad, Bombay: Marg Publications 1980

Traditional Ornaments of Kerala, Kerala: The Kerala State Handicrafts Apex Cooperative Society, Ernakulam; Department of Industries and Commerce, Kerala. 1970

Treasures of Indian Textiles: Calico Museum, Ahmedabad, Bombay: Marg Publications 1980

Tana, Pradumna and Rosalba Tana, *Traditional Chikankari Embroidery Patterns of India*, Owings Mills, MD: Stemmer House Publishers Inc. 1988

Tana, Pradumna, *Traditional designs from India for artists and craftsmen*. New York: Dover Publications, 1981

Tarlo, Emma, *Gujarati embroidery: a stitch in time revives an old skill*, India Magazine, 1990-91, 11(3).

Umesh Charan Patnaik, Aswini Kumar Mishra, 1997. *Handloom industry in action*. 1997.

Verma, Nisha, *The Terracottas of Bihar*. Delhi: Ramanand Vidya Bhawan 1986

Vetu Pillai, T K,*The Travancore State Manual* (Volume 1 and 2).1906

Victoria and Albert Museum, London, *Art and the East India Trade*, London: Her Majesty's Stationary Office 1970

Victoria and Albert Museum, London, *Art and the East India Trade*. London: Her Majesty's Stationery Office 1970

Victoria and Albert Museum, London, Indian Section, *Bibliography of Indian Textiles*, London: Victoria and Albert Museum 1975 or 1976

Vidyarthi, L. P., *Cultural Contours of Tribal Bihar*, Calcutta: Punthi Pustak 1964

Walker, John. "Psychedelic Art". *Glossary of Art, Architecture & Design since 1945*, 3rd. ed. (1992)

Watson, John Forbes, *Collection of Specimens and Illustrations of the Textile Manufactures of India*, 4 vols. fol., 13 vols. London: 1873-1880

Wacziarg, Francis, ed., *Arts and Crafts of Rajasthan*. Ahmedabad: Mapin Publishing 1989

Wadhwani, H. R. ,"*Bewitching brocades of Banares.*" Indian silk, vol. 4, no. 11, (1965)

Waldschmidt, E.; Translated by D. Wilson, *Nepal - Art Treasures from the Himalaya*, Calcutta: Oxford & IBH Publishing Co. 1967

Walker, Anthony R., *The Toda of South India: A New Look*, Delhi: Hindustan Publishing Corporation 1986

Walker, Daniel, Pride of the princes: Indian art of the Mughal era, Hali, vol 28, 1985

Walker, Daniel, Flowers *Underfoot: Indian Carpets of the Mughal Era*. London: Thames and Hudson 1998

Walter, R.Cassels, *An accountof the culture of the Bombay Presidency*, Collected from the government of India records

Ward, Philip, *Gujarat, Daman and Diu*. Hyderabad: Orient Longman 2000

Wardle, Thomas, *Kashmir: its new silk industry, with some account of its natural history, geology, sport, etc. and with forty-five, full-plate illustrations of Kashmir scenery, and of sport etc.. Also notes of a visit to the silk-producing district of Bengal 1885*-6. London: Simpkin, Marshall, Hamilton, Kent. 1904

Wardle, Thomas, *Royal Commission and Government of India silk culture court, descriptive catalogue*.London: W. Clowes, 1886

Wardle, Thomas, *Handbook of the collection illustrative of the wild silks of India in the Indian Section of the South* Kensington Museum. London: HMSO, 1881

Wardle, Thomas, *Monographs on the tusser and other wild silks of India... and on the dyestuffs and tannin matters of India and their native uses, descriptive of the collection in the India section of the Paris Exhibition*. London: 1878

Wardle, Thomas, *Silk: its entomology, history & manufacture, as exemplified at the Royal Jubilee Exhibition, Manchester*', 1887. London: Edward Bumpus, 238p. 1887

Warmington, E. H., *The Commerce between the Roman Empire and India,* New York: Octagon Books, rev. ed. 1974

Warner, Marina, *Woven winds : the infinite variety of the sari. Connoisseur*, vol. 216, April pp. 84- 91. 1986

Watson, John Forbes, *A Classified and Descriptive Catalogue of the Indian Department*, London: W. H. Allen & Co. 1873

Watson, John Forbes, *Indian costumes and textile fabrics*, Edinburgh Review, 1867, 126

Watson, John Forbes and John William Kaye, eds., *The People of India: A Series of Photographic Illustrations...*, 8 vols. London: India Museum 1868-75

Watt, George, *A Dictionary of the Economic Products of India*, 10 Vol., Calcutta: Office of the Superintendent, Government Printin, The Art of Kantha Embroidery, Dhaka: 1993

Zealey, Philip, *Masters of an age-old craft: the weavers of Sambalpur*, March of India, 1957, IX

Zealey, Philip, *The folk painters of Jaipur*, March of India, 1956, VIII(6)

Zebrowski, Mark, *The Hindu and Muslim elements of Mughal art with reference to textiles - In Quest of Themes and Skills, Asian Textiles,* Krishna Riboud, ed., Bombay: Marg Publications 1989.

Zimmer, Heinrich, *The Art of Indian Asia: Its Mythology and Transformations*, 2 vols. Princeton, NJ: Princeton University Press 1983

Index